The Eberly Library
Waynesburg University

Waynesburg, Pennsylvania

UNIVERSITAS WAYNESBURGIENSIS · FIAT LUX · MDCCCL

194 D438Zn

Derrida

Christopher Norris

Derrida

Harvard University Press
Cambridge, Massachusetts
1987

10 9 8 7 6 5 4 3 2 1

Library of Congress Cataloging-in-Publication Data
Norris, Christopher.
  Derrida/by Christopher Norris.
    p. cm.
  Bibliography: p.
  Includes index.
  ISBN 0-674-19823-9 (alk. paper).   ISBN 0-674-19824-7 (pbk. :
alk. paper)
  1. Derrida, Jacques. I. Title.
B2430.D484N66 1987
194—dc19   87-22922
             CIP

For Alison, Clare and Jenny

Contents

Acknowledgements

This book is the result of readings, teachings, conversations and fortunate encounters too numerous to place on record. A semester at Berkeley in the summer of 1986 gave me a chance to try out some parts of it in a graduate seminar whose members provided an ideally responsive and critical audience. My thanks to Art Quinn and Susan Shahzade for introducing me to the Rhetoric Department and making those occasions possible. Also to Bob and Renate Holub, Joan Hammes, Chris Saxton and Hans Sluga, for their friendship and lively exchange of ideas on and off campus. Further back, I am aware that many of the arguments in this book took shape during sessions of the Cardiff Critical Theory seminar, most often in dialogue with Terence Hawkes, Catherine Belsey and (more recently) Ian Whitehouse. My students in the English Department at UWIST also helped a great deal by criticizing lectures based on an early draft and demanding clarification at various points.

But the longest-standing debt is to Frank Kermode, since my interest in Derrida began with the series of postgraduate seminars that he chaired at University College London in the early 1970s. I am certainly not alone in thinking of those occasions as marked by an all too rare spirit of communal excitement and discovery. Now I can thank him also for commissioning this volume and seeing it through to press as General Editor of the Modern Masters series.

Chapters 6 and 7 are modified versions of material that first appeared in the journals *Paragraph* and *Philosophy and Literature*. Chapter 8 also incorporates some arguments first developed in an essay for the *Southern Review* (Adelaide). I am grateful to the editors and publishers concerned, especially Ken Ruthven and Noel King of the *Southern Review* for all their interest and encouragement over the past few years.

Cardiff, Wales   June, 1987

1. Introduction

'Ah, you want me to tell you things like "I was born in El-Biar in the suburbs of Algiers in a petit-bourgeois Jewish family which was assimilated but . . ." Is this really necessary? I just couldn't do it, you'll have to help me.'[1] Thus Jacques Derrida in an interview for *Le Nouvel Observateur,* attempting to head off the usual questions about childhood and 'personal background'. In fact the interview was conducted in 1982, just a few months after Derrida's arrest in Czechoslovakia on a trumped-up charge of possessing drugs. While in Prague he had participated in an 'unofficial' seminar, visited Kafka's grave and worked on a paper whose title — 'Before the Law' — took on a certain retrospective irony.[2] Derrida obligingly recounts these events, but not for their newsworthy or anecdotal value. What he finds most perplexing in this sad episode is the fact that it simply doesn't bear narrating in the way his interviewers want him to describe it. 'What am I supposed to say? "You know, I have raised certain questions relative to the state, the substructure, and the function of discourse as it concerns the rights of man today"? Or, rather: "The essential thing is what is being discussed over there, in this forbidden seminar, on the political question of the 'subject' and other familiar issues"? Or, even: "What I really underwent over there would demand other forms of narration, another poetics than that of the 12.45 news"?'[3] His experience in Prague is no more 'relevant' to an understanding of his work than it is to learn, for instance, that one of Derrida's earliest, most haunting memories was his sense of extreme isolation as the child of a largely 'assimilated' Jewish family during a time of mounting persecution and racial violence. Such facts are important but not in the sense that they 'explain' what Derrida has subsequently written. His Jewishness, his sense of

11

belonging to a marginal, dispossessed culture — these were undoubtedly formative influences and may therefore be placed on record. Indeed, one of Derrida's chief concerns is to break down that rigid demarcation of realms which holds that 'philosophy' is an autonomous discipline, a pursuit of timeless, self-validating truths, having nothing to do with politics and everyday experience. But these influences cannot be simply read off from Derrida's texts as so many 'themes' or motivating factors. They only become relevant to his *writing* insofar as they take the form of a relentless interrogation of philosophy by one who — for whatever reason — shares rather few of philosophy's traditional beliefs. Hence Derrida's reluctance to supply that familiar kind of background information which relates 'life' to 'work' through a presupposed logic of one-way causal influence.

Still it may be useful — with these caveats in mind — to review the main facts of Derrida's career. Born in 1930, he achieved his baccalavreate, went to France as a nineteen-year-old student and then chanced to hear a broadcast about Camus, which led to his enrolling for philosophy classes at the École Normale. The main early 'influence' was Sartre, though in retrospect Derrida is puzzled to explain how anyone who was *wrong* on so many issues — for instance, in his readings of Hegel, Husserl, Heidegger — could nonetheless achieve such extraordinary prominence as the intellectual conscience of his age. By 1957 Derrida was planning a state doctorate whose title — 'The Ideality of the Literary Object' — later struck him as decidedly strange. In fact this work was never completed, and it was not until 1980 that Derrida conducted his 'thesis defence', based on published writings that included *Speech and Phenomena, Writing and Difference, Of Grammatology* and other texts. In the published version of this oral defence ('The Time of a Thesis: Punctuations') Derrida explains some of his reasons for not having completed the original project. Crucially, it was the intensive reading of Husserl that led him to perceive certain problems in the way of phenomenological enquiry, problems which had to do with writing, inscription and what might be called the 'literary' aspects of philosophy. Such issues could scarcely be raised, let alone resolved, in the style and form of a doctoral thesis. On the one hand they resulted in Derrida's book-length Introduction to Husserl's essay *The Origin of Geometry,* where he identifies the 'unthought axiomatics' of Husserlian method in its recourse to various *irreducible* metaphors of writing and graphic transmission. Here he was advancing a philosophical case, though one decidedly at odds with the orthodox interpretation of Husserl's project. But on the other hand this emphasis on writing led Derrida to question the founding assumptions of philosophical discourse. 'For I have to remind you [his jury of examiners], somewhat bluntly and simply, that my most constant interest, coming before even my philosophical interest I should say, if this is possible, has been directed towards literature, towards that writing which is called literary.'[4] And this — one might conjecture — was yet another obstacle to his completing any work which took as its eminently *philosophical* theme the 'ideality' of the literary text.

The reception of Derrida's work since then might seem to provide a striking confirmation of this estimate. It was a paper he gave in 1966 at a conference organized by Johns Hopkins University that marked the emergence of 'literary' deconstruction as a force in American criticism. Since then Derrida has divided his time between teaching in Paris and the United States, as well as collaborating with American translators in the production of numerous texts. In 'The Time of a Thesis' he refers to 'deconstruction' as a 'word whose fortunes have disagreeably surprised me' (p. 44). Those fortunes have certainly been more bound up with literary criticism than with philosophy, at least in the current (institutional) sense of those terms. One result has been the refusal by many philosophers in the mainstream Anglo-American tradition to take Derrida seriously, or to read his texts with anything like the requisite care and attention.

Meanwhile, Derrida's 'philosophical' interests — and the main focus of his teaching activity in France — have moved toward the wider political bearings of what might be called 'applied deconstruction'. He is closely involved with GREPH (Groupe de Recherches sur l'Enseignement Philosophique), a collective set up to examine the ways in which philosophy has been taught in the French school and university system, and the various institutional pressures that have shaped its curricular role.[5] In part this research is an effort to demystify philosophy, to show how it has developed, especially since Kant and Hegel, in a complex relation to the structures of official (state-sponsored) discourse. But it is also a defence of philosophical teaching, specifically in the face of proposals to remove it from the range of subjects available to students in the final-year *lycée* class. GREPH has set out to challenge the idea that younger pupils are incapable of thinking philosophically; that there is an age-barrier which makes it a less-than-suitable discipline for those still at school. Authority flows from the possessor of knowledge to the one who is of an age to receive that knowledge, being neither too young ('immature') nor too old (and thus beyond reach of proper instruction). Inscribed in this scene is a politics of learning and of cultural transmission which Derrida and his colleagues find everywhere implicit in the texts of philosophy, from Plato to the present. Deconstructing those texts is therefore an activity which calls into question some of the basic ideas and beliefs that legitimize current institutional forms of knowledge.

In 'The Time of a Thesis' Derrida gives this as one more reason for his not having taken the usual path of academic preferment. That his work has been *marginal* to the dominant concerns of present-day philosophy – consciously and strategically so – is a fact he scarcely wishes to deny. Deconstruction is *not*, he says, 'primarily a matter of philosophical contents, themes or theses, philosophemes, poems, theologemes or ideologemes, but especially and inseparably [of] meaningful frames, institutional structures, pedagogical or rhetorical norms, the possibilities of law, of authority, of representation in terms of its very market' (pp. 44-5). In the course of this sentence Derrida effectively repudiates just about everything that has been carried on in the name of 'deconstruction' by his various exegetes and disciples. Above all it seems intended as a distancing gesture with regard to the massive *institutional* success of deconstructive criticism in American departments of English and Comparative Literature.

That he should now figure as an addition to the Modern Masters series is yet another irony of Derrida's ascent to intellectual stardom. No philosopher has done more to disown the idea that his writings embody some kind of masterly or authoritative wisdom. And the irony is compounded by the fact that Derrida goes out of his way to resist any kind of adequate treatment in a book like this. Take the word *différance*, a neologism that Derrida coined in order to suggest how meaning is at once 'differential' and 'deferred', the product of a restless play within language that cannot be fixed or pinned down for the purposes of conceptual definition.[6] It is a cardinal precept of modern (structural) linguistics that signs don't have meaning in and of themselves, but by virtue of their occupying a distinctive place within the systematic network of contrasts and differences which make up any given language. And this picture is complicated, in Derrida's view, by the fact that meaning is nowhere punctually *present* in language, that it is always subject to a kind of semantic slippage (or deferral) which prevents the sign from ever (so to speak) coinciding with itself in a moment of perfect, remainderless grasp. In French, the anomalous *a* of *différance* registers only in the written form of the word, since when spoken it cannot be distinguished from the commonplace, received spelling. And this is precisely what Derrida intends: that *différance* should function not as a concept, not as a word whose meaning could be finally 'booked into the present', but as one set of marks in a signifying chain which exceeds and disturbs the classical economy of language and representation.

To explain *différance* like this is already to lift it out of Derrida's text – where it is given very specific work to do – and treat it as a species of key-word or master concept. The term is most frequently deployed in *Speech and Phenomena* (1967) where it marks the point of encounter between Husserlian phenomenology (the dream of self-present, intelligible meaning) and a radically structuralist account of the sign which challenges Husserl's most basic premises. In short, *différance* is the upshot of a long and meticulous process of argument, such that it cannot (or should not) be wrenched out of context for the purposes of ad hoc definition. This is why Derrida insists that there is no substitute for the hard work of reading and re-reading texts (his own texts included); that it is pointless to ask what

15

différance means, or indeed what 'deconstruction' amounts to, unless one is prepared (in every sense of the phrase) to find out the difficult way. On the one hand this involves an adequate grasp of the complex philosophical background to Derrida's writings. On the other it demands that his texts be read with uncommon attentiveness to those features – too loosely termed 'stylistic' or 'literary' – that mark their distance from received philosophical tradition.

Anyone who writes about Derrida must be uncomfortably aware that such warning preambles easily reduce to a species of pious self-deception. Richard Rorty has made the point in his recent essay 'Deconstruction and Circumvention'.[7] Perhaps it is possible, as Derrida suggests, to work with terms like *différance* whose non-self-identical play of sense prevents them from rejoining the 'logocentric' order of Western metaphysics. Such terms will then be thought of as permanently 'under erasure' (*sous rature*), deployed on the page for tactical reasons but subject to a dislocating textual force that denies them any kind of semantic or conceptual stability. But in Rorty's view these tactics must finally become self-defeating. Perhaps *différance* had no definite, assignable sense when it first came to light as an offbeat neologism in the texts of one Jacques Derrida. But now, as Rorty says, there is little hope of tenure for any bright young theorist who can't come up with a handy definition of *différance*. The mere fact of its belonging to a shared language – at no matter what rarefied level of discourse – is enough to give the word a certain conceptual currency. And the same would apply to all those other deconstructive key-terms – 'supplement', 'pharmakon', 'writing' etc. – whose role in Derrida's arguments will occupy a major part of this book.

Rorty has a strong point here, but one that Derrida himself concedes on numerous occasions. It is only possible to criticize existing institutions from *within* an inherited language, a discourse that will always have been worked over in advance by traditional concepts and categories. What is required is a kind of internal distancing, an effort of defamiliarization which prevents those concepts from settling down into routine habits of thought. 'In literature, for example, philosophical language is still present in some sense; but it produces and presents itself as alienated from itself, at a remove, at a distance . . . it was my preoccupation with literary texts which enabled me to discern the problematics of writing as one of the key factors in the deconstruction of metaphysics.'[8] But this is *not* to argue – as Rorty would have it – that we simply collapse the difference between philosophy and literature, since they are both 'kinds of writing' with nothing to distinguish them in point of method or legitimate concern. Rather, it requires that one should follow as closely as possible that process of mutual interrogative exchange which Derrida has conducted from his earliest texts to his latest, more overtly 'literary' productions. So – without wishing to draw immodest comparisons – I would suggest that this book be treated much as Wittgenstein proposed at the end of his *Tractatus*: as a ladder to be unceremoniously kicked away once it has served its purpose.

2. Philosophy/Literature

Any attempt to define 'deconstruction' must soon run up against the many and varied obstacles that Derrida has shrewdly placed in its path. To begin with, at least, one can perhaps best proceed by way of a series of negative descriptions. Deconstruction is *not*, he insists, either a 'method', a 'technique' or a species of 'critique'. Nor does it have anything to do with textual 'interpretation', of the kind developed to a high pitch of subtlety and refinement by literary critics from Coleridge to Eliot and beyond. Certainly it has tended to take one or another of these forms when applied by disciples of Derrida who have found in deconstruction a useful means of saying new things about literary texts. Sometimes Derrida disclaims all responsibility for such misreadings, regarding them as a kind of *déformation professionelle*, the result of grafting deconstruction on to an activity (that of literary criticism) with its own very specific needs and requirements. This would then be a case of that powerful institutional pressure that works to domesticate new ideas and reduce them to the stock-in-trade of a seasonal academic novelty. Elsewhere Derrida is more tolerant of this so-called 'American deconstruction'. It has grown up, he remarks, in a very specific cultural context, one that includes both American literature (especially in its complex relation to European Romanticism) and the history and varieties of American religious experience.[1] These factors he has no wish to analyse in any great depth. But they do suggest reasons, Derrida thinks, why 'deconstruction in America' should have assumed a form distinctly alien to his own interests and preoccupations.

Let us pursue this *via negativa* and ask more specifically just why deconstruction is neither 'method' on the one hand nor 'interpretation' on the other. In fact it is not too difficult to come up with a concise formula that would make it sound very much like a 'method' and yet describe quite accurately some of Derrida's most typical deconstructive moves. What these consist in, very briefly, is the dismantling of conceptual oppositions, the taking apart of hierarchical systems of thought which can then be *reinscribed* within a different order of textual signification. Or again: deconstruction is the vigilant seeking-out of those 'aporias', blindspots or moments of self-contradiction where a text involuntarily betrays the tension between rhetoric and logic, between what it manifestly *means to say* and what it is nonetheless *constrained to mean*. To 'deconstruct' a piece of writing is therefore to operate a kind of strategic reversal, seizing on precisely those unregarded details (casual metaphors, footnotes, incidental turns of argument) which are always, and necessarily, passed over by interpreters of a more orthodox persuasion. For it is here, in the margins of the text − the 'margins', that is, as defined by a powerful normative consensus − that deconstruction discovers those same unsettling forces at work. So there is at least a certain *prima facie* case for the claim that deconstruction is a 'method' of reading with its own specific rules and protocols. And indeed, as we shall see, the above brief account of Derrida's deconstructive strategy does provide at least a fair working notion of what goes on in his texts.

Nevertheless Derrida has good reason for resisting any attempt, on the part of his disciples and commentators, to reduce deconstruction to a *concept* definable in terms of method or technique. For it is precisely this idea − this assumption that meaning can always be grasped in the form of some proper, self-identical concept − that Derrida is most determinedly out to deconstruct. The issue is stated concisely in his recent 'Letter to a Japanese Friend' concerning certain cardinal problems of translation. Could Derrida suggest at least some approximate definitional equivalents for his usage of the term 'deconstruction'? To which he responds: 'All sentences of the type "deconstruction is X" or "deconstruction is not X", *a priori*, miss the point, which is to say that they are at least false. As you know, one of the principal things at stake in what is called in my texts "deconstruction", is precisely the delimiting of ontology and above all

of the third-person present indicative: S is P.'[2] The full implications of this passage would need a good deal of unpacking. For
the moment, however, its point can be drawn quite simply. To
think of deconstruction as a 'method' is to pull it back into the
orbit of those traditional concepts and categories which (as
Derrida argues) have organized the discourse of Western reason
from the time of its ancient Greek inception. It is to set aside the
detailed and specific *activity* of deconstructive reading in favour
of a generalized *idea* of that activity, an idea assumed to
comprehend all its differences of local application.

In which case one might expect that Derrida's vigilant scepticism as regards deconstructive 'method' would lead him to
embrace precisely that form of wholesale interpretative freedom
that marks the absence of methodical constraints by throwing
off every last vestige of critical rigour. Certainly this is how
Derrida has been read by those (mainly American) admirers who
find in deconstruction a welcome pretext for breaking with 'old'
New Critical ideas of hermeneutic tact and decorum. Nor can
this response be written off simply as a case of wilful misappro-
priation, since there are indeed texts of Derrida – mainly those
written with a view to translation for American readers – which
exploit such a rhetoric of 'freeplay' and limitless interpretative
licence. But to take those texts at face value is, I shall argue,
nonetheless a failure to engage fully and responsibly with
Derrida's arguments. What such readings have to ignore is the
rigorous *work* of deconstruction that occupies the other, more
substantial and significant portion of his work. This may have
the ultimate effect of undermining – or rendering intensely
problematic – most of what passes for 'rigorous' thought in
philosophy and literary theory alike. But this effect is not
achieved by dispensing with the protocols of detailed, meticulous argument, or by simply abandoning the conceptual ground
on which such arguments have hitherto been conducted. To treat
deconstruction as an open invitation to new and more adventurous forms of interpretative criticism is clearly to mistake whatever is most distinctive and demanding in Derrida's texts.[3]

It is important to make these points at the outset, since there is
a widespread notion – among philosophers especially – that

Derrida is some kind of mischievous latter-day sophist bent upon reducing every discipline of thought to a species of rhetorical play. Certainly he argues that philosophy is prone — peculiarly prone — to repress or to sublimate its own written character; that in some sense the 'philosopher' may even be *defined* as the one who habitually forgets that s/he is writing. In *Of Grammatology* Derrida traces the history and the logic of this repression, from its ancient Greek roots to its latest show-ings in Husserl, Saussure and Lévi-Strauss. And the effect is not simply to rehabilitate writing as against the superior truth-claims of speech, but also — through a deconstructive logic of reversal — to insist that all thinking about language, philosophy and culture must henceforth be conceived within the context of a massively extended 'writing'. Of course I shall return to this text later on and explain in more detail how Derrida arrives at these seemingly exorbitant claims. For the moment what I want to make clear is that Derrida's stress on textuality and writing is *not* in any sense a break with philosophy, or a declaration of interpretative freedoms hitherto undreamt under the grim rep-ressive law of conceptual clarity and truth. That this impression is so widespread is partly the result of philosophers' having shown little willingness to *read* Derrida but an uncommon zeal to denounce him on the strength of second-hand acquaintance with his work. But it also has to do with that desire among literary critics to annex deconstruction as a kind of anti-philosophy, a justification (as they see it) for rejecting the superior truth-claims of philosophers from Plato to the present day. Hence their strongly marked preference for those texts where the deconstructive groundwork (so to speak) is very largely taken as read, and where Derrida most thoroughly exploits the resultant opportunities for experiments in style.

All the same it would be simplifying matters very grossly to suggest any hard-and-fast distinction between the rigorous ('phi-losophical') and non-rigorous ('literary') forms of deconstructive activity. As we shall see, Derrida has often seized upon just this kind of entrenched opposition in order to demonstrate how deep and far-reaching are the prejudices ranged behind it. I should therefore be striking a slightly absurd posture if I insisted on

21

reading his texts against what is manifestly one of their key
strategies. But the fact remains that Derrida has been widely
misunderstood on account of that opposite simplification which
sets him up as a crafty rhetorician with not the least regard for
'philosophic' protocols of reason and truth. So it is a part of my
purpose in this book to redress the damagingly one-sided
'reading' of Derrida that has gained wide credit among disciples
and opponents alike. Put simply, I am more interested in the
philosophical consequences of deconstruction than in its current
high prestige among literary critics. This is *not* to ignore what
Derrida has shown to such striking effect: that all attempts to
keep philosophy separate from literature – to maintain it as a
privileged, truth-speaking discourse, immune from the vagaries
of writing – are bound to run up against the salient fact of their
own textual constitution. Rather, it is to insist that any adequate
reading of Derrida will have to go by way of that prolonged,
meticulous encounter with the texts of philosophy that has
brought him to the point of suspending (not annulling) such
time-honoured distinctions.

Derrida has an essay on Paul Valéry (in *Margins of Philosophy*) that may help to clarify these issues. For Valéry remarkably
anticipated Derrida in conceiving of philosophy as a 'kind of
writing', and as that particular kind, what's more, that habitually sought to efface or dissemble its own written character. So it
is predictable that Derrida should read him as an elective
precursor, a deconstructionist *avant la lettre,* one whose scrupulous meditations on poetry and language led him to the point of
formulating some of Derrida's cardinal insights. And indeed this
is the gist of Derrida's essay so long as one reads it with an eye to
the more familiar landmarks. Thus according to Valéry, 'we can
easily observe that philosophy as defined by its product, which is
in writing, is objectively a particular branch of literature . . . we
are forced to assign it a place not far from poetry' (quoted by
Derrida in *Margins*, p. 294). And the essay goes on to cite
Valéry's equally prescient remarks on the pervasiveness of
figural language in philosophy, the effects of uncontrolled
semantic slippage and the ways in which philosophic *concepts* –
the very touchstones of intellectual rigour and truth – are often

found to rest on buried or forgotten metaphors. Most striking of all is Valéry's insistence on the sheer impossibility of grounding knowledge and truth in that idea of authentic, self-present awareness achieved by the speaking subject. 'The strongest of them [philosophers] have worn themselves out in the effort to *make their thoughts speak* . . . Whatever the words may be — Ideas or Being or Noumenon or Cogito or Ego — they are all *ciphers*, the meaning of which is determined solely by the context . . .' (quoted in *Margins*, p. 292). This passage from Valéry makes precisely the point that Derrida will make in his deconstructive readings of the 'logocentric' bias that inhabits our thinking about mind, language and reality. The assumed priority of speech over writing goes along with the idea of a pure, self-authenticating knowledge, such that the intrusion of written signs — mere arbitrary marks upon a page — could only represent a deplorable swerve from truth. It is in the face of this deep-grained metaphysical prejudice that Valéry, like Derrida, asserts the ubiquity of writing and the fact that philosophy is simply *unthinkable* outside this encompassing textual domain.

Up to this point, Derrida's reading of Valéry appears to fit in well enough with the currently prevailing view of deconstruction as literature's revenge upon philosophy. For it is the poet in Valéry — most refined and self-conscious of verbal artificers — who asks us to read philosophical texts with an eye to their formal or stylistic attributes. But it is here precisely that Derrida enters his characteristic cautionary note. Has not Valéry simply *turned the tables* on philosophy by treating it as just another kind of literature, reading it in the light of his own ultra-refined post-symbolist aesthetic and ignoring whatever escapes or resists that account? 'I said one day before philosophers: philosophy is an affair of form.' Thus Valéry, with Derrida's (at this stage) provisional agreement. But to think of philosophy as *exclusively* an 'affair of form' — or of style, poetic diction or other such 'literary' qualities — is in truth not to think about philosophy at all, but to refuse it in the name of an all-embracing literature. And here we can perhaps see the point of Derrida's repeated insistence: that deconstruction should not be content simply to *invert* certain cardinal oppositions (speech/writing, philosophy/

literature) so as to leave the 'inferior' term henceforth firmly established on top. For this is nothing more than a notional gesture, a reversal that leaves the opposition still very much in place without beginning to shift the conceptual ground wherein its foundations are securely laid. Valéry pitches the claims of a 'literature' (conceived in the purest of formalist terms) against those of a 'philosophy' likewise treated as some kind of uniform adversary discourse. He thus fails to take the further, decisive step that would question these self-sufficient concepts ('philosophy' and 'literature'), explore their mutual crossings and involvements, but *not* simply collapse the one into the other by denying everything specific to the discourse of philosophic reason and critique.

There are two passages from Derrida's essay on Valéry that I shall now quote at length because they help to locate this crucial shift of emphasis. The first describes the way that philosophical writings would need to be read if treated in accordance with Valéry's programme for a full-scale poetics of the genre. 'A task is then prescribed: to study the philosophical text in its formal structure, in its rhetorical organization, in the specificity and diversity of its textual types . . . drawing upon the reserves of a language, cultivating, forcing, or making deviate a set of tropic [metaphorical] resources older than philosophy itself' (*Margins*, p. 293). At the end of such a reading, philosophy would stand revealed as *nothing more* than a 'particular literary genre', shorn of its grandiose truth-claims and henceforth received – unresistingly absorbed – into the field of a generalized poetics. As I have said, there is an aspect of Derridean deconstruction – predominant in certain of his texts – that would seem to go all the way with this distinctly one-sided gesture. But the second passage from his essay on Valéry insists on a further, complicating stage in the argument, one that would respect the particular demands of philosophical writing and not take refuge in a literary formalism naively opposed to 'philosophy' as such. 'This elaboration would pass through the re-reading of all these texts [those of Valéry himself and the philosophers he thinks to have played off the field] . . . It demands that one become engaged in it without endlessly circling round the form of these texts, that

one decipher the law of their internal conflicts, of their heterogeneity, of their contradictions, and that one not simply cast an
aesthete's glance over philosophical discourse . . .' (*Margins*, p.
305). The terms in which this passage argues its way – 'law',
'conflicts', 'contradictions', 'heterogeneity' – belong to *philosophy* insofar as they implicitly invoke its normative standards of
logic, consistency and the 'law' of non-contradiction. Elsewhere
Derrida may deny these standards any absolute or binding force,
and suggest (after Nietzsche) that their authority rests upon our
not perceiving the extent and the dissimulating power of certain
root metaphors raised into concepts. But in the present instance
there can be no doubt that Derrida is turning philosophy's
conceptual resources back against a premature move to annul
them in the name of a thoroughgoing 'literary' formalism. And
this same double gesture is repeated every time that Derrida
detects the simplifying strategies of a 'deconstruction' that
would thus avoid the rigours of thinking through its own
problematical status *vis-à-vis* philosophy.

This brief account of Derrida on Valéry may help to focus
some of the difficulties involved in defining what precisely such
deconstructive 'rigour' might entail. Certainly it has a good deal
in common with Valéry's meticulous attention to poetic forms
and devices, his insistence that philosophy (and thinking in
general) cannot be conducted at full self-critical stretch without
the kind of disciplined awareness that poets bring to language.
Hence the many passages in Derrida that effectively reproach
philosophers for not having read the central texts of their
tradition with an adequate sense of their full rhetorical complexity. What is called for is a 'prudent, differentiated, slow,
stratified' reading (*Dissemination*, p. 33), one that takes account
of certain 'literary' refinements probably more familiar to critics
than philosophers. But with each of these adjectives Derrida
insists that deconstruction keep its eye on the specific *differences*
of logic and sense that mark off one text from another, and
which also demand some answering awareness of generic distinctions on the reader's part. Texts are 'stratified' in the sense
that they bear along with them a whole network of articulated
themes and assumptions whose meaning everywhere links up

with other texts, other genres or topics of discourse. This is what Derrida calls the 'disseminating' force always at work within language, written or spoken. It is enough (he argues) to disqualify any reading that would confine its attentions to 'philosophy' or 'literature' and seek to close off all contaminating influences from outside its own subject-domain. Writing, in short, is *intertextual* through and through. But this should not be taken as a licence for that other kind of wholesale 'intertextuality' that rejoices in simply riding roughshod over all such generic distinctions. For it is precisely this 'stratified' character of language — the fact that it has been endlessly worked over by *specific* genealogies and logics of sense — which now demands such a corresponding effort of 'prudent, slow, differentiated' reading. And among those traces, as Derrida argues, are the various 'philosophemes', or ways of thinking which by now have impressed themselves so deeply on our language that we take them as commonsense truths and forget their specific (philosophical) prehistory.

This is why Derrida holds out against the move to dissolve 'philosophy' as a discipline of thought and open it up to a henceforth unlimited intertextuality. His reasons are given most clearly in a recent interview where the question is posed: 'Would you count yourself a philosopher above all else?' Derrida's response is carefully nuanced but not, I think, in the least evasive. 'I have attempted more and more systematically to find a non-site, or a non-philosophical site, from which to question philosophy. But the search for a non-philosophical site does not bespeak an anti-philosophical attitude. My central question is: how can philosophy as such appear to itself as other than itself, so that it can interrogate and reflect upon itself in an original manner?'[4] And he goes on to justify this double stance, not only in terms of what might be called its 'technical' viability, but also on account of its power to effect real changes in the present institutional structures of power, knowledge and politics. I shall have more to say about these claims for deconstruction as a form of ideological critique. For now it suffices to remark that Derrida thinks of philosophy, not only as a site of institutional struggle, but also as a highly specific discipline of thought whose central texts may indeed be 'deconstructed' but *not* given up to any kind of intertextual or undifferentiated 'freeplay'.

What I have written so far has been intended partly as a brief introduction to Derrida's work, and partly as a means of forewarning the reader that this book has its own case to argue. There would not be much point in just summarizing Derrida's ideas, especially in view of his repeated insistence that decon-struction is a *process*, an activity of reading, irreducible to concept or method. On the other hand there are, of course, restrictions to be reckoned with, including a tight limitation on length and the need to make this book accessible to readers with no very wide or specialized knowledge of recent Continental philosophy. So I have combined passages of detailed close-reading with others that mix exposition and critique in more or less equal proportions. And this is not just a matter of tailoring my approach to the general series format. As I have argued already – and will argue again – deconstruction is ill-served by those zealots of a limitless textual 'freeplay' who reject the very notions of rigorous thinking or conceptual critique. It is a premise of this book that the central issues of deconstruction can be set forth and defended in such a way as to engage the serious interest of philosophers in the 'other', Anglo-American or analy-tical tradition. To be sure, it would take a fairly drastic shift of attitude on the part of that tradition if Derrida's texts were to enter the mainstream of debate. But to clear away just a few of the deep-seated prejudices which have so far prevented this encounter is an effort well worth making.

3. Derrida on Plato: Writing as Poison and Cure

A good place to start is with 'Plato's Pharmacy', the reading of Plato's dialogue the *Phaedrus* which occupies Derrida for some hundred pages of closely argued textual and analytic commentary.[1] It is an obvious jumping-off point for several connected reasons. First, because Derrida is here engaged with something like a mythic inaugural moment in the 'logocentric' epoch whose effects (as he argues) reach down from Plato to the present day. To put it this way is to fall back on a simplifying shorthand, since Derrida expressly avoids such talk of origins, regarding it as closely bound up with that same metaphysical mystique. Nevertheless, it is in Plato – and in the *Phaedrus* most strikingly – that Derrida discovers a certain prototypical scene of instruction, one that concerns the priority of speech over writing and the dangers (philosophical, moral and political) of thinking to invert that priority. Then again, this is of all Derrida's essays the most challenging to traditional philosophy and scholarship in its rigorous protocols of argument, its detailed attention to the text and its close engagement with other, more orthodox readings. Derrida is not simply out to provide a brilliant new interpretation of Plato's dialogue. Nor is he attempting to confound the philosophers with a 'literary' reading that ignores the plain drift of Plato's argument and delights in discovering odd turns of metaphor. On the contrary, it is those others – the mainstream interpreters – who have often found the *Phaedrus* an ill-constructed dialogue, especially when it comes to Plato's mythical excursion into the origins and dangers of writing.[2] Had they but read more attentively, Derrida suggests, then they would have seen not only how this episode fits in with the local context of argument, but also how it follows *of necessity* from Plato's governing system of assumptions.

This might be called the 'principle of charity' at work in Derrida's reading. With the *Phaedrus*, it is a matter of choosing between two possible lines of approach, the one apologetic (explaining or excusing certain 'faults' of construction), the other assuming a far greater likelihood that the text will make sense — albeit problematical sense — through a reading sufficiently alert to its complicated tensions of logic and rhetoric. It is this latter possibility that Derrida holds to, at the outset as a kind of working faith, but then increasingly on a basis of demonstrative argument. 'The hypothesis of a rigorous, sure, and subtle form is naturally more fertile '(*Dissemination*, p. 67). That is to say, it is a better, more productive starting-point than the various hypotheses advanced by scholars who seek to excuse Plato's apparently loose or digressive sequence of topics. Thus tradition once held that the *Phaedrus* was his first extended attempt at the dialogue form, and should therefore be judged by standards fitting to a piece of apprentice-work. Later there developed an odd counter-argument: that the *Phaedrus* was in fact a product of Plato's last years, so that commentators should not be surprised if it manifested symptoms of failing narrative or organizational powers. And so a modern scholar is able to pronounce, with an air of invincible logic, that 'the inability to accomplish what has been well conceived is precisely a proof of old age' (quoted in *Dissemination*, p. 67). The perfect circularity of reasoning here is what Derrida proposes to break by assuming that Plato's text has a 'rigour', a 'sureness' and a 'subtlety' of organization somehow invisible to orthodox commentators.

Some major points emerge from this contest of readings. For one thing, it raises the question of philosophical *maturity*, of the age at which educated minds are supposed to complete their juvenile period of apprenticeship and take upon themselves the genuine, self-authorized quest for wisdom and truth. And conversely, there is the notion that this period has a definite end-point, that maturity is distinguished from incipient second childhood precisely by exhibiting proper respect for what *counts* as a well-formed philosophical argument. And these assumptions are connected in turn with the various ideas about teaching philosophy — where, how, by whom and to whom, at what 'proper' age and through what 'proper' kinds of teacher-pupil relationship — that Derrida and his associates in GREPH have recently set out to analyse.[3] For there exist close links between the truth-claims of philosophy and the complex, hierarchical framework of instruction by which those claims are preserved, transmitted and (on rare occasions) exposed to a reading which unsettles their age-old complicity. Central to this handing-down of tradition is the idea of philosophy as an access to truths whose authority derives from that privileged relationship between teacher and good, receptive student. And the pattern thus established is a form of patriarchal inheritance, a situation where the father retains full powers until the son comes of age and is able to exercise reason on his own behalf. It is in Hegel's writings on philosophy, education, the family and the state that Derrida finds these principles most clearly expounded. But they are also present — as we shall now see — in that otherwise diversionary episode from the *Phaedrus* where Plato resorts to an exotic mythology in order to explain why writing threatens the interests of morality and truth.

The myth in question tells of the Egyptian King Thamus, to whom there comes a visitor, a god named Thoth (or Theuth), believed to have invented — among other things — the arts of geometry, mathematics, astronomy and writing. Thoth makes the offer of writing as a gift to King Thamus, but the latter, having weighed up its virtues and vices, decides that man is better off *without* writing and therefore firmly declines the offer. His reasons (to which Plato evidently subscribes) are set forth in detail through the King's considered response. Writing is a dangerous gift because it substitutes mere inscriptions — alien, arbitrary, lifeless signs — for the authentic living presence of spoken language. It may be in some sense a cultural advance, since with it mankind can build up a documentary archive, a written 'memory' far in excess of any oral tradition. But again there is a danger lurking within this apparently beneficent invention. For with the access to writing, says the King, men's *real* powers of memory will rapidly decline, since they will no longer need to *remember* anything at all — inwardly and actively get it by heart — when they can simply look things up on

demand. And from this particular evil flow others more grave
and far-reaching. 'Thanks to you and your invention, your
pupils will be widely read without benefit of a teacher's instruction' (quoted in *Dissemination*, p. 102). The effect of writing
will thus be to break those peculiar ties − of paternal sanction
on the one side and filial obligation on the other − that serve to
ensure the passage of authentic truth from each generation to the
next. For it is only by respecting the authority vested in the
teacher, an authority achieved through mature self-knowledge
and *not* just acquired by reading other men's books, that the
pupil can arrive at genuine wisdom on his own account.

What is in question here is the crucial difference, as Derrida
phrases it, between 'knowledge as memory and non-knowledge
as rememoration' (p. 135). The one (good) kind of memory is
that to which Plato applies the word *anamnesis*. It involves,
literally, an act of 'unforgetting', a recollection of spiritual truths
which the soul has forgotten in its fallen state, its confinement to
the prison-house of the senses, but which can still be summoned
to mind through wise teaching and the disciplines of self-
knowledge. The other (bad) kind of memory is the kind that
substitutes mnemonic devices for genuine, living wisdom; that
simulates knowledge by a crafty resort to the short-cut remedy
of writing. King Thamus (like Ammon, the supreme God whose
earthly representative he is) has of course no need to compromp-
ise his state by adopting such dangerous expedients. 'He speaks,
he says, he dictates, and his word suffices' (p. 76). And in this
respect, Egyptian mythology agrees with that other, Judaeo-
Christian account of God's creating word and the power of the
logos to manifest itself directly in thought-made-deed. In *Of
Grammatology,* Derrida cites numerous instances of this
logocentric will to devalue written language in contrast to the
natural, the authentic or spontaneous nature of self-present
speech. 'The letter killeth, but the spirit giveth life.' Such
statements may be found (as Derrida records in *Of Grammatology*) across a quite extraordinary range of the world's religions
and systems of thought. And this is no coincidence, he argues,
any more than it is by chance or through the absence of a
'logical' groundplan that Plato introduces the topos of writing

and the legend of Thoth and Thamus. What is at work in these instances is a rigorous logic of exclusion, a logic determined by the need to protect the sovereign claims of truth against the bad, degenerate effects of writing.

Scholars have gone various long ways around to explain why Plato should have had recourse to that curious episode from Egyptian mythology. Its presence is all the more unsettling for the fact that Plato mostly treated myths as an inferior kind of cultural production, useful (the best of them) for teaching simple lessons to ignorant minds, but otherwise totally unsuited for the purposes of genuine enlightenment. The contest between *mythos* and *logos* is commonly seen as one of the great transitional stages in the evolution of Greek thought and culture. It is dramatized in Plato's writing through the various set-piece dialectical encounters where Socrates — voice of reason and truth — comes up against the sophists, poets, rhetoricians and other such purveyors of a false wisdom. Mythology stands condemned because it rests on a credulous appeal to mere fables and second-hand legends, rather than following the true path of knowledge represented by Socratic reasoning. The dialogues are always so constructed as to give the last word to Socrates, since he — Plato's master and guide in the ways of dialectical argument — has the power to demonstrate reason properly and actively at work. Thus Socrates is able to convict his opponents of not really *knowing* what they claim to know; of putting forward various plausible truth-claims without the least substance of authentic wisdom. The retailers of mythology are guilty of this, because they merely repeat whatever fabulous events come down from tradition or happen to catch the public fancy. The sophists show up in a yet worse light, since (as Socrates argues) they rely on mere rhetoric and persuasive skills to impose upon ill-trained vulgar minds. But it is *writing* again — if one pursues this case to its logical conclusion — that most easily enables such frauds to take place. For writing is the readiest means to acquire all those forms of unearned or gratuitous wisdom which the sophists and mythologists then pass off as the genuine goods. 'What Plato is attacking in sophistics, therefore, is not simply recourse to memory but, within such recourse, the substitution of the mnemonic device for live memory . . . the passive, mechanical "by heart" for the active reanimation of knowledge, for its reproduction in the present' (*Dissemination*, p. 108). It is through writing that the *logos* is deflected from its proper, truth-seeking aim and abandoned to a state of hazardous dependence on the vagaries of *unauthorized* transmission.

So the scholars have cause to be puzzled by Plato's resort to a *myth* about writing in order to demonstrate writing's undesirability. For writing and myth are effectively lined up on the same, bad side of that natural kinship which seems to exist between the various forms of untruth, sophistry and fraud. The response, it seems, has been either to treat this episode indulgently, as a piece of atavistic whimsy on Plato's part, or to launch into remote speculations as to whether Plato might actually have *visited* Egypt and picked up the myth at first hand. Derrida records these discussions in a series of dutiful footnotes, but his interest lies elsewhere. The 'regression' to myth is an aspect of that generalized uncertainty that overtakes Plato's arguments as soon as they touch upon the dangerous topic of writing. And this uncertainty is no mere accident, no momentary lapse or simple absent-mindedness in Plato's handling of the theme. Rather, it obeys an order of necessity inscribed in every detail of Plato's text, though an order whose logical upshot and effects are very nearly kept from view.

For the fact is − to put the case at its simplest − that Plato is *inescapably* condemned to writing, even as he seeks to denounce its effects and uphold the authority of self-present (spoken) truth. And this predicament repeats itself wherever philosophy refuses to acknowledge its own textual status and aspires to a pure contemplation of truth independent of mere written signs. Far from standing out as a mere freakish episode, Plato's treatment of writing in the *Phaedrus* sets a pattern for similar encounters down through the history of Western thought. It is this pattern that Derrida will trace so intently in the texts of that tradition, from Plato to Kant, Hegel, Husserl and other representative thinkers. If Plato is something of a special case, it is not just because his writings are in at the outset of this logocentric epoch, or because they inaugurate a certain way of thinking about language, truth and reality. Such ideas of *origin* – of an authentic first instance, thereafter subject to mere repetition – are among the effects of that same, potent mythology whose symptoms are there to be read in Plato's dialogue. Writing is preeminently the realm of repetition, of a language that mimics the true form of knowledge by exploiting the resources of a dead, mechanical notation. To think of Plato as a 'source' for such ideas is again to fall back on that loaded system of binary distinctions – speech/writing, presence/absence, origin/ supplement – which marks the discourse of logocentric reason. And indeed, it is a main part of Derrida's argument that there can be no thinking back to origins and sources, no escaping from the 'logic of supplementarity' upon which these crucial opposi- tions finally break down. As he will show in his reading of the *Phaedrus* – an exemplary but in no sense a privileged case – this desire to fix an origin for truth and knowledge must always get entangled in textual complications beyond its power to predict or control.

All the same, there is a sense in which Plato's dialogue sets itself up for deconstructive treatment in a paradigmatic way. This has to do with the presence of Socrates as master in a scene of instruction to which Plato, who obediently *writes it down,* is both admiring witness and guilty party. For there is one signal fact about Socrates which Plato can record only by acknowledg- ing his own clear failure to meet the same standards of philo- sophic probity and truth. Socrates (as Plato informs us) never once committed his thoughts to writing, and could thus maintain an authority proof against the risks of textual misadventure. It was Plato to whom there fell the dubious honour of preserving his teacher's wisdom, and that by the only means available: by faithfully transcribing the dialogues. So there is, one could say, a *prima facie* case for suspecting that Plato's stance on this question will manifest signs of perplexity and doubt. But it is not just a matter of pointing out the logical inconsistency or sheer bad faith of Plato's arguments. What is required of a genuinely deconstructive reading is the patient, meticulous working- through of those cardinal oppositions which define the very nature and limits of Plato's thought. And this will entail, as Derrida writes, a 'slipping away' from all received models of textual commentary or interpretation. It will involve a certain violence to the text, but a violence that comes not so much from 'outside' − from a reading bent upon its own perverse design − but rather from within the text itself, in those strains and contortions of sense that characterize its language. For this latter opposition ('inside'/'outside') belongs once again to a larger system which includes, among its main philosophical supports, the exclusion of writing from a proper, self-sufficient speech.

We must now look more closely at the detailed operations of this strategy in Derrida's reading. What he reveals is a failure of the text to *achieve* what its arguments expressly require: the priority of speech, *logos* and presence over writing, sophistics and everything opposed to the truth-claims of Socratic reason. This failure is inscribed throughout the *Phaedrus* in a series of metaphors and figural substitutions that prevent the dialogue from settling down into a clear-cut logic of sense, a logic that would fully comprehend or regulate its own rhetorical field. And this is not a question of simply *inverting* the received order of priorities, so that henceforth 'writing' will somehow take precedence over 'speech' and its various associated values. More than this, it involves the dismantling of all those binary distinctions that organize Plato's text, to the point where opposition itself − the very ground of dialectical reason − gives way to a process where opposites merge in a constant *undecidable* exchange of attributes. Thus Plato is unable to define what should count as the 'good' (philosophical) employment of language, memory, reason and so forth, without falling back, by a strange compulsion, upon metaphors drawn from writing. These metaphors are present even in the passages where Socrates 'speaks' with maximum force against the dangers of writing as a thing that contaminates the wellsprings of wisdom and truth.

There is thus a perpetual double movement in Plato's text by which positive values (speech, self-presence, living memory) are defined only by contrast to whatever threatens or invades their privileged domain. So speech is represented, not only as the opposite of writing, but as a 'good' kind of writing that is inscribed in the soul by revealed or self-authorized truth. Living memory is that which avoids the bad detour through writing (mere marks on a page), but which is still very often defined by metaphors of engraving, deciphering, inscription and other such textual figures. And it is only in terms of a *presence deferred* — of a truth that still awaits its fulfilment in speech, much like the character of writing — that Plato can explain the power of dialectics to draw the philosopher endlessly on toward a vanishing-point of ultimate wisdom. 'Only words that are deferred, reserved . . . only hidden letters can thus get Socrates moving. If a speech could be genuinely present . . . offered up in person in its truth, without the detours of a signifier foreign to it, if at the limit an undeferred *logos* were possible, it would not seduce anyone' (*Dissemination,* p. 71).

These are not (Derrida argues) just casual metaphors or incidental turns of phrase. Nor do they represent an added (but optional) range of semantic possibility, a wealth of meaning which the interpreter may choose to exploit while the scholar or philosopher can safely declare it off-limits. Rather they belong to a whole intricate system of logico-semantic links and entailments which must be taken into account by any adequate reading of the text. That such readings have not (until now) been forthcoming is a measure, not merely of the 'novelty' of deconstruction, but of the power long vested in those logocentric values and assumptions that determine what shall count as 'adequate'. Hence Derrida's counter-resolve to deconstruct the bases of that massive self-evidence that seems to decree the natural priority of speech over writing. And this means eliciting details of the text — metaphors, 'mythemes', chains of implication — which are demonstrably *there* to be read but standardly ignored on account of their 'marginal' relevance. It is what the *Phaedrus* cannot know (or explicitly acknowledge) in its own textual make-up that furnishes the materials of a deconstructive reading.

Here again, there is a curious double logic at work, a sense in which the *Phaedrus* preempts such readings precisely by defining the *written* as that which fails to achieve real knowledge. 'One thus begins by repeating without knowing — through a myth —

the definition of writing, which is to repeat without knowing. This kinship of writing and myth, both of them distinguished from *logos* and dialectics, will only become more precise as the text concludes. Having just repeated without knowing that writing consists of repeating without knowing, Socrates goes on to base the demonstration of his indictment, of his *logos*, ... upon structures that are readable through a fabulous genealogy of writing' (*Dissemination*, p. 75). In this situation one is obliged to push beyond those structured oppositions (*logos/mythos*, origin/repetition, speech/writing) that govern the express argumentative design of Plato's dialogue. But in so doing one is *not* giving up all claim to consistency and rigour of argument. Thus Derrida insists that 'the spontaneity, freedom, and fantasy attributed to Plato in his legend of Thoth were actually supervised and limited by rigorous necessities' (p. 85). And the same applies to Derrida's reading of the *Phaedrus,* insofar as it seeks out that obscure yet inescapable logic by which the text deconstructs its own most rooted assumptions.

We have seen that it is through certain double-edged metaphors, certain oddly reversible figures of thought, that Derrida pursues this covert textual logic. Most crucial here is the Greek word *pharmakon,* a word whose ramifications of sense are everywhere apparent in the dialogue. *Pharmakon* is not just an 'ambiguous' term, such that one could list its various meanings and appreciate the richness, subtlety or scope that it lends to Plato's text. For its two chief senses are 'poison' on the one hand and 'remedy' or 'cure' on the other, meanings which one might think could hardly come together in any single utterance or context of usage. Yet this is precisely Derrida's point: that these two antithetical senses of the word are everywhere co-present in Plato's text, defeating all attempts (on the part of tidy-minded scholars and translators) to choose one or other according to context. And it is not by chance, he argues, that the *pharmakon* inserts this strange double logic into Plato's text at the point where writing is explicitly on trial, along with all its manifold associated terms. Writing is both poison *and* cure, on the one hand a threat to the living presence of authentic (spoken) language, on the other an indispensable means for

anyone who wants to record, transmit or somehow commemo-
rate that presence.

Faced with such intractable problems, the scholars and translators will inevitably opt for whichever documented meaning of
the word best 'makes sense' in a given passage. 'All translations
into languages that are the heirs and depositaries of Western
metaphysics thus produce on the *pharmakon* an *effect of
analysis* that violently destroys it, reduces it to one of its simple
elements by interpreting it, paradoxically, in the light of the
ulterior developments that it itself has made possible' (*Dissemination*, p. 99). That is to say, translation is governed by the ideal
of an adequate transfer of sense between languages, a transfer
that respects the priority of the signified (of meaning itself) over
the mere written signs that necessarily serve to communicate its
presence. So when translators tend to reduce the *pharmakon* to
one or other of its violently disjunctive senses, what is in
question is not just a localized example of semantic insensitivity,
but a need to ignore the problematical effects of a writing that
nonetheless resists such reduction. Certainly Derrida is not
blaming the translators for simply having missed these complexities of sense through an oversight amounting to professional
incompetence. Rather, he is suggesting that what is really 'on
trial' in these efforts to cope with the *pharmakon* of writing is an
ethics of language that has always privileged authentic, self-
present speech over the vagaries of textual inscription. No
translation could possibly do justice to this text while continuing
to respect the classical ideals that govern the self-conceived
nature and project of 'translation'.[4] For there is simply no
reckoning, on logocentric terms, with an instance like Plato's
pharmakon that disrupts the very logic of self-identity, that
opens up a play of semantic substitutions beyond all hope of
assured conceptual grasp.

These problems of translation are exactly reproduced at the
level of thematic commentary. Thus when Phaedrus asks Socrates to define the form of wisdom that is superior to anything
acquired from written texts, Socrates replies: 'the sort that goes
together with learning and is written in the soul of the learner'
(*Dissemination*, p. 148). As Derrida comments, it is remarkable

here 'that the so-called living discourse should suddenly be described by a metaphor borrowed from the order of the very thing one is trying to exclude from it, the order of its simulacrum' (p. 149). And this is no isolated instance but a sample of the crucially ambivalent discourse upon writing that Derrida reveals, not only in the *Phaedrus* but in many other texts of Western tradition. There is the 'good' writing, engraved in the soul, whether (as Socrates would have it) through the living remembrance of truths now revealed by the exercise of philosophic wisdom, or (as in Christian doctrine) through God's vouchsafing His word to those in a state of spiritual grace. And there is the other, 'bad' writing that must always corrupt or pervert such wisdom, since it can only exist in the debased form of inscriptions, material marks, the 'dead letter' of a mere supplement to speech. Yet as Derrida shows with remorseless regularity, this contrast must always undermine its own logic by opposing 'good' and 'bad' on the basis of a single term – that of writing itself – whose primary (literal) sense is undeniably that of textual inscription. So the 'good' writing, imprinted on the soul, can only be conceived as a metaphor derived from its supposedly derivative opposite term. 'Metaphoricity is the logic of contamination and the contamination of logic' (p. 149). And this reversal comes about, not just as a result of Plato's peculiarly awkward situation in the *Phaedrus,* but wherever philosophy defines itself against the lures and the falsehoods of writing.

Derrida suggests a rather nice comparison here with the so-called 'kettle-logic' which Freud discovered in his work on dreams, jokes and their relation to the unconscious. Thus the subject may think to defend or excuse some action by advancing a whole series of wildly contradictory claims. (1) I never borrowed your kettle; (2) it was in perfect condition when I gave it back to you; (3) it already had those holes in the bottom when I borrowed it. To which Derrida compares the following logocentric moves: (1) writing is 'rigorously exterior and inferior' to living speech, which it can therefore not threaten in any way; (2) writing may indeed be harmful, since it can put speech and reason 'to sleep', and hence 'infect their very life'; and (3) 'if one has resorted to . . . writing at all, it is not for [its] intrinsic value, but because living memory is finite, it already has holes in it before writing ever comes to leave its traces' (p. 111). This 'kettle-logic' is the means by which the *Phaedrus* both persistently raises the question of writing and just as persistently manages to evade, suppress or contain its larger implications. And these effects extend into every main topic of the text, wherever some privileged idea takes command (or, as Derrida would argue, *fails* to take command) by setting itself up in determined opposition to some other, debased or 'supplementary' term. For there is a *politics* and an *ethics* that are closely bound up with the insistence on speech as a model for the wise and responsible conduct of human affairs. This is why Derrida goes on to compare the 'trial of writing' in the *Phaedrus* with the 'trial of democracy' that occupies Plato intermittently throughout the *Republic*. What is required of the good citizen (like the good son) is that he should come to maturity through an exercise of reason that has taught him to acknowledge — in his own best interests — the *logos* of paternal wisdom and law. Not that this law is solely in the keeping of fathers, kings or master-philosophers who can jealously withhold it from their sons, subjects or eager disciples like Plato. Rather it is a joint possession, shared among the members of a proper, legitimate family or a community of rational citizens whose sharing can thus never threaten its self-authorized power.

So it is that the ethics of speech as self-presence affects the constitution of Plato's ideal Republic. Within such a system there would always be the ultimate reference back to an authority residing outside and beyond specific differences of age, class or political interest. These differences could then be subsumed — like the problematic instance of writing — under a *logos* that would always already be established in the place of self-present truth. And if writing ever presumed to challenge this truth, to deny the paternal law of speech, then it would have to be accounted a bastard son, or an orphan deprived of all natural, hereditary rights. For it is the passage of authority from fathers to sons — rightful, legitimate sons — that ensures the continuity of tradition and the maintenance of properly exercised power in family and state. '*Logos* is a son, then, a son that would be

40

destroyed in his very *presence* without the present *attendance* of his father. His father who answers. His father who speaks for him and answers for him' (*Dissemination*, p. 77). Such is the self-perpetuating logic that guarantees truth and social stability alike. Its representative voices are those of Socrates and good King Thamus, both of them wise enough to reject the proffered gift of writing, whose bad effects they so shrewdly perceive. So what exactly *is* the position of writing with regard to this legitimate family line? Its status, Derrida writes, is that of an 'orphan', one whose 'welfare cannot be assured by any [paternal] attendance or assistance'. It thus resembles nothing more than the character of a *graphein* {a written trace} 'which, being nobody's son at the instant it reaches inscription, scarcely remains a son at all and no longer recognizes its origins, whether legally or morally' (p. 77). The only kind of writing to escape this hapless predicament is the kind that abjures all claims to independence, accepts the authority of a sovereign *logos* and therefore no longer poses any threat to the established order of discourse.

This same essential logic of exclusion serves to define the laws and the limits of Greek communal life. The ideal *polis,* as Plato describes it in the *Republic,* is one where the citizen (free-born male) takes upon himself the full responsibilities of an active political involvement. And again, the precondition for assuming this role is that the citizen not only obey the laws but assent to them, knowingly and willingly, as a self-acting rational intelligence. The community is therefore defined, not only by those who properly belong inside it, but also by the rigorous prohibitions that apply to aliens, criminals and non-competent members. These latter − external *and* internal émigrés − are not without their own representative figures. For it seems (according to Sir James Frazer, whom Derrida cites) that the Athenians maintained 'at the public expense' a number of 'degraded and useless beings' who could always be treated as scapegoats, or sacrificial victims, in a time of threatening catastrophe. A strange logic seems to operate here, a logic established by that same pattern of reversed or cross-related senses that marked the word *pharmakon* and − inseparably − the emergence of writing as a

41

topic in Plato's dialogue. 'The city's body *proper* thus reconstitutes its unity, closes around the security of its inner courts, gives back to itself the word that links it with itself within the confines of the agora, by violently excluding from its territory the representative of an external threat or aggression' (p. 133). Yet there is also the scapegoat, maintained within bounds – 'chosen, fed, kept etc., in the very heart of the inside' – apparently as an extra, supplementary means of warding off this 'outside' threat. Like the *logos* conceived as pure, self-present speech, the *polis* seems able to sustain its identity only by allowing a certain admixture of the alien, the 'debased' or 'useless'. And as metaphors of writing invade the very discourse of logocentric reason, so the scapegoat becomes that indispensable 'other' by which the Greek city-state defines its own powers and constitution.

Now it cannot be by chance, Derrida argues, that there exists a Greek word that both captures this entire range of meanings bound up with the scapegoat-figure, and that furthermore suggests, through its lexical resemblance, a connection with the *pharmakon* of writing. In fact the two words are distinguished by a single letter, which implies not only that they are related through a common etymology, but that somewhere, in the play of structured oppositions that makes up Plato's text, their meanings must enter a certain regulated exchange of semantic attributes. The Greek word in question is *pharmakos,* for which scholars record the various senses 'magician', 'wizard', 'poisoner' and 'the one sacrificed in expiation for the sins of a city' (p. 132n). And the same dictionary that Derrida refers to here gives these following entries for *pharmakon*: 'charm, philtre, drug, remedy, poison'. So Derrida would seem to have good philological warrant for his thesis that writing is in some sense a *scapegoat,* a necessary evil that society tolerates only in the hope of preventing worse ills. Both terms belong to that same paradoxical system that can take a single word (whether *pharmakos* or *pharmakon*) and invest it with meanings so sharply opposed as to render its senses undecidable in any given context.

But there is a problem in the way of Derrida's reading, one that might seem – by any normative standard of textual commentary – to count very decisively against it. For the word 'pharmakos' never actually occurs in the course of Plato's dialogue. That is to say, it is not *present* as a lexical item, though its effects can be traced (so Derrida would argue) through the logic of displacement or 'supplementarity' that everywhere governs the text. In the case of *pharmakon* one is dealing with a word which, 'for all its hiddenness, for all that it might escape Plato's notice, is nevertheless something that passes through certain discoverable *points of presence*' (*Dissemination*, p. 129). Such a reading is still within the bounds of lexical self-evidence, no matter how remote or unsettling the effects that it begins to induce. But with *pharmakos*, seemingly an 'absent' term, there is no last appeal to the 'words on the page' as support for one's various conjectures. Here, Derrida argues, we shall need once again to suspend those structured oppositions (inside/outside, present/absent) which standardly serve to define or delimit the operations of textual commentary. After all, the word 'pharmakos' is demonstrably *there* among the lexical resources of the Greek language, and would moreover seem to have played a vital role in Greek thought and culture. So how can we account for its absence in a text where everything points to the *pharmakos* as key to that text's most essential and intricate logic of sense?

Derrida's response to this question will take us a good way toward grasping what is at stake in the deconstructive enterprise. It rests upon the notion of intertextuality, but *not* the kind of open-ended textual 'freeplay' – the farewell to rigorous protocols of reading – that literary critics often make of it. What Derrida is concerned to bring out is the rigorous logic of exchange and substitution that links these 'pharmaceutical' metaphors in a chain extending well beyond the limits of a single text or corpus of writings. 'Not that one must then consider that it is leaking on all sides and can be drowned confusedly in the undifferentiated generality of its element' (p. 130). Such a reading would break with certain well-established notions of scholarly and critical method. For instance, it would challenge the formalist idea – raised into a high point of principle by the American New Critics – that poems must be treated as 'verbal icons', as self-enclosed structures of rhetorical implication, so that any appeal to 'extrinsic' sources or contexts would simply not *count* as a genuine reading.[5] No doubt it was partly in reaction to this kind of strict self-denying ordinance that American critics embraced deconstruction in the guise of a henceforth unlimited textual 'freeplay'. But this is clearly not the path that Derrida follows in his reading of the *Phaedrus,* a reading that demands much more in the way of disciplined philological argument.

To be sure, he very definitely rejects the idea that 'there exists, in all rigour, a Platonic text, closed upon itself, complete with its inside and its outside' (p. 130). Nor can the limit be simply pushed back a stage, extended to embrace the entirety of Plato's writings or the lexicon of words that he is known to have used on this or that specific occasion. For the fact that certain terms may be *absent* yet *present* – inscribed through a different, 'supplementary' order of necessity – requires that one look beyond the lexical system to the various 'sub-units' (the phonemes or minimal distinctive components of meaning) that enter the chain of substitutions. It would then become apparent that 'what we call a word' is far from determining the limits of assignable sense. The elements of a term like *pharmakos* may exert their force at a distance, so to speak, creating all manner of pathways and connections that inevitably lead 'outside' the text. 'With respect to the weight of such a force, the so-called "presence" of a quite relative verbal unit – the word – while not being a contingent accident worthy of no attention, nevertheless does not constitute the ultimate criterion and the utmost pertinence' (p. 130). But it is equally important to recognize that this breaking-down of textual and semantic boundaries cannot be accomplished by a style of free-wheeling commentary that simply ignores the requirements of disciplined reading. Thus Derrida declares himself 'less interested in breaking through certain limits' than in 'putting in doubt the right to posit such limits in the first place' (p. 130). And this means rejecting any simplified version of intertextuality that would 'leak on all sides', obliterate every distinction to begin with, and thus place the question of those *de jure* limits beyond reach of any serious critique. It is only by respecting the intricate logic of Plato's text — albeit a 'logic' of logical anomalies — that deconstruction can arrive at the point of suspending such powerful normative constraints. And then it will appear that the *pharmakos* has indeed been exerting its remarkable powers, though not by any means that could be 'booked into the present' by pointing to a simple instance on the page. 'Rather, provided the articulations are rigorously and prudently recognized, one should be able to untangle the hidden forces of attraction linking a present word with an absent word in the text of Plato' (p. 130).

I have offered this relatively detailed account of Derrida on the *Phaedrus* since the essay helps· to pinpoint exactly what is involved in the deconstructive reading of canonical texts. It could well be taken — superficially at least — as belonging to the species of textual commentary, or as offering just one 'interpretation' of a work that invites endless re-readings from alternative points of view. And indeed there is a sense in which the *Phaedrus*, like so many of his chosen texts, lends itself ideally to Derrida's purpose by insisting on those various crucial antinomies (speech/writing, presence/absence etc.) which can then be deconstructed and held to characterize the discourse of 'logocentric' reason at large. That is to say, these topics are expressly *thematized* in Plato's dialogue, present in the foreground of debate and all the more striking for that. But Derrida is assuredly claiming something more; that the forces at work within a text like the *Phaedrus*, in its uncanny 'logic' of figural substitution, are forces that are found in every text of every language marked by that same ubiquitous 'metaphysics of presence'. In this case the 'thematic' reading of Derrida on Plato would have missed the main point in a certain quite specific and highly predictable way. It would have worked to assimilate deconstruction to familiar ideas about language, truth and reference. We can now turn to 'The Double Session' — an essay on Plato and Mallarmé also included in *Dissemination* — to see just how far such (mis)readings can be checked by a determined counter-strategy on Derrida's part.

45

Versions of *mimesis*: Plato and Mallarmé

'The Double Session' is one example of a technique that Derrida
frequently uses to bring home the effects of intertextuality, the
ways in which writing cannot be contained within the limits of a
book, an authoritative discourse or self-enclosed system of
meaning.[6] This technique takes the form of a graphic reminder,
of printing two very different texts on a single page and virtually
forcing the reader's eye to shuttle incessantly between them. By
far the most ambitious exercise in this vein is Derrida's *Glas,* his
'commentary' (for want of a better word) upon texts of Hegel
and Genet. On the one hand is the philosopher, dialectician,
arch-theorist of the family and state, of law, ethics, universal
reason and Christianity as the highest form of revealed truth. On
the other stands Genet, homosexual thief-turned-writer, trans-
vestite, celebrant of all that would threaten or subvert those
sovereign Hegelian values. And along with these texts goes one
masquerading under Derrida's name, a gloss that reflects
(among numerous other topics) on the play and place of proper
names in writing, on the infinite permeability of text and context
and the various laws – of genre, copyright, authorial signature,
'literal' versus 'metaphorical' sense – that would seek to contain
these disseminating forces. I shall not have very much to say
about *Glas* since it is a work (like *Finnegans Wake*) that defeats
the best efforts of descriptive analysis or summary. I mention it
here in order to suggest what lies at one extreme of Derrida's
project: a writing that would finally *enact* the break with all
received ideas of the 'proper' relationship between author, text
and commentary.[7]

In 'The Double Session' it is Plato and Mallarmé whose texts
are juxtaposed on the opening page and whose writings are
thenceforth involved in a contest of intertextual feints and
allusions. Of Plato, it is a passage from his dialogue the *Philebus*
where Socrates raises, among other things, the question of
mimesis, of the means by which painting – and analogous forms
of graphic inscription – can best convey genuine truths to the
mind properly attuned. The good painter is he who reproduces
images always already engraved in the soul, pictures whose

authenticity is proved by appealing to a wisdom that naturally *precedes* the mere instance of graphic reproduction. What the painter must strive to attain is an adequate approach to the known forms of mimetic fidelity and truth. Thus Socrates speaks of this good artist as one who brings about 'the conjunction of memory with sensations', and who can therefore be said to 'write words in our souls' with the result that 'true opinions and true assertions spring up in us' (cited by Derrida, *Dissemination*, p. 175). And in this case 'our soul is like a book', in the sense that truth is there to be read through the signs (or images) that faithfully transcribe what we are properly given to know. So there is a good *mimesis*, common to the arts of painting and writing, that requires a due submission to the ultimate authority of a *logos* which precedes all mere supplementary inscriptions. And of course there is also a bad *mimesis*, the kind that results when the 'internal scribe' has deluded ideas of his own independence and therefore, quite simply, 'writes what is false' (p. 175).

This scene of instruction has a range of lessons to impart. They include (1) the authority of *the book* as a source of plenary wisdom; (2) the *decidability* of truth, as something arrived at through carefully distinguishing the 'good' from the 'bad' kinds of writing; and (3) the equation of truth as self-presence with a genuine *mimesis* that always reproduces what the soul must already (however remotely) have known. So the analogy with painting — with images pictured in the soul — makes it possible for Socrates to convince his opponent, as always, that writing (or sophistics) is a false knowledge, redeemable only through its wisely acknowledging the priority of self-present truth. Thus the theory of *mimesis*, or artistic representation, falls in with that same genealogy of thought that Derrida has analysed in the *Phaedrus*. 'It is through recourse to the truth of that which is, of things as such, that one can always decide whether writing is or is not true, whether it is in conformity or in "opposition" to the true' (*Dissemination*, p. 185). And this mimetic regime finds its ultimate authority in the *book*, in that idea of a self-enclosed totality of meaning where the *logos* can preside and impose firm limits on the play of textual inscription. Hence Plato's metaphor of a writing in the soul, an inspired writing that contrasts with the fallen, degenerate nature of material marks and signs.

Sharing the page with this passage from Plato is a prose-text by Mallarmé which also has to do with the topics of writing, *mimesis* and graphic representation. It is entitled 'Mimique' and describes – though this word will come to seem hardly adequate – a mime whose gestures 'imitate' no model, whose perform-ance appears to be wholly 'unscripted', yet whose actions, as Mallarmé recounts or imagines them, are caught up in a chain of supplementary inscriptions after the event. The drama can be summarized quickly enough, but not so the complicated *mise-en-scène* that develops as Mallarmé reads about the mimic, composes an elusive and remarkable text on the subject, and thus sets in play that strange dialectic of absence and illusion that has come between himself, as imaginary spectator, and the scene that he strives to recreate. The act involves a Pierrot who has murdered his unfaithful wife by the horrible expedient of tying her down to a bed and tickling her feet until she expires in an ecstasy of laughter. Mallarmé encountered the story in a text ('this suggestive and truly rare booklet') written by one Fernand Beissier, who had witnessed the mime and recounts it with a mixture of disgust and speculative intrigue. So there is a first complication evident here: that Mallarmé is deriving his own version from a written source (as it happens, a second edition of Beissier's pamphlet) composed some five years after the mimic performance took place. 'Whether Mallarmé ever did actually go to *see* the "spectacle" *too* is not only hard to verify but irrelevant to the organization of the text' (p. 198). And this because the mime is played out in Mallarmé's re-telling through a series of oblique derivations and swerves from origin that block all attempts to refer it back to some proper first instance of mimetic truth. What we have is a scene of multiplied writings and readings, a scene that is repeated at every stage in the chain of textual transmission. And this chain goes right the way back to where everything began, since the Mime himself (so Mallarmé records) was subject to the same injunction, required to act as though inventing his gestural 'script' momentarily as the scene unfolded.

Derrida's point in all this – to put the matter very simply – is

that Mallarmé has hit upon an excellent device for deconstructing the Platonic idea of *mimesis,* origins and truth. What we read
in 'Mimique' is the non-availability of any first principle, ground
or cause that would exercise control over the play of 'supplementary' writings and representations. Any reading that
thought to locate such a ground in the 'original' mime itself
would fail to take account of the problems that multiply as soon
as one reads Mallarmé's text. For if the mimic performance had
no prior model, if its extraordinary character consisted in
precisely this ('the order given to the Mime to imitate nothing
that in any way preexists his operation'), then there is simply no
appealing to a concept of *mimesis* that would always point back
to a truth or reality beyond the mere play of textual inscription.
The Mime will always already be caught up in a different
economy of meaning, one that substitutes an improvised 'script'
for the lost security of origins and presence. 'The Mime ought
only to write himself on the white page he is; he must *himself*
inscribe *himself* through gestures and plays of facial expression'
(p. 199). And in this respect the Mime is in the same position as
Beissier, Mallarmé, Derrida and readers of 'The Double Session',
since for all of them the 'original' performance is an idea only, an
idea created through multiplied inscriptions on a series of white
pages.

And so Derrida asks: is it strictly possible to speak of a
'referent' for Mallarmé's text, any object or event that would
ultimately serve to reconstitute *mimesis* in its classic form? Not,
certainly, the mimic performance which he had probably not
even seen, and had anyway written up to begin with from a
'secondary' source. Perhaps one could argue that the 'true'
referent was in fact that very booklet that Mallarmé discovered
and kept open before him while writing 'Mimique'. But here
again, as Derrida shows, there are sizable problems that emerge
if one troubles to examine the textual history of that same little
volume. For Beissier had in fact written the 'Preface' only to a
longer work (*Pierrot Murderer of His Wife*) which the mime
Paul Margueritte, a distant relative of Mallarmé, planned to
complete and publish. And then one has to reckon with questions of chronology, of whether it is possible, by dating these

projects, to establish any clear-cut temporal sequence, so that the mime could be shown (logically enough) to precede and set in train a series of supplementary glosses. That such attempts must fail — and, in failing, raise questions as to the very concept of mimetic truth — is the upshot of a paragraph in Derrida's essay which needs quoting at length. 'The temporal and textual structure of "the thing" (what shall we call it?) presents itself, for the time being, thus: a mimodrama "takes place", as a gestural writing, preceded by no booklet; a preface is planned and then written *after* the "event" to precede a booklet written *after the fact*, reflecting the mimodrama rather than programming it. This Preface is replaced four years later by a Note written by the "author" himself, a sort of floating outwork' (p. 199). Given these perplexities, it is hard to conceive of the booklet as in any sense supplying a 'referent' for Mallarmé's discourse. What we are instead forced to entertain, so Derrida argues, is the notion of an endless series of inscriptions, a perpetual redoubling of text upon text, such that the 'original' act of *mimesis* will always be lost beyond recall. The Mime himself will already have set this process in train, since the act requires that he must 'double' in the roles of Pierrot (the jealous husband) and Columbine (his faithless wife). Then again, his performance can only be conceived as a supplement that lacks any ultimate origin, a writing in gestures that 'represent' nothing, since his mimicry begins and ends with the act itself.

So what can be said of our own predicament as readers of Mallarmé's text, our attention constantly drawn to it, as Derrida ensures, by the fact of its existing there on the page, along with the passage from Plato's *Philebus*? Perhaps after all we are no worse off than Mallarmé who likewise had to start from scratch, so to speak, and improvise a writing with no recourse to the authority of truth or origins. And again — to push the argument back a stage — we are only repeating that 'order' given to the Mime himself, that he 'not let anything be prescribed to him but his own writing', and 'not reproduce by imitation any action or any speech' (p. 198). So Mallarmé is in this sense faithful to the Mime's performance, though not by any kind of *mimetic* fidelity that could claim to reproduce its original. What he does, rather, is faithfully transcribe the predicament of a mimic writing that itself has no model, no authentic source to fall back on. Thus 'Mallarmé (he who fills the function of "author") writes upon a white page on the basis of a text he is reading in which it is written that one must write upon a white page' (p. 198). And Mallarmé's reader can only repeat this aboriginal swerve from origins, since the text of 'Mimique' — though indeed it is there to hand, like the 'booklet' that Mallarmé consulted — can give no assurance of anything more solidly grounded than a play of multiplied textual inscriptions.

We will return to the more 'philosophical' questions raised by this elaborately staged encounter between Plato and Mallarmé. Before that, I should like to cite a couple of passages from Angela Carter's recent novel *Nights at the Circus* (1983), a book much concerned with the topics of *mimesis*, repetition and the non-originality of origins. It belongs — insofar as such labels serve any useful purpose — to the species of 'magical realism', doubling back and forth between naturalistic detail and a 'post-modern' stress on those elements of fabulous narrative contrivance that resist the strong pull toward mimetic illusion. And it also has to do (as the title would suggest) with clowns, mimics and a whole weird 'circus' of effects brought about by this suspension of realist norms. There is a young American, Walser, who starts out as a down-to-earth cynical observer of the scene, but who then finds himself increasingly drawn into its magical orbit. When he first joins the circus and puts on his clown's make-up then, we are told, 'he experienced the freedom that lies behind the mask, within dissimulation, the freedom to juggle with being, and, indeed, with the language which is vital to our being, that lies at the heart of burlesque.'[8] I would guess, from this and other passages, that Carter has read 'The Double Session' and read it, what is more, with a keen sense of its fictional possibilities. But there is perhaps no need for such conjecture, since (as Derrida remarks in his readings of Plato and Mallarmé) texts may be linked by an order of 'structural' necessity that has little to do with questions of direct influence. And the effect of reading *Nights at the Circus* alongside 'The Double Session' is to bear out Derrida's cardinal claim: that we

51

are dealing with the signs of a movement that is always there, repressed but decipherable, in the discourse of mimetic realism.

There is a passage later in the novel which could also be adduced or, better still, inset within 'The Double Session', as Derrida does with the texts of Plato and Mallarmé. It is spoken by the great clown Buffo, and occurs in the course of a remarkable set-piece monologue. Clowning is a wretched, a sordid occupation, not in the least what appearances suggest. And yet, says Buffo, the clowns have one privilege, one special distinction, that makes of their 'outcast and degraded' state something ultimately precious and rare. 'We can invent our own faces! We *make* ourselves . . . The code of the circus permits of no copying, no change. However much the face of Buffo may appear identical to Grik's face, or to Grok's face . . . it is, all the same, a fingerprint of authentic dissimilarity, a genuine expression of my own autonomy. And so my face eclipses me. I have become this face which is not mine, and yet I chose it freely.'[9] I have no wish to press too hard on what may be — as conventional wisdom would have it — a fortuitous coincidence of 'themes'. But these passages from *Nights at the Circus* do catch precisely the logic and the effects of that 'dissimulating' movement that Derrida finds at work in Mallarmé's cryptic text. His Mime, like Angela Carter's clown, is an adept of deconstruction before the letter, of a gestural writing that effaces all signs of origin and exists only in the moment of its own production. And *Nights at the Circus* can be read — indeed, asks to be read — as a text which deconstructs the conventions of mimetic realism, resisting all attempts to naturalize its various extravagant scenes and episodes.

But what would be the consequence for 'philosophy' if its texts were subjected to this same kind of rigorously anti-mimetic reading? Such is the question that Derrida poses in 'The Double Session' and pursues through his graphic juxtaposition of the passages from Plato and Mallarmé. It would *not* amount to simply treating philosophy as a sub-genre of literature, reading it henceforth with an eye to its purely rhetorical aspects and without the least regard for logic, consistency or truth. Rather, it would involve the most scrupulous attention to those moments of stress in the philosophic text where writing perceptibly exceeds and disturbs the order of *mimesis*, of presence and origins. At such points the discourse of philosophy is shadowed by a mimic writing whose effect is the obverse of everything envisaged in Socrates' model of speech as the authentic unveiling of truth. Thus Derrida writes of the 'double mark', the supplementary inscription which 'escapes the pertinence or authority of truth', not simply by *rejecting* such ideas wholesale but by showing how they rest on a certain metaphysics, an ontology of language and being whose absolute reign must henceforth at least be open to doubt. And this is what Derrida asks us to read in the series of subtle 'displacements' brought about in the language of Platonism by its contact with Mallarmé's 'Mimique'. It is not — he insists — a question of breaking altogether with that language, of coming out once and for all on the far side of everything pertaining to an old, discredited mimetic regime. Such claims could only be self-deluding, since there is simply no alternative ground on which to stand, no language that has not been endlessly worked over in its deepest conceptual resources by the logical grammar of Platonism. To regard deconstruction in this light — as declaring an imminent 'end' to the epoch of 'Western metaphysics' or logocentric thinking — is to misread some crucial passages in Derrida's work.

This point is worth taking up in rather more detail, since 'The Double Session' is especially concerned to preempt and deflect such readings. For there are, Derrida says, a great many ways of recuperating Mallarmé's texts, restoring them to a *different* mimetic order which would seem to respect their peculiar character yet still, in the end, annex them to a thoroughly traditional economy of word and thought. And one of these ways, paradoxically enough, is to take it for granted that they have *achieved* a radical break with all forms of mimetic representation, so that henceforth commentary need only repeat and celebrate the signal achievement. This tendency is encouraged by a certain rather facile strain in current post-structuralist thinking, one that passes directly from the 'arbitrary' nature of the sign (the lack of any natural or determinate link between signifier and signified) to the notion that texts cannot possibly 'refer' to any world outside their own rhetorical domain. On the contrary, Derrida argues: language is marked through and through by referential (or mimetic) assumptions, and there is no way of simply breaking their hold by a kind of deconstructionist fiat. What he *does* seek to show – most patiently and meticulously in 'The Double Session' – is that classical ideas of this referential function have greatly simplified its nature, ignoring whatever gets in the way of a direct return to *mimesis*, origins and truth. There is, in short, an *ideology* of representation which bears all the marks of its philosophical descent, from Plato to the present day. And any reading of Mallarmé that fails to reckon with this long and complex prehistory is not, in fact, a genuinely deconstructive reading but one that ineffectually gestures in that direction.

To understand more exactly how Derrida is arguing here we need to distinguish the two main concepts of truth (or *mimesis*) that have governed philosophical enquiry. One is the strictly *referential* idea of truth as an adequate matching-up, a correspondence between words and the things they can properly be used to represent. The precise nature of these 'things' – whether sense-data, real-world objects or factual states of affairs – has given rise to long-running debate among epistemologists.[10] But their versions have at least this much in common: they all assume that truthful statements can be tested or verified as such by determining their 'fit' with an outside reality. It is this correspondence-theory of truth – taken in its least sophisticated form, as a simple *adequation* between words and things – that is chiefly under attack from post-structuralism. But there is another concept of *mimesis*, equally entrenched in Western philosophical tradition, which can always be appealed to in cases where language resists or evades such referential treatment. This is the Platonic doctrine of truth as a form of inward revelation, as a 'writing in the soul' that makes itself visible to the mind in a state of receptive wisdom. Such knowledge, as Plato conceives it, would be more authentic – closer to the origin and the nature of things – than any truth attainable by a mere copying of external reality. For it is a cardinal precept of Plato's philosophy that wisdom consists in seeing beyond the world of material objects and events, the world we inhabit so long as we are enslaved to the predominance of sensory perception. There is a higher reality of essences, 'forms' or ideas which are locally embodied in the things we perceive but which can only be *known*, in their essential nature, through a process of inward seeking-after-truth. This is the concept of truth as *aletheia*, as the moment of epiphany or inward 'unveiling', vouchsafed to the soul through an exercise of reason transcending all forms of sensory perception. And it is the unique authority of Socrates' teaching — a teaching conducted exclusively through dialogue, through the *spoken word*, without recourse to the bad art of writing — that enables this truth to take hold in the minds of his genuine disciples.

A more careful reading of 'The Double Session' will show that Derrida is far more concerned with this second, distinctively Platonic notion of *mimesis* as revealed truth. And it is on this account that he rejects those 'advanced' interpretations of Mallarmé that plume themselves on having somehow transcended, at a stroke, the naive assumptions of a referential reading. For one can reach this point very easily and yet leave room for a line of counter-argument that would save 'Mimique' for the purest form of Platonist interpretation. The Mime would then be seen as 'the very movement of truth', imitating nothing (in the referential sense) but 'opening up in its origin the very thing he is tracing out, presenting, or producing' (*Dissemination*, p. 205). And this would be the upshot of any sophisticated reading that dispensed altogether with the illusion of mimetic realism while continuing to talk of Mallarmé's 'themes' or 'ideas' as if these existed in some Platonic heaven of ideal forms, quite apart from the detailed activity of his writing. 'One could indeed push Mallarmé back into the most "originary" metaphysics of truth if all mimicry (*mimique*) had indeed disappeared, if it had effaced itself in the scriptural production of truth' (p. 206). For it is only by conserving some residual notion of reference — even if reduced to a 'mimic' dimension far removed from classical *mimesis* — that thought can hold out against the logocentric drift toward origins and self-present truth.

These few paragraphs from 'The Double Session' would bear a much more detailed analytical commentary than I've room for here. But they do bring out that essential feature of a deconstructive reading that consists, not merely in *reversing* or *subverting* some established hierarchical order, but in showing how its terms are indissociably entwined in a strictly undecidable exchange of values and priorities. Thus the move to redeem Mallarmé's text from all taint of referential meaning must finally fall prey to a different order of mimeticism, one that rejoins the Platonist tradition at a deeper, more self-deluding level of complicity. And this because it fails to take the necessary step of *redoubling* that initial move, perceiving how the obverse of a crude realism is a return to classic idealist themes of *aletheia* and a good mimetic 'writing in the soul'. 'Any attempt to reverse mimetologism or escape it in one fell swoop by leaping out of it *with both feet* [Derrida's italics] would only amount to an inevitable and immediate fall back into its system: in suppressing the double or making it dialectical, one is back in the perception of the thing itself, the production of its presence, its truth, as idea, form, or matter' (p. 207). Dialectics (whether in Plato or in Hegel) is the form of thinking that attempts to master the effects of difference in language by playing them off in a carefully ordered sequence of arguments that *must* − by all the laws of dialectical reason − lead up to some ultimate truth. And the reading of Mallarmé that stakes its claim on a straightforward *abolition* of referential sense is a reading that lends itself very readily to the Platonist conception of an ideal *mimesis* beyond mere marks on the page.

This is why Derrida insists that deconstruction is a process of 'displacement' endlessly at work in Mallarmé 's text, rather than an act of critical intervention that would come, so to speak, *from outside* and simply apply the standard technique for reversing some 'logocentric' order of priorities. The activity in question is, he writes, 'more subtle and patient, more discreet and efficient' (*Dissemination*, p. 207). It is not by any means the distinctive operation of a 'method' devised by Derrida himself or one that had to wait until modern critical theory had provided the necessary tools. Nor is it peculiar to that stage of intensely self-conscious reflection on language and poetics that the later French Symbolists (and Mallarmé especially) raised to a high point of principle. For this would be to fall back once again into a form of dialectical thinking, one which — precisely in Hegel's manner — equated the unfolding of literary history with the emergence of a truth at last delivered up in the fullness of its own reflective grasp. For deconstruction is *always already* at work, even in those texts that would seem most expressly committed to a 'logocentric' order of assumptions. And conversely, as Derrida often repeats, it is impossible for a deconstructive reading to escape that ubiquitous system of ideas, impossible to leap outside it and land 'with both feet' on some alternative ground.

It is exactly this 'subtle and patient' operation — this 'displace-ment without reversal of Platonism and its heritage' — that Derrida calls to our attention in Mallarmé's text. And not only there but also, it would seem, in those very texts that appear most strenuously to resist it. What we find in 'Mimique', Derrida writes, is 'a simulacrum of Platonism or Hegelianism which is separated from what it simulates only by a barely perceptible veil, about which one can just as well say that it already runs — unnoticed — between Platonism and itself, between Hegelianism and itself' (p. 207). Or indeed, he goes on, 'between Mallarmé's text and itself', since of course there is no question of 'Mimique' having *achieved* the strictly unthinkable and placed itself 'beyond' logocentrism in all its forms. So again we have a double movement here, on the one hand deploying the resources of Mallarmé's text against the hold of entrenched metaphysical ideas, while on the other insisting (1) that those ideas were *already* thus affected in the writings of Plato and Hegel, and (2) that their persistence must yet be acknowledged in Mallarmé's own productions. It is this latter, 'supplementary' but essential move that Derrida asks us to keep very firmly in mind as his reading proceeds. For it will otherwise amount to nothing more than a novel twist in what remains after all a familiar dialectical routine.

It is now possible to see more clearly why Derrida claims *not* to be engaged in any form of 'thematic' commentary. To seek out themes in Mallarmé's text — even if they happen to be themes of writing, displacement or mimetic doubling — is always to imply that the text points back to some originary complex of meanings or ideas. What Derrida has in mind is a certain style of *phenomenological* criticism, one whose interest focuses on the reflexive or self-referential qualities of Mallarmé's writing. These interpreters — Jean-Pierre Richard among them — are far from endorsing any naive mimeticism or straightforward 'metaphysics of presence'. On the contrary, they are always willing to acknowledge the elusiveness of Mallarmé's themes, the points at which his poetry exceeds and perplexes the efforts of analytic thought. In fact this is precisely what they *value* in Mallarmé: the extreme self-conscious refinement and subtlety of a language that reflects on its most intimate resources of meaning and style. Thus Richard locates a whole series of key metaphors — 'wings, pages, veils, sails, folds, plumes etc.' — which suggest the same process of figural doubling, of the text folded back upon itself, so to speak, in an endless chain of 'supplementary' meanings or inscriptions. But by this he means to celebrate the extraordinary *wealth,* the complexity and depth of poetic implication that must finally defeat all critical attempts to exhaust the Mallarméan text. And it is here that Derrida defines the crucial point of divergence between deconstruction and all such phenomenological readings. For if commentary is in some sense defeated by Mallarmé's writing, it is not because his texts are so impossibly rich, so laden with meaning, as to show up the poverty of critical language. Nor is it by virtue of that self-reflexive subtlety that leads toward depths of poetic under-standing where mere interpretation must fear to tread. This way of thinking, says Derrida, 'confirms the classical reading of Mallarmé and confines his text within an atmosphere of intim-ism, symbolism, and neo-Hegelianism' (*Dissemination*, p. 271). For it will always point back to some authenticating source, some point — or series of points — in the text where its meanings can be anchored to a 'key-word' or theme. And it must therefore repeat that gesture of containment by which commentary seeks to close off the play of textual inscriptions and restore writing to an order of self-present truth.

This is why Derrida is so careful to mark his distance from the idea — virtually a truism among modern literary critics — that poetry differs from 'ordinary' language on account of its unique complexity of meaning, irreducible to plain prose statement. The critics have adopted various strategies to cope with this awkward predicament. Some (like William Empson) rise to the challenge by first seeking out poetic 'ambiguities', then offering all kinds of oblique multiple paraphrase in order to *suggest* — without claiming to *exhaust* — the poem's rich variety of sense.[11] Others (the American New Critics in particular) erect a whole system of doctrinal checks and sanctions, forbidding any recourse to paraphrase since this could only blur the ontological distinction between poetry and other kinds of language.[12] The best that criticism can do is equip itself with a lexicon of privileged analytic terms ('irony', 'paradox' etc.) which supposedly give access to this separate domain while respecting its imperative boundary-conditions. Critics may indulge the most elaborate methods of rhetorical close-reading so long as they acknowledge that these are heuristic devices only, with no power to express or comprehend the full range of poetic meaning.

These assumptions run deep across just about every modern school of literary-critical thinking. And it is here that Derrida establishes his own very different set of priorities. 'If polysemy is infinite, if it cannot be mastered as such, this is so not because a finite reading or a finite writing remains incapable of exhausting a superabundance of meaning' (p. 253). For what deconstruction finds at work in Mallarmé's text is the very reverse of a rich multiplicity of sense attaching to certain privileged 'themes'. It is the effect of an endless *displacement* of meaning, one that constantly baffles and frustrates the desire for some assurance of thematic unity or grasp. And this is nowhere more apparent than in Mallarmé's reiterated images of folds, veils, marks, absences and 'blank' (unwritten) spaces on the page. A phenomenological reading would assimilate these words to a complex of *themes* which could then be traced back — at the end of many fascinating detours and delays — to some ultimate source of interpretative unity and truth. But this is to ignore the problems that arise as soon as one follows out the intricate logic that

59

relates each of these terms in a series of endlessly self-effacing gestures. 'As they play within this differential-supplementary structure, all the marks must blend to it, taking on the fold of this blank. The blank is folded, is (marked by) a fold . . . For the fold is no more of a theme (a signified) than the blank, and if one takes into account the linkages and rifts they propagate in the text, then *nothing* can simply have the value of a theme any more' (p. 253). It is only by a certain 'conceptual' strategy — a move to repress or contain these effects — that writing can be held within the limits laid down by any kind of thematic or phenomenological approach.

What Derrida is out to resist as far as possible is the Platonizing drift that would restore interpretation to a quest for self-present meaning and truth. And this not simply in order to demonstrate that 'philosophy' has always been deluded in its high truth-claims, and that 'literature' (or literary criticism) must henceforth rightfully have the last word. For it soon becomes clear in reading 'The Double Session' that Derrida is far from endorsing such a straightforward reversal of established priorities. Interpretation — of the kind that literary critics most commonly practise — is itself caught up in a structure of assumptions which philosophy continues to dominate, as it were, at one remove. The entire Platonic order of *mimesis, aletheia* and truth as self-presence is still operative in these modern sophisticated readings of Mallarmé, for all that they appear to challenge or subvert it.

Here perhaps it is worth recalling more exactly the terms on which that order is established in Plato's famous allegory of the cave (*Republic*).[13] We fallible human knowers are, he suggests, like creatures of the dark, sitting inside an underground cavern with our backs firmly turned to the world of daylight reality. All that we perceive are the shadows cast upon the wall of this prison by a moving puppet-show of figures projected by a flickering artificial fire. To face the sun directly is more than our senses can bear, accustomed as they are to this benighted state of transient physical perception. Only by directing our minds *inward and back* towards the knowledge of a higher (non-sensuous) reality can we at last break out of this wretched enslavement and achieve genuine wisdom. It is on these grounds that Plato argues his case against poetry, along with other forms of aesthetic *mimesis*. For what the mind is taken in by when it credits such manifest illusions is in truth the mere *copy of a copy*, the representation of a physical world whose substance is itself nothing more than the shadow-play projected by our own state of ignorance. This bad *mimesis* thus operates at a double remove from reality. For if art cannot truthfully convey what presents itself in the world of mere physical appearances, still less can it achieve that superior knowledge that lies beyond the sensory realm.

It is against this whole Platonic scene of instruction that Derrida enlists the resources of Mallarmé's 'Mimique', of a writing that 'outwits and undoes all ontologies, all philosophemes, all manner of dialectics' (*Dissemination*, p. 215). And this means rejecting any version of Mallarmé that aims to reconstitute the 'themes' of his text through a totalizing process that would finally subscribe to some ultimate truth behind or beyond the play of mimetic inscriptions. Thus Derrida takes Mallarmé very much at his word when he calls himself 'profoundly and scrupulously a syntaxer' (p. 224). What a deconstructive reading draws out in 'Mimique' are those disturbing effects upon the *logic* of sense (the 'logic', that is to say, of origins, *mimesis* and representation) that baffle criticism by inducing complications beyond all hope of assured thematic grasp. There is no 'transcendental signified', no concept or meaning that would serve to arrest this chain of aboriginal supplements. And the same applies to those 'key-words' in the lexicon of Mallarmé's poems − those folds, blanks, images of textual concealment and deciphering − that commentary reduces to an ideal (imaginary) coherence. For there is always, Derrida writes, 'one trope too many or too few', one element in the chain that insists on its exorbitantly *literal* status and so disrupts this perfect economy of words and ideas. 'While belonging in the series of valences, it always occupies the position of a supplementary valence, or rather, it marks the structurally necessary position of a supplementary inscription that could always be added to or substracted from the series' (p.

252). Such is the effect of removing the 'transcendental privilege' that allows criticism to decide which terms shall be taken as the key-words, the organizing themes or metaphors of Mallarmé's text. Only by ignoring this differential play — this 'syntax' or logic of figural displacement — can criticism discover an ideal plenitude of sense. And in so doing it must always, at some point, repeat that Platonic gesture which indicts poetry as 'bad' *mimesis*, subjugates writing to a self-present speech, and yet — by a strange twist of metaphor — commemorates truth as a 'writing in the soul' superior to all other forms of knowledge.

4. Speech, Presence, Origins: from Hegel to Saussure

Of Grammatology[1] looks and reads very much like a book with a theme. An imposing, copiously annotated book whose topic (roughly stated) is the prejudice against writing among philosophers, linguists, anthropologists and others down through the history of Western 'logocentric' thought. I have already suggested some of the reasons why Derrida would want to reject any such generalized or summary account. The conceptual operation that extracts 'themes' from writing has its counterpart in the notion that *books* exist as self-enclosed systems of meaning and reference, their signifiers all pointing back toward some 'transcendental signified' or source of authentic and unitary truth. The traditional idea of the book is of a writing held within bounds by the author's sovereign presence; a writing whose integrity of purpose and theme comes from its acceptance of these proper, self-regulating limits. To question the authority of the book is also to challenge the priority of speech over writing, presence over absence, the origin over that which merely repeats, reduplicates or inscribes the origin. 'The good writing has therefore always been *comprehended . . .* within a totality, and enveloped in a volume or a book. The idea of a book is the idea of a totality, finite or infinite, of the signifier; this totality of the signifier cannot be a totality, unless a totality constituted by the signified preexists it, supervises its inscriptions and its signs, and is independent of it in its ideality' (*Of Grammatology*, p. 18). Thus a whole metaphysics of 'the book' is closely bound up with the logocentric will to privilege a self-present (spoken) truth above the endless duplicities of written language.

This idea is one that Derrida has sought to deconstruct by all manner of graphic and rhetorical means. In 'The Double Session', as we saw, it is a matter of reading Plato alongside

Mallarmé in a textual *mise-en-scène* that begins with their appearing on the same printed page, and is then pursued through a process of mutual interrogative dialogue and exchange. In the essay 'Living On: Border-lines' the effect is achieved by a running footnote that accompanies the text for its entire length and raises certain questions (about meaning, genre, translation, context) which cannot be regarded as in any sense 'marginal', since they bear at every point upon the problems involved in writing, translating and reading this essay.[2] And in *Glas* the technique is carried yet further, since the double columns of text (from Hegel and Genet) are engaged in a play of limitless 'supplementarity' which can nowhere be reduced to some privileged voice, some self-present source of meaning and truth. It is pointless to ask who is *speaking* in any given passage of this text, whether Hegel, Genet, Derrida *ipse* or some other ghostly intertextual 'presence'. For there is no last word, no metalanguage or voice of authorial control that would ultimately serve to adjudicate the matter. The portions of *Glas* that (apparently) issue under Derrida's name are just as involved in this ceaseless play of intertextual citation and allusion. So *Glas* is not a 'book', at least in the traditional sense of that word: a volume whose unifying principle consists in its always referring us back to some privileged source of authorial intention. It thus enacts what Derrida implies through his title for the opening chapter in *Of Grammatology*: 'The End of the Book and the Beginning of Writing'.

But the fact remains: *Grammatology* not only looks very much like a book but argues its way with a notably book-like persistence and fixity of purpose. So it is not entirely on grounds of expedience – my own obvious need to make sense of its arguments – that I shall set aside Derrida's cautionary remarks and treat *Grammatology* as a book with a theme. For this is, of all his texts, the one most amenable to the kind of expository treatment which Derrida elsewhere does so much to problematize or to play off the field. So let me offer, to begin with, some further suggestions as to what this book is 'about'. Then, having grasped the main outlines of his argument, we can move on to qualify this (admittedly inadequate) account by seeing where exactly its limits show up in the face of Derrida's more complex strategies of reading. But I would want to claim more than this: that the only way to approach a work like *Of Grammatology* is to press as far as possible in the effort to make good sense of it on familiar (thematic and logical) terms. Otherwise there is always the risk of simply acquiescing in its various paradoxical assertions; taking them on board (so to speak) without a due sense of the problems they create, not only for some vastly generalized 'Western metaphysics' but for all our deep-laid normative ideas about language, logic and truth.

But if writing is not a 'theme' in any normal sense, then what exactly is it? We can perhaps best start with Derrida's most explicit passage that links written signs with the logic of supplementarity. Writing, he says, is 'the supplement *par excellence* since it marks the point where the supplement proposes itself as supplement of supplement, sign of sign, *taking the place* of a speech already significant' (p. 281). Such is the classical definition of writing, spelled out by Aristotle in his *De Interpretatione*. Spoken words are the signs we adopt to communicate thoughts or ideas. Written words are the secondary symbols that stand in for speech and so — at one further remove — assist in the process of communication. Already there is the outline of a hierarchy here, a descending order of priority in which writing ranks a very poor third on account of its irrevocable distance from origins, truth and self-present meaning. For ideas, says Aristotle, are common to all men and can hence be the subject of a genuinely universal knowledge. One might suppose that the sheer variety of tongues would place spoken language in much the same bad predicament as writing. But this is not quite what Aristotle's reasoning implies. 'Just as all men have not the same writing so all men have not the same speech-sounds, but the mental experiences, which these directly symbolize, are the same for all, as also are those things of which our experiences are the images' (cited in *Of Grammatology*, p. 73). It is because spoken words are thought of as symbolizing ideas 'directly' — without the further passage through a supplementary medium of written signs — that speech can be safely maintained within the zone of a privileged relation to truth. Thus writing is the inferior term in this series, the term that is marked by its *exclusion* from the intimate circuit of exchange set up between ideas and speech.

For Derrida, this is the founding gesture of a whole philosophical tradition, one that will henceforth invest spoken language or its analogues (presence, origins, meaning) with the value of a positive and self-authenticating truth. Writing will appear in the opposite role: as a supplement, an accessory or substitute sign, twice removed from source and therefore a prey to all manner of dangerous misunderstanding. Writing is not merely a second-best recourse but an accident that somehow befalls language and threatens its very well-being. For writing, though defined as the 'supplement of a supplement', has a way of intruding upon that privileged relation between truth and speech. As we saw in the case of Plato's *Phaedrus*, it may prove difficult — even impossible — to conceptualize language without falling back on covert metaphors of writing. Hence the 'undecidable' meaning of the *pharmakon* in Plato's text: at once cure and poison, wisdom and folly, 'good' writing in the soul that commemorates truth, and 'bad' writing which debases that truth through a shadow-play of mimic signs and inscriptions. There is an order of structural necessity here, one that inscribes writing 'at the source' even in those texts which most vigorously assert the absolute priority of speech.

Now this would create very sizable problems, not only for Aristotle's theory of language but for any attempt to make good the claims of philosophy by identifying knowledge with self-present truth. For there are two senses of the word 'supplement', only one of which squares with this traditional idea of the relation between speech and writing. The relation would continue undisturbed if writing was the kind of *mere* supplement or optional feature that may or may not be added as required. Then we would have a self-sufficient entity (speech) which could make use of writing, whatever its known limitations, as an aid to memory or mass-communication. But a 'supplement' is also that which is required to *complete* or *fill up* some existing lack, some hiatus in the present order of things. And in this case writing would no longer be a strictly dispensable or ancillary technique. On the contrary, it would have to be treated as a precondition of language in general, a necessary supplement in the absence of which speech itself could scarcely be conceived. What Derrida calls the 'logic of supplementarity' is precisely this strange reversal of values whereby an apparently derivative or secondary term takes on the crucial role in determining an entire structure of assumptions.

It is clear enough why writing has been denied this role by philosophers in so many (seemingly diverse) traditions of thought. For if speech is conceived as giving access to truth through its proximity to a self-present consciousness, then writing can only obstruct that access by obtruding its opaque, material inscriptions in the place of an ideal transparency. It is the speaking subject, the voice of experience, whose being is threatened by this alien mode of language. Writing, says Derrida, 'displaces the *proper place* of the sentence, the unique time of the sentence pronounced *hic et nunc* by an irreplaceable subject, and in return enervates the voice' (p. 281). Such at least is the suspicion, the strong (sometimes violent) prejudice that writing has aroused among those thinkers whose texts Derrida examines in *Of Grammatology*. Nor can it be called exactly an 'irrational' prejudice, since so much of the history of Western reason, from Plato to Husserl, is bound up with this view of the relation — the strictly one-sided relation of dominance — between spoken and written language. A perverse double logic seems to operate here as Derrida reads these cardinal texts with an eye to their figural twists and complications. The more firmly writing is denied or demoted, the more clearly it leaves its problematic mark on the metaphors, allegories and detours of argument resorted to by thinkers in the mainstream (logocentric) tradition. Such, Derrida writes, is its position in the history of Western metaphysics: 'a debased, lateralized, repressed, displaced theme, yet exercising a permanent and obsessive pressure from the place where it remains held in check. A feared writing must be cancelled because it erases the presence of the self-same (*propre*) within speech' (p. 270).

Of Grammatology sets out to show that this uncanny reversal, this 'return of the repressed', is no mere accident or momentary lapse but a *rigorous necessity* inscribed in the nature of all 'metaphysical' thinking. On the one hand it is a fact that writing as we know it — as practised in all Western cultures — is a form of phonetic-alphabetical transcription. That is to say, written language is naturally conceived as a second-order system of signs based on the primary material of the spoken word. So it is clearly not by chance that philosophies of language — including the spontaneous philosophy of everyday, commonsense belief — should regard speech as the norm, and writing as a purely derivative function. Derrida is far from wishing to deny the appearance of self-evident truth possessed by this feature of natural language. Thus: 'to be sure this factum of phonetic writing is massive; it commands our entire culture and our entire science, and it is certainly not just one fact among others' (p. 31). But this fact, he goes on, 'does not correspond to any necessity of an absolute and universal essence'. That is to say, there is no justification, in the strictest logical terms, for treating this priority attached to spoken language as a ground for further claims about the nature of truth, meaning or language in general.

It is worth pausing to examine the form of this argument, since it is repeated on many occasions in Derrida's writing. It rests on the distinction between two kinds of truth-claim or forms of argumentative self-evidence. The one is a matter of *de facto* truth, of appealing to what is actually the case in any given realm of enquiry. Thus it cannot be doubted, in the present context, that phonetic-alphabetical writing is a straightforward fact of our cultural experience which is sure to have a certain pervasive influence on the way we habitually think about language. That is to say, we are 'naturally' disposed to accept the priority of speech over writing and the idea that writing is *de facto* confined to a 'supplementary' role in the process of linguistic exchange. But this is not to be confused with the *de jure* argument that would take this kind of factual self-evidence as a basis for claims about the logical *necessity* of thinking as we do. Quite simply, it might have been otherwise, since of course there exist other languages — pictographic or hieroglyphic languages — where there is no question of this privileged bond between sound and sense, such that meaning is thought of as directly embodied in the forms of spoken utterance. That our

own linguistic experience is inevitably shaped by such assumptions is a fact to be reckoned with, certainly. But it is *not* the kind
of fundamental truth about language that would justify raising
an entire metaphysics — a generalized theory of meaning and
truth — on the basis of that experience. And this is the kind of
illegitimate extension that Derrida finds persistently at work in
the thinking of philosophers and linguists from Plato and
Aristotle to Husserl and Saussure. They assume either that
language is always and everywhere based on 'phonocentric'
principles, or that language in its highest, most articulate form is
necessarily so based. And from this it follows that writing will be
cast in one of two possible 'supplementary' roles. On the one
hand it can be seen as a more or less faithful transcription of
spoken sounds, a derivative and secondary medium, to be sure,
but a useful technique none the less. On the other it is perceived
as a positive *threat,* as an alien, parasitical order of signs that can
work to destroy the natural relation between sound, meaning
and truth. Writing then appears as the 'non-phonetic moment'
that lurks within language and creates all manner of dangerous,
disruptive effects. For what is threatened here is not simply
language in its 'natural', spoken state but the whole associated
system of values upheld by this root supposition.

So the 'logocentric' bias in Western thought goes along with
the idea of phonetic-alphabetical writing as the only form that
can possibly approach the dignity of truth and origins. Other
kinds of writing — for instance, the ancient Egyptian or Chinese
— operate according to a wholly different logic, one that goes
straight from the idea itself to a graphic inscription on the page.
And as Derrida shows, notably in an essay on Hegel, philosophers have often treated such writing with contempt, since it
doesn't pass by way of the vital link between articulate *sound*
and intelligible *sense*.[3] 'Alphabetical writing is on all accounts
the more intelligent,' Hegel argues. And again: 'the Eastern form
must therefore be excluded from the History of Philosophy'
(quoted by Derrida, *Margins of Philosophy*, pp. 95 and 101).
For Hegel, the history of philosophy is narrated from the
viewpoint of Absolute Reason, of a consciousness that can now
look back and retrace the progress of its own triumphal

evolution.[4] This progress is marked by an increasing power of reflexive self-understanding, so that Reason finally arrives at a point where its entire past history becomes ideally intelligible in the light of present knowledge. And it is here that Hegelian logic requires the link between philosophy as a quest for self-present truth and the assumed superiority of phonetic writing as the only medium properly equipped to preserve and transmit that truth. Hegel was fascinated by new advances in the deciphering of Egyptian ideographic script. But he firmly denies that such alien forms of writing can lay the least claim to serious *philosophical* importance. And this because they lack — or simply pass over — that vital stage in the economy of writing that obliges it to pass by way of voice, presence and authentic (spoken) utterance.

Derrida's essay on Hegel ('The Pit and the Pyramid') helps to elucidate some otherwise very cryptic passages from *Of Grammatology*. These have to do with the interlinked themes of history, truth and origins, each of them threatened (as Derrida argues) by a certain idea of writing and its dangerous effects. Thus: 'history and knowledge . . . have always been determined . . . as detours *for the purpose* of the reappropriation of presence' (*Of Grammatology*, p. 10). It is in Hegel that this 'detour' finally achieves its most sweeping and grandiose form. Hegelian dialectic claims to speak the truth of history as well as the history of truth. That is to say, it offers not only a narrative account of certain stages on the path to Absolute Reason, but a *meta-narrative* or God's-eye view that would finally transcend all mere relativities of place and time. And to bring off this argument Hegel has to insist that language should properly bear within itself the power to revive past meanings and intentions, to communicate truths that would otherwise fall into the realm of inert, dead inscriptions. The viability of Hegel's great project must ultimately rest on this presence within language of a live, self-authenticating truth which allows us to read and, in reading, to pass through and beyond the mere written signs to a knowledge of their animating purpose. Otherwise there would be no grounds for assurance, no warrant that history made good sense or that Reason was now securely placed to make sense of it.

This — very briefly — is what Derrida means when he writes of 'history and knowledge' alike as being 'detours for the reappropriation of presence'. It is not (as some would have him say) that history doesn't exist, that there is no reality (past or present) outside the written text. Rather it is a question of that powerful *ideology*, most strikingly exemplified in Hegel, which assimilates all forms of history and knowledge to the unfolding of a teleological scheme whose end-point is self-present truth. And this is why Hegelian logic requires 'the privilege of speech over writing and of phonetic writing over every other system of inscription, particularly over hieroglyphic or ideographic writing' (*Margins*, p. 88). For it is only in the case of spoken language — or in a writing that respects the natural priority of speech — that there occurs this apparently ideal coincidence of meaning and present intent. When we speak there is a sense of some peculiarly intimate relation between the words that we utter and the meaning that animates those words. In French there is a phrase, *s'entendre-parler*, that nicely suggests the intuitive logic of this natural attitude to speech. 'Entendre' means both 'to hear' and 'to understand', with the strong implication that hearing is in some way a privileged or uniquely authentic form of understanding. *S'entendre-parler* might thus be translated: 'hearing oneself speak and immediately grasping the sense of one's own utterance'. This idea has the force, the persuasive power of a primordial intuition. It is certainly not to be argued away by some decision henceforth to think differently, to break with such 'phonocentric' habits of mind and thus invert the traditional logic that subjugates writing to a self-present speech. Hearing/understanding oneself talk is a *de facto* truth in our experience of language that appears so massively self-evident as almost to brook no question.

But it is a different matter when philosophers like Hegel construct an entire metaphysics of history and truth on the basis of this same phonocentric prejudice. Then it becomes clear — through a deconstructive reading — that the system rests not only on the privileges accruing to a self-present speech but also on the active *suppression* of other motifs that might call this concept into doubt. Hegel's dialectic claims to transcend all previous philosophies of mind and nature by showing how their

71

various problems or antinomies are finally resolved through the movement of speculative thought. This movement is epitomized in the famous Hegelian triad of 'thesis', 'antithesis' and 'synthesis'. Reason proceeds by positing an initial idea which then turns out to have further, contradictory implications beyond its power to explain or control. The only way out of this logical impasse is through the leap to a higher, dialectical plane of reasoning where the old contradiction no longer applies since its terms have been transformed in the process. This moment of conceptual *Aufhebung* − the emergence of a logic or an order of meaning undreamt of previously − is the heart of Hegel's idealist metaphysics. It claims to represent not only the highest form of logical thinking but also the dynamics of change at work both in nature and in the unfolding of world-historical events. These processes can only be grasped, Hegel argues, through an act of dialectical synthesis, an act whereby the mind self-consciously narrates and interprets the history of its own stages on the road to present understanding.

Thus the three main branches of Hegelian thought (logic, philosophy of mind, philosophy of nature) are all at last brought together in the name of Absolute Reason. And to achieve this *dénouement* − as Derrida shows − Hegel must establish two main facts about the character and proper capabilities of language. First, it is vital that speech (authentic, self-present speech) should represent the natural condition of language. Only then will it be possible for thought to re-live the various episodes of its own evolution, from the earliest forms of unreflective sensuous experience to the highest, most complex or 'mediated' stage of self-conscious philosophical grasp. And if *writing* necessarily plays a large role in this account − both as source of historical evidence and as the mark of a decisive phase in the cultural evolution of mind − then it has to be a writing which duly acknowledges its own subservient status *vis-à-vis* speech. And so it is that Hegel finds himself compelled to refuse 'philosophical' significance to those other kinds of writing − the Egyptian and Chinese − that altogether bypass the privileged tie between voice, self-presence and truth.

Now Derrida's point − to put it very simply − is that Hegel's arguments cannot sustain this idealized concept of language and representation. He is confusing a *de facto* 'natural' attitude (the logic of *s'entendre-parler*) with an *de jure* system of regulative concepts which would claim to dictate the very nature and limits of rational thought. But if there is indeed an order of necessity governing the relations between speech and writing in Hegel's text, it is one that creates some rather awkward complications for his whole metaphysics of language. In fact the opposition *de facto/de jure* turns out to have a different pertinence here, one that would require a meticulous re-reading of Hegelian logic and all its associated values. 'Writing', says Derrida, 'can never be totally inhabited by the voice. The non-phonetic function, the operative silences of alphabetic writing, are not factual accidents or waste products one might hope to reduce . . . The *fact* of which we have just spoken is not only an empirical fact, it is the example of an essential law that irreducibly limits the achievement of a teleological ideal' (*Margins,* pp. 95-6). For it is a matter of necessity, not only that writing includes such 'non-phonetic' forms or components, but also that Hegel should inevitably come up against them in his efforts to comprehend the nature of language. And it is here that the title of Derrida's essay ('The Pit and the Pyramid') takes on a certain graphic force of suggestion. For there now begins to emerge, in Hegel's writing, a series of thematic oppositions which stage the encounter between Western metaphysics and its alien, disturbing counterpart. These images point on the one hand to the deep, dark reserves of a consciousness ideally present to itself in the authentic act of speech, and on the other to a monumental order of inscriptions raised, as it were, like a pyramid in the desert, confronting the traveller with meanings that can only be *deciphered,* not restored to anything like a state of original, pristine intelligibility.

It is Hegel's purpose to keep these two orders of language firmly separate. Thus he hopes to prevent mere writing (in its non-phonetic form) from working its disruptive effects upon the logic of meaning, identity and truth. But this proves impossible for a number of reasons. First, there is the *fact* that such 'other' languages do exist, not only in different (past and present) cultures but also in the various formalized systems of signs adopted by philosophers such as Leibniz, by modern mathematicians, cryptographers and proponents of symbolic logic. To say that these are not 'natural' languages, and therefore need not be taken into account, is of course to beg the main question of Derrida's case. For what has always counted as 'natural' language, at least with philosophers like Plato, Aristotle and Hegel, is language that confirms the priority of speech (or phonetic writing) over anything that takes an alternative route from inscription to intelligible sense. And Derrida's second point is the logical corollary of this: that writing cannot be 'totally inhabited by the voice' because it always contains, along with those phonetic components, a further, necessary range of resources (punctuation, spacing, diacritical marks and so forth) which exist only in the form of graphic inscription.

That Hegel is disturbed by this fact about language is manifest, Derrida thinks, in his brief and dismissive dealing with Leibniz. Here is the case of a 'practical mind' (Hegel's words) whose lack of philosophical sophistication led him to 'exaggerate the advantages which a complete written language would have as a universal language for the intercourse of nations and especially of scholars' (quoted by Derrida, *Margins*, p. 96). What the 'practical mind' fails to grasp is the necessity for concepts to pass by way of the natural link between sound and sense as preserved in phonetic-alphabetical writing. And it is precisely the speculative bent of Hegel's philosophy — its quest for an order of ideal, self-present truth beyond the grasp of mere 'practical' reason — that set him at odds with Leibniz. In Hegelian logic, the sign is understood 'according to the structure and movement of the *Aufhebung*, by means of which the spirit, elevating itself above the nature in which it was submerged, at once suppresses and retains nature, sublimating nature into itself, accomplishing itself as internal freedom, and thereby presenting itself to itself for itself, *as such*' (*Margins*, p. 76). Thus the written sign can only serve Hegel's purpose insofar as it transcends its material condition, uniting language and thought in a moment of ideal, self-present understanding. And it is for this reason that Hegel devalues any writing, or any project for a writing, which would somehow dispense with the passage through voice and phonetic-

alphabetical transcription. Such sign-systems can have nothing
to do with *philosophy*, Hegel insists, since philosophy's business
is always to envisage some higher, more advanced dialectical
stage of the antinomies between mind and nature, freedom and
necessity, intelligible truth and sensuous immediacy. And if
written language is to mark the point of this *Aufhebung* – if it is
to be, as Derrida's translator nicely puts it, *relevant* – then the
detour through voice and phonetics is an absolute necessity. For
it is precisely in the idea of self-addressed speech – in the
moment of *s'entendre-parler* – that these two realms, the
sensible and the intelligible, are brought into greatest proximity.

What Derrida draws to our attention in Hegel's text are the
strains and contradictions produced by this attempt, first to
subordinate writing to speech, and secondly to distinguish a
'good' (phonetic) writing from its 'bad' (ideographic or non-
phonetic) counterpart. There is a remarkable paragraph in his
essay which again picks up the implications of its title. 'A path,
which we will follow, leads from this night pit . . . resonating
with all the powers of the voice which it holds in reserve, to a
pyramid brought back from the Egyptian desert which will soon
be raised over the sober and abstract weave of the Hegelian text,
there composing the stature and the status of the sign' (*Margins*,
p. 77). The pyramid represents a feared, alien form of writing, a
monument to everything that eludes the order of natural,
self-present speech. It teases interpretation out of thought, like
the statue whose ruins confront the desert traveller in Shelley's
sonnet 'Ozymandias'. Indeed, that mysterious poem might serve
as an epigraph to Derrida's essay on Hegelian semiotics. The
'shattered visage' remains, half-sunk in sand, to bear witness
'that its sculptor well those passions read/Which yet survive,
stamped on these lifeless things,/The hand that mocked them,
and the heart that fed'. But this sense of intimate communion
with the dead is sharply undermined by the poem's insisting that
these are indeed the ruins of time, placed beyond reach of living
recall by the muteness of dead inscriptions on stone.

> 'My name is Ozymandias, king of kings:
> Look on my works, ye Mighty, and despair!'

Nothing beside remains. Round the decay
Of that colossal wreck, boundless and bare,
The lone and level sands stretch far away.

Such writing provokes the utmost of speculative thought without the least promise of leading back to some assurance of
origins and presence. The traveller's reaction is akin to that of
Hegel when confronted with the fact of a language that exists in
the form of irreducibly *written* signs, a hieroglyphics devoid of
the animating spirit that belongs to phonetic-alphabetical writing.

Thus for Hegel, hearing is the ideal form of sensory perception, that which comes closest to transcending the hateful
antinomies of subject and object, mind and nature, reason and
experience. For the act of hearing has a special virtue, a power to
bring sensations home, so to speak, through the intimate awareness of sounds from outside which nonetheless register deep
within the aural cavities. It is this virtue that is raised metaphorically into a notion of ideal self-presence, of the mind perfectly
attuned to interpret the incoming data of sensory perception.
There is a strain of neo-Platonist mysticism that seems to reassert
its hold upon philosophy through this privilege granted to
hearing. Blake thought of the five senses as the 'chief inlets of
soul in this age' for creatures deprived of more immediate access
to the truths of imaginative vision. From Plato to Hegel,
philosophy inherits this will to transcend the limitations of
mortal experience in the quest for a knowledge ideally independent of mere sensory acquaintance. But Hegel cannot afford to
go all the way with this Platonic contempt for worldly appearances. His project, after all, is to write a full-scale phenomenological history of Mind in its various manifestations, from the
primitive stages of unreflective sensuous experience to the
highest, most complex forms of self-conscious thought. His
philosophy must therefore take full account of the senses, but
only on terms laid down in advance by the need to transcend
them dialectically, to incorporate their material witness into a
higher, spiritual form of understanding. And it is precisely
through the privilege attached to hearing that Hegel achieves this

totalizing movement of thought. Hearing, as he writes in the *Aesthetics*, is 'like sight, one of the theoretical and not practical senses, and is still more ideal than sight'. For the ear 'listens to the result of the inner vibration of the body', a peculiarly intimate experience which cannot be reduced to any merely physical order of stimulus-response (quoted in *Margins*, p. 92).

In this passage one finds compactly stated the entire dialectical strategy by which Hegel seeks to sublimate or spiritualize the nature of sensory experience. But it is also, as Derrida argues, a classic example of the logocentric prejudice which always identifies truth and reason with the instance of self-present (spoken) language. His preface to *Margins* sets out to question this prejudice by asking what techniques might exist for disturbing the tranquillity of a self-assured discourse intent upon hearing/understanding itself speak. It is entitled 'Tympan', a reference to (among other things) the *tympanum*, or part of the inner ear that vibrates in response to changes in atmospheric pressure and transmits these vibrations to the cerebral cortex. The tympan is also a component in certain kinds of manual printing press, a framework (or more often two, of wood and iron) used to clamp the sheets and maintain a proper layout of margins and spaces. So the word brings together a range of senses, all of which have to do with the *topoi* of limits, enclosures and that which *comes between* some original impression and the mark it leaves. Derrida's text plays on the idea of a liminal writing that would pass clean through the boundaries and buffer-zones traditionally set up between philosophy and other, less reputable forms of discourse. What has kept these distinctions firmly in place is the image philosophy has of itself as a language somehow uniquely attuned to those inward vibrations of truth and knowledge. Where it does have to deal with the 'outside' world of sensory experience, philosophy can always keep itself pure by insisting on the absolute priority of concepts and the power of dialectics to transcend the enslavement to mere physical perception. And so it is that hearing takes on its privileged role as the 'ideal' organ of sense, since it offers the required assurance that nothing need escape the sovereign order of self-present meanings and concepts. 'Indefatigably at issue is the ear, the distinct, differentiated, articulated organ that produces the effect of proximity, of absolute properness, the idealizing erasure of organic difference' (*Margins,* p. xvii).

But the ear is also 'at issue' in another sense, one that disturbs this perfect inner tranquillity and sets up a different, more troublesome chain of repercussions. For hearing is not confined, as Derrida writes, to the 'sheltered portico of the tympanum', to a sound that would resonate inwardly without the least risk of external, contaminating influence. What this idealizing metaphor leaves out of account is the whole convoluted apparatus of canals, pathways and passages that envelop the tympanum, as it were, *on both sides,* and complicate its working beyond any question of a straightforward, decidable contrast between inner and outer ears. To reflect on these hidden liabilities of its own most cherished metaphor would perforce lead philosophy beyond the closed circle of self-communing voice and presence. So this is the question Derrida poses at the outset of *Margins.* 'Under what conditions, then, could one *mark,* for a philosopheme in general, a *limit,* a margin that it could not infinitely reappropriate, *conceive* as its own, in advance engendering and interning the process of its expropriation?' (p. xv; Derrida's italics). This can best be achieved by attending to the margins of a dominant discourse, those points at which thought 'repercusses its absolute limit only in sonorous representation' (p. xix). For it is here that the tympanum begins to play a different, more unsettling role in the general metaphorics of philosophy. Rather than delimiting a self-enclosed space where thought can settle down to hear itself speak, the diaphragm appears undecidably stretched between philosophy and everything that threatens or subverts the philosophic enterprise.

In its printing-press employment, one of the essential uses of this device was 'the regular calculation of the margin'. And likewise in the case of our hearing apparatus, where the membrane can be thought of – from one point of view – as that which *mediates* between external impressions and inward understanding, but which still remains firmly in place as the integral boundary, the marker of limits, that separates these two distinct realms. But the polysemous character of this word is such as to prevent it from operating strictly in accordance with this well-defined logic of 'inside' and 'outside'. As Derrida asks: 'will the multiplicity of these tympanums permit themselves to be analyzed? Will we be led back, at the exit of the labyrinths, toward some *topos* or commonplace named *tympanum?*' (p. xxvii). If not — if the word should prove ultimately resistant, like Plato's *pharmakon,* to any reading that would pin down its sense to a clear-cut logical distribution — then philosophy might be forced to rethink the basis of its own privileged truth-claims. More specifically, the 'margins' of philosophic discourse would begin to encroach upon the main text, since the tympan would no longer serve in its role as a firm marker-out of limits and boundaries. Or again, to vary the metaphor: what might be the effect upon philosophy's 'inner ear' — its self-assured ethos of *s'entendre-parler* — if the tympanum turned out to lack any stable identity of meaning, any power to hold itself properly in place as a mark of the inwardness achieved by thought on its way to authentic truth?

These questions are raised in what will strike most philosophers — at least those in the dominant Anglo-American tradition — as a style of extravagant metaphorical whimsy. Such wordplay, they are likely to argue, is at most a kind of sophistical doodling on the margins of serious, truth-seeking discourse. But Derrida can always respond by pointing out that philosophy has constantly sustained itself on metaphors, notably those which assimilate truth and reason to the idea of a pure, self-present speech. What he does in *Margins* is pursue such tropes beyond their usual, self-regulating limits, to the point where philosophy is confronted with the evidence of its own more devious textual ruses. These essays, Derrida writes, 'interrogate philosophy beyond its meaning, treating it not only as a discourse but as a determined text inscribed in a general text, enclosed in the representation of its own margin' (p. xxiii). Hence his strategic recourse to metaphors like the ubiquitous *tympanum,* figures of thought which refuse to settle down into a stable order of concepts or clear-cut logical oppositions. The stage is then set for that long-deferred encounter between philosophy and everything that threatens to subvert or decon-struct the sovereignty of philosophic reason. Thus Derrida can ask: 'what is the specific resistance of philosophical discourse to deconstruction?' (p. xix). And he can argue that the ground of this resistance is precisely its refusal to countenance a writing that allows full play to the disseminating powers of language, the 'undecidability' of terms like *tympanum* that suspend philoso-phy's most crucial working distinctions.

Thus the essays collected in *Margins of Philosophy* make a point of being marginal to everything that has hitherto counted as 'serious' philosophical discourse. Typically they approach their subject-text by latching on to metaphors, footnotes, pass-ing analogies or turns of argument which philosophers would regard as scarcely meriting such detailed attention. But this is exactly Derrida's point: that philosophy has maintained its longstanding prerogative in matters of ultimate truth by always dictating in advance what shall *count* as worthwhile topics of debate. To return to the printing-press metaphor: 'philosophical discourse intends to know and to master its margin, to define the line, align the page, enveloping it in its volume' (p. xxiv). What Derrida broaches in *Margins* is a deconstruction of the limits that have always determined philosophy's elective self-image. And this by way of showing that the privileged metaphors of philosophy are open to a radically different reading, one that would sound out their further 'repercussions' in a play of rhetorical exchange and substitution that exceeds any straight-forward logical accounting.

We can now perhaps return to *Of Grammatology* with a keener sense of the issues at stake in Derrida's 'rehabilitation' of writing against the superior truth-claims of speech. At least we will not be so tempted to reduce this strategy to a matter of localized topics or 'themes' in the texts he singles out for deconstructive treatment. It is not only that the repression of writing goes deep and far back in Western philosophical dis-course. There is also the fact that this repression is tied up with everything that philosophy has hitherto marshalled on the side of reason, dialectics and truth. Writing is conceived as the 'dangerous supplement' that philosophy must at all costs subdue to its purpose by maintaining a whole complex system of assumptions based on the priority of self-present speech. Just *why* this prejudice has taken hold, and to what extent deconstruction can resist its effects, are the main questions that Derrida addresses in *Of Grammatology*.

Linguistics or grammatology?

In Plato, as we have seen, there is a 'good' writing, a figurative writing-in-the-soul, which leads back to truth and has nothing in common with its bad, literal counterpart. Nothing, that is, apart from the awkward fact that it can only be described, conceived or brought to book through the metaphor of writing itself. *Of Grammatology* starts out by collecting various examples of this singular compulsion to degrade literal writing by declaring it a supplement to something more authentic or inwardly related to truth. Thus Christian tradition speaks of the 'book of nature', of God's purpose vouchsafed to the soul in a receptive state of grace through all manner of occult signs and tokens. The same metaphor is to be found in the texts of Jewish tradition, in the writings of various neo-Platonist adepts and in thinkers of seemingly the most diverse persuasion, from Descartes and Kant to Heidegger, Saussure and Lévi-Strauss. So this is the basic question that Derrida poses in *Of Grammatology*. How has it come about that writing is subject to this strange reversal of values, its *literal* meaning everywhere spoken against while its *figural* sense takes on a whole range of occult or mystical overtones?

Any answer to this question will need to do more than simply invert the established opposition and declare the priority of literal writing over its various metaphorical adjuncts. For the very idea of 'literal' sense is itself a species of root metaphor, bound up with the notion that straightforward (non-metaphorical) meaning inheres in the *letter* of the text. If this were indeed the case − if metaphor could always be defined as a swerve from the literal norm − then philosophy would have no great cause for concern. And indeed, this has been the dominant assumption among linguists, philosophers and others who have

81

sought to conceptualize metaphor on terms laid down by the assumed priority of literal meaning. Metaphor is essentially a *deviant* figure, a non-standard usage that achieves its effects precisely by subverting the normal economy of sense, or refusing the established (literal) relation between signifier and signified. Such was Aristotle's definition of metaphor, and such has always been the dominant theory, maintained still by formalist critics who value metaphor as a means of 'defamiliarizing' the language of commonplace routine perception.

So it is tempting to misread Derrida as saying simply that this theory has got things upside down; that metaphor is there from the start, since 'literal' meaning (the *letter* of the text) is itself nothing more than a kind of aboriginal trope. But this is to neglect a further and crucial stage in Derrida's argument. For it is precisely such a straightforward reversal of values − the elevation of metaphor in place of literal meaning − that has characterized the mystical discourse of 'writing in the soul'. If one simply accepts that everything is metaphor − including the idea of 'literal' writing − then there is no hope of breaking this charmed (or maybe vicious) circle of sublimated meaning. 'It is not, therefore, a matter of inverting the literal meaning and the figurative meaning but of determining the "literal" meaning of writing as metaphoricity itself' (*Of Grammatology,* p. 15). What deconstruction has to show is the ultimate *undecidability* of all these deep-laid conceptual oppositions. And it can only do this by refusing to content itself with the simple demonstration that all philosophical concepts come down to metaphor in the end. For it would then be repeating the same aboriginal gesture that assimilates writing ('literal' inscription) to a higher, metaphorical order of truth which nonetheless depends upon writing as the means of making itself understood. 'All that functions as *metaphor* in these discourses confirms the privilege of the logos and founds the "literal" meaning then given to writing: a sign signifying a signifier itself signifying an eternal logos' (p. 15). What is in question here is not just a generalized sense of metaphorical drift but a specific movement that repeats itself wherever thought tries to fix some 'literal' ground on which to establish its superior claims-to-truth. So deconstruction must seize upon those moments in the text where writing *resists* this seductive process; where something escapes, exceeds or perplexes the sovereignty of logocentric reason. If 'literal' writing has been determined as a supplement — as a secondary, fallen, derivative order of signs — then deconstruction will bring out the perverse double logic involved in this strange operation.

Such is the task of an applied 'grammatology', in Derrida's massively extended sense of the term. Of course there exist many studies of writing in its various stages of historical and technical evolution.[5] What these studies all take for granted, Derrida finds, is first the absolute, self-evident priority of speech over writing, and secondly — following from that — the superior status of phonetic-alphabetical script. We have seen already how these assumptions dominate Hegel's thinking about language and history. They support his view that reason has achieved its highest, most refined or sophisticated forms only in those cultures where writing is a faithful *transcription* of self-present speech. And the same holds true of those histories of writing which trace its evolution from a 'primitive' (pictographic) script to the stage where it learns to reproduce or articulate the sound-structure of 'natural' language. Now of course Derrida is not denying that these changes have indeed taken place. Nor is he suggesting — absurdly — that writing 'preceded' speech in the process of linguistic evolution. Rather, he asks what is really at stake in this question of priorities; whether there is not more involved than an issue of straightforward historical precedence. For it is precisely when it tries to *think the origin* of language, when it goes beyond matters of documentary record, that grammatology repeats the Hegelian gesture of repressing or sublimating the written. At this point, as if by some perverse compulsion, writing is both appealed to (inescapably, since it offers the only possible evidence) and yet always treated as a bad, degenerate system of signs. The grammatologist cannot avoid asking the question, 'What is writing?' or 'Where and when does writing begin?' But this question is never pressed beyond a certain sticking-point prescribed by the nature of logocentric thinking. As Derrida remarks, 'the responses generally come very quickly. They circulate within concepts that are seldom criticized and move within evidence which always seems self-evident' (*Of Grammatology*, p. 28). In short, such histories of writing as we have are deeply complicit with the assumption that language achieves its predestined *telos* or goal in the form of phonetic-alphabetical script.

So Derrida is not challenging this massive consensus on the grounds of its factual or historical accuracy. What he is trying to pinpoint is the questionable nexus of ideas that leads from a contingent fact (the priority of speech, historically considered) to a wholesale mystique (the ethos of speech as self-presence and the consequent devaluation of writing). And the signs of this confusion between *de facto* and *de jure* truth are there, Derrida claims, in all the standard histories of writing. 'A philosophical and teleological classification exhausts the problem in a few pages; one passes next to an exposition of facts' (p. 28). What grammatologists have so far failed to think through is their relation to writing as that which makes possible not only their particular discipline but every kind of scholarly, scientific or critical tradition. For it is through writing alone that knowledge is transmitted and achieves whatever can be achieved in the way of objectivity and truth. Those who expressly deplore this fact — who take to writing, like Plato, as a bad expedient forced upon them by the need to preserve or communicate ideas — are therefore placed in a peculiarly false position. And their predicament is repeated, as Derrida will show, in the writing of numerous philosophers, linguists, anthropologists and others, too many for this to be regarded as merely a passing phase in the history of European thought. What Derrida says of traditional grammatology applies far beyond the specialized domain of the 'science of writing' as such. In these historians there is a singular contrast between 'the theoretical fragility of the reconstructions and the historical, archaeological, ethnological, philosophical wealth of information' (p. 28). Deconstruction — or Derridean grammatology — will seek out the blindspots of this logocentric discourse, the points at which writing as it were returns to haunt the scene of its own repression.

This deconstructive strategy involves a double challenge to the commonplace treatment of writing. On the one hand — as we have seen with Derrida on Plato – there is a scrupulous attention to the *letter* of the text, a rejection of the idea that 'philosophy' is a matter of absolute concepts or truths, so that any attempt to analyse its language, in the style of rhetoricians and literary critics, would seem just a kind of perverse category-mistake. Thus Derrida will catch at those moments of 'undecid-ability' where writing complicates the meaning of a text beyond its express intentions or its self-authorized logic of sense. 'There is a point in the system', he writes, 'where the signifier can no longer be replaced by its signified, so that in consequence no signifier can be replaced, purely and simply' (p. 266). The classical definition of writing – as found in thinkers from Plato and Aristotle to Hegel, Husserl and Saussure – takes it as axiomatically the 'sign of a sign', a mere supplementary inscription, twice removed from origins and truth. Derrida will not so much reject this definition as extend it to cover *every* kind of discourse, spoken language included. For it is a major precept of modern structural linguistics that meaning is not a relation of identity between signifier and signified but a product of the differences, the signifying contrasts and relationships that exist at every level of language. Such was Saussure's cardinal insight: that only by conceiving language 'synchronically', as a network of interrelated sounds and meanings, could linguistics become a genuine, self-respecting science.[6] We will soon have occasion to look more closely at the logic and the wider repercussions of Saussurean linguistics. For the moment it is enough to see how Derrida draws out its radical implications for the science of writing. For if language is *always and everywhere* a system of differential signs – if meaning subsists in various structures of relationship and *not* in some ideal correspondence between sound and sense – then the classical definition of writing would apply to every form of language whatsoever. 'From the moment that there is meaning there are nothing but signs. We think only in signs' (p. 50). To think logocentrically is to dream of a 'transcendental signified', of a meaning outside and beyond the differential play of language that would finally put a stop to this unnerving predicament. Deconstruction defines its own project by contrast as a perpetual reminder that meaning is always the 'sign of a sign'; that thought cannot escape this logic of endless supplementarity; and that *writing* is in at the origin of language, since that origin cannot be conceived except by acknowledging the differential nature of signs.

So this is Derrida's first challenge to the 'massive self-evidence' gathered on the side of traditional (logocentric) reason. He will take the classical idea of writing – 'sign of a sign' – and show that it exceeds all the bounds of its 'proper', restricted application. It will then appear that all philosophy, all reflection on thought and language, is caught up in a play of graphic concepts or metaphors. 'A writing within which philosophy is inscribed as a place within a text which it does not command.' And again: 'philosophy is, within writing, nothing but this movement of writing as effacement of the signifier and the desire of presence restored, of being, signified in its brilliance and its glory' (p. 286). This is where deconstruction begins: by locating the stress-points where writing resists any attempt to reduce it to an order of univocal (single-*voiced*) truth. Hence Derrida's meticulous attention to the *letter* of the text, to those apparently 'marginal' details or twists of implication that philosophers have mostly ignored in the interests of preserving a conceptual status quo. If writing – *literal* writing – has up to now been treated as a mere supplement to that other, good, metaphorical 'writing in the soul', Derrida will turn the argument round and insist on a rigorous literalism of the text. From which it will emerge that philosophy, linguistics, anthropology and the 'human sciences' at large have hitherto been based on a covert ideology of voice and self-presence, a metaphysics which in turn has worked to prevent their texts from being read with anything like an adequate attention to detail.

But this is still to understand 'writing' in the narrow, familiar sense of graphic inscriptions or literal marks on a page. If deconstruction involved nothing more than this then it would simply be a kind of meticulous close-reading technique whose methods derived from rhetoric or literary criticism and whose only novelty lay in its extending those methods to other, less hospitable subject-disciplines. But in fact, as Derrida argues, writing has played a role in traditional thought which cannot be confined to its restricted (graphological) sense. Writing is the name metaphorically attached to whatever eludes, subverts or opposes the discourse of logocentric reason. 'Writing, the letter, the sensible inscription, has always been considered by Western tradition as the body and matter external to the spirit, to breath, to speech, and to the logos' (p. 35). And it is not that writing is just one metaphor among others, a metaphor that happens to line up predictably on the side of everything alien to Being and truth. On the contrary, Derrida asserts: 'the problem of body and soul is no doubt derived from the problem of writing from which it seems to borrow its metaphors' (p. 35). No matter how far back one pushes the enquiry — whether to Plato, to Aristotle, to Jewish, Christian or other scriptural sources — there always appears this root opposition between the *letter* and the *spirit* of the text, between a debased, merely literal way of understanding and a privileged access to revealed truth. The same applies to those enlightened moralists like Kant who equate human virtue with the sovereignty of reason over instinct, and who therefore identify sin — in Derrida's words — as 'the inversion of the natural relationship between the soul and the body through passion' (p. 34). Clearly there are some large issues bound up with the attempt to hold writing firmly in place as a sup-plementary adjunct to speech.

We can now turn back to Saussure and his project of structural linguistics, since this provides perhaps the best point of entry to Derrida's labyrinthine text. And we can start, like Derrida, with the simple question: why is it that Saussure treats *writing* — the fact and the idea of writing — with such evident suspicion and reserve? Certainly the signs are there in Saussure's *Course in General Linguistics,* as Derrida shows through a series of striking quotations. 'Writing', says Saussure, 'though unre-lated to its inner system, is used continually to represent language. We cannot simply disregard it. We must be acquainted with its usefulness, shortcomings and dangers.' And again: 'Writing veils the appearance of language; it is not a guise for language but a disguise.'[7] Elsewhere Saussure's metaphors sug-gest all manner of evil, degenerate effects brought about by this exposure of language to the dangers of writing. His rhetoric goes far beyond the kind of cautionary note that would serve to warn linguists not to place *too* much confidence in written sources, or to listen wherever possible to spoken language. And it is precisely this strain of rhetorical excess which should therefore alert us, Derrida thinks, to the issues at stake in Saussure's prejudicial treatment of writing. What Saussure wants to do is to insulate 'natural' language against all the mischiefs created by a writing that gets in the way of that privileged relation between voice and self-present thought. This latter is for Saussure a 'natural' bond, one that defines the very *nature* of language and saves it from contamination by the alien, external, corrupting power of written signs. As with Kant and the older Christian moralists, so here: the good is whatever is lined up on the side of reason, spirit or soul, while the bad is either what rejects that alignment or − worse still − renders such distinctions simply *undecidable*.

For this is indeed Derrida's point: that Saussure denounces writing precisely on account of its unsettling effects on the logic of his own argument. After all, what could be the 'natural bond' between sound and sense if language is a system without 'positive terms', its structure (as Saussure tells us) entirely a matter of differential contrasts and relationships? One result of this theory is the doctrine of the 'arbitrary' sign, the denial that there could possibly exist any *natural* relation between signifier and signified, since each occupies its own distinctive place in a separate economy of signifying elements. Certainly Saussure went some way toward qualifying this doctrine, conceding (for instance) that there might be *degrees* of naturalization brought about by established or conventional usage.[8] But the notion of the 'arbitrary' sign is a crucial component of Saussurean linguistics and of all those developments in the wake of Saussure commonly known as French structuralism. It was this idea that led on to the adoption of linguistics as model discipline, one that would enable anthropologists like Claude Lévi-Strauss or literary critics like Roland Barthes to reformulate the purpose of their enterprise. For it opened the way to thinking of these various second-order 'languages' (myth, kinship-systems, literary styles, narrative grammars) as based on the same structural ground-rules that Saussure had laid down for the study of 'natural' language. If the sign is indeed an 'arbitrary' relation between signifier and signified, then it leaves room for all kinds of secondary elaboration in the spheres of cultural and literary study. Hence Barthes's argument in his early book *Mythologies* (1957): that bourgeois 'myth' was best understood as a signifying system that took its materials from a first-order language, attached various cultural values to them, and then tried to pass off these artificial constructs as belonging to some timeless *natural* order of meaning, rather than to mere cultural fashion.[9] The object of a radical structuralist critique was to expose the workings of this bogus mythology by insisting on the thoroughly arbitrary character of the sign.

It may be argued that some of these developments went further than anything Saussure intended by his own, more qualified treatment of the theme. But there is certainly no grasping the principles of structural linguistics without perceiving the importance he accords to the arbitrary nature of the sign. And it is this that gives rise to Derrida's question: how can Saussure nonetheless make such a point of the 'natural bond' between sound and sense? And why is it always *writing* that is cast in the role of an alien, perverting influence? One further passage from Saussure may help to bring out the sheer force of this indictment. It speaks of the 'tyranny' of writing; the way that, 'by imposing itself on the masses, spelling influences and modifies language'. These modifications 'lead to wrong (*vicieuses*) pronunciations', and such mistakes are truly 'pathological' in nature (quoted in *Of Grammatology*, p. 41). Writing is conceived as a perversion of the natural order of language, an influence that operates always *from outside* to corrupt or destroy the pure spontaneity of self-present speech. And so, in Derrida's words, 'this natural bond of the signified (concept or sense) to the phonic signifier would condition the natural relationship subordinating writing (visible image) to speech. It is this natural relationship that would have been inverted by the original sin of writing' (p. 35). But what are we to make of this attitude, given that Saussure can only conceive of language as a system of interrelated differences, a network of structural relations that nowhere reduces to 'positive terms'? And the problem is compounded by Saussure's tendency to fall back on covert metaphors of *writing* − of trace, inscription and suchlike imagery − when he comes to explain this differential system. For otherwise it is strictly impossible to think how a sign can have meaning not in and of itself but by virtue of its always already being inscribed in a network of articulated sense. The only model that serves to conceptualize this character of language is that which resorts to an inscriptionalist idiom by way of making good its claims.

Thus Derrida can ask: 'What is the evil?' and 'What has been invested in the "living word" that makes such aggressions of writing intolerable?' (p. 41). And his response takes the form of a sustained meditation on everything that writing has come to represent in a culture so deeply wedded to the joint ideals of speech and authentic self-presence. In Saussure this prejudice is linked to the fact that *phonology* − the study of sound-structures in language − has seemed to provide the most authoritative model for a genuine science of linguistics. For it is here that one can point to those crucial distinctions at the level of the signifier (as between 'cat' and 'bat', or 'cat' and 'can') which articulate the whole complex network of meanings in any given language. So phonology has gained a certain natural prestige as the aspect of language most readily amenable to objective, scientific study. And indeed, this assumption is shared by other linguists of a structuralist persuasion, including Roman Jakobson who did a great deal to extend and refine Saussure's treatment of the subject.[10]

Once again, Derrida is not questioning the fruits of their research, or suggesting that phonology doesn't deserve its currently privileged status. 'I hope my intention is clear,' he interjects. 'I think Saussure's reasons are good. I do not question, *on the level at which he says it,* the truth of *what Saussure says*' (p. 39). What Derrida does want to challenge is the logic that extends this privilege to a wholesale metaphysics of language based on the priority of self-present speech. And the grounds for this objection are not just some perverse counter-prejudice on Derrida's part in favour of 'writing' over 'speech'. His point is that Saussure cannot *think* the differential nature of language without contradicting his own premise as regards the 'natural' bond between sound and sense. And this because the logic of Saussure's argument commits him to a more far-reaching and radical notion of 'difference' than he expressly wants to maintain. Once this logic takes hold, it prevents Saussure's concepts from settling down into a firm, well-regulated system, such as might provide the exemplary basis for a structuralist science of language. For difference is not so much a self-possessed 'concept' as a fissile term whose introduction into *any* theoretical discourse will induce all manner of disturbing, contradictory effects. The logic of difference is a non-self-identical logic, one that eludes all the normative constraints which govern classical reason. If language is marked by the absence of 'positive terms' − if meaning is differential through and through − then any theory which attempts to conceptualize language will find itself up against this ultimate limit to its own explanatory powers.

Derrida cites a number of passages from Saussure where one can see quite clearly how the logic of his argument is overtaken by this problematizing drift. Thus Saussure draws a sharp distinction between the 'material substance' of language − its physical embodiment in sound − and the signifying system which alone enables those sounds to make articulate sense. To confuse these levels of description, Saussure argues, is to lose sight of the elementary fact that meaning is composed of manifold *differences,* rather than identities between signifier and signified. 'It is impossible for sound alone, a material element, to belong to language. It is only a secondary thing, substance to be put to use. All our conventional values have the characteristic of not being confused with the tangible element which supports them . . . the idea or phonic substance that a sign contains is of less importance than the other signs that surround it.'[11] But if this is the case then it is hard to see how Saussure can maintain his insistence on the privileged (natural) bond between spoken language and thought. And indeed, the whole drift of Saussure's thinking on the topic of linguistic difference is to undermine the hold of those traditional metaphors turned back toward speech as self-presence. Insofar as language can only be grasped as a system of differing (non-self-identical) terms, it moves beyond reach of phonocentric concepts and thus falls prey – as Derrida will show – to a generalized grammatology, or science of writing. For it is precisely at those points where Saussure pushes furthest toward a purely differential theory of meaning that he also falls back, as if by necessity, on grammatological images and metaphors.

Thus writing comes in as a useful analogy when Saussure tries to explain how meaning subsists in a structure of distinctive oppositions *always already* at work within language. If writing is classically determined as the 'sign of a sign', this would equally apply to that system of differences 'without positive terms' that Saussure puts forward as the conceptual basis of a general linguistics. The readiest means of describing this system is through recourse to the metaphor of writing. It may then become clear how the individual speech-act (*parole*) presupposes a grasp of those signifying contrasts and relationships which make up the structure of language as a whole (*la langue*). Speech, that is to say, is already inscribed in a differential system which must always be in place before communication begins. And this system is very like writing, in the sense that written signs have traditionally been thought of as marks of difference, supplementarity or non-self-present meaning. And so it comes about that Saussure, for all his manifest suspicion of writing, nonetheless adopts it – 'metaphorically' at least – as a type-case of language in general. 'Since an identical state of affairs [i.e. the differential nature of meaning] is observable in writing, another system of signs, we shall use writing to draw some comparisons that will clarify the whole issue.' To which Derrida responds with a query that encapsulates his entire critical project in *Of Grammatology*. By what strange logic (or perversion of logic) can Saussure both seek to exclude writing from the purview of a general linguistics *and* exploit it, when required, as a means of support for his own most crucial turns of argument? Or, to put it rather differently: what could be at stake in this marked determination to conceal or repress writing's constitutive role in the development of a general linguistics?

Derrida suggests an answer by taking one more passage from

Saussure and exploiting some ingenious tricks of verbal substitution. This has to do with Saussure's vision of a future semiotic enterprise that would base itself on the model of a first-order structural linguistics, but then extend this model to *every* kind of cultural activity, everything that lent itself to treatment as a system of signs or social representations. It is a well-known passage, not least because it looks forward so strikingly to the widespread structuralist activity of later decades. But for Derrida it possesses a rather different order of significance. Where Saussure points toward this larger programme – that of an applied semiology – which will eventually subsume linguistics as such, Derrida suggests that in fact it is *writing* that marks the as yet scarcely glimpsed horizon of Saussurean method. We can, he says, substitute the word 'grammatology' for 'semiotics' in this passage from Saussure, and thereby begin to grasp the project opened by a radical critique of the sign. 'I shall call it [grammatology] . . . Since the science does not yet exist, no one can say what it would be; but it has a right to existence, a place staked out in advance. Linguistics is only a part of [that] general science . . .; the laws discovered by [grammatology] will be applicable to linguistics' (p. 51). This would follow from what Derrida has shown already: that Saussure's attempt to conceptualize language as a system of purely *differential* signs leads him to the point where only writing could serve as a basis for this generalized theory. And we should then have to re-think the concept of writing, since clearly its pertinence and field of operation would extend far beyond the standard, restricted sense of literal 'marks on a page'.

So it is here, at the close of these densely argued pages on Saussure, that Derrida broaches the project of an applied grammatology, or science of writing in its widest, most comprehensive sense. 'Arche-writing' is the term he now proposes for whatever exceeds those traditional ideas that have hitherto maintained the restricted economy of language and representation. It is *not* – he insists – to be treated as a 'concept', as a word to which there must correspond some fixed or definite idea, such that its meaning could in principle be exhausted by careful definition. Rather, it is a term that will come into play at certain crucial points of Derrida's text, those points moreover where something can be shown to escape or exceed all the bounds of classical reason. If deconstruction proposes to re-formulate the accepted idea of writing, it is not by means of some *other* idea which could then be set up in its place. Grammatology has hitherto worked on the assumption that writing is one among many objects of enquiry; that its develop-ment can be studied from various familiar angles (historical, philological etc.); and that certainly there need be – or should be – nothing in the nature of writing that resists conceptual understanding. In Hegel, as we have seen, the strength of these ideas is such as to dictate the absolute superiority of one form of writing (the alphabetical-phonetic) at the expense of all others. And it is this preconception, along with all its manifold entail-ments, that Derridean grammatology will henceforth place in doubt.

His argument can be stated most simply in the following terms. If writing is the very *condition* of knowledge – if, that is to say, it can be shown to precede and articulate all our working notions of science, history, tradition etc. – then how can writing be just one object of knowledge among others? What Derrida is using here is the form of 'transcendental' reasoning which Kant first brought to bear upon the central problems of philosophy. In fact I shall go on to argue that deconstruction is a Kantian enterprise in ways that few of its commentators have so far been inclined to acknowledge. For the moment it is enough to register the force of this particular turn in Derrida's argument. A 'transcendental' question takes the form: what exactly are the *presuppositions* of our reasoning on this or that topic if the upshot is to make any kind of intelligible sense? Philosophers were mistaken, Kant thought, when they challenged the claims of epistemological scepticism (i.e. the argument that we can have no sure, objective knowledge of reality, or no way of knowing that we have such knowledge) by attempting to prove that a real world existed and, moreover, that it matched up exactly with our perceptions of it. Such reasonings were circular at best and always open to a knock-down sceptical rejoinder. What philo-sophers had much better do, he argued, was examine the inbuilt presuppositions of their own and (implicitly) of *all* cognitive enquiry, the intellectual ground-rules in the absence of which our thinking would have no sense, no logic or purpose. And then, according to Kant, they could start to rebuild the whole edifice of human knowledge on rational foundations that were placed beyond doubt by the fact that they belonged to a simply inescapable, *a priori* structure of concepts.

Derrida's version of this Kantian argument makes writing (or 'arche-writing') the precondition of all possible knowledge. And this not merely by virtue of the fact − the self-evident fact − that writing is the form in which ideas are passed down, preserved in a constantly expanding archive, and thus made available to subsequent debate. His claim is *a priori* in the radically Kantian sense: that we cannot *think* the possibility of culture, history or knowledge in general without also thinking the prior necessity of writing. Thus 'writing is not only an auxiliary means in the service of science − and possibly its object − but first, . . . the condition of the possibility of ideal objects and therefore of scientific objectivity' (*Of Grammatology*, p. 27). Thought is deluded if it thinks to comprehend the nature of writing from a standpoint securely outside or above the field that writing so completely commands. And it is philosophy − for reasons we can now perhaps recognize − that most often falls prey to this delusion. Philosophy is perennially subject to that desire for self-present origins and truth that would make writing merely a tool in the service of its own higher purpose. And this would also apply to those histories of writing which uncritically adopt the same logocentric rationale. For if it is the case, as Derrida claims, that history itself is 'tied to the possibility of writing' (p. 27) − of writing, that is, in the extended, Derridean sense − then there is reason to doubt any historical treatment which fails to reckon with this *a priori* constitution of the field.

What such histories cannot entertain is the notion of a writing that precedes and delimits their every last conceptual resource. To recognize this would be to call into question that rooted 'metaphysics of presence' which subjugates writing to speech. And it would likewise cast doubt on the implicit *teleology* − the organizing concept of historical advance − which derives from that same powerful set of ruling assumptions. But according to Derrida the doubt is already there, its symptoms to be read in those very same texts that expressly assert the traditional view. 'I believe that generalized writing is not just the idea of a system to be invented, an hypothetical characteristic or a future possibility. I think on the contrary that oral language already belongs to this writing' (p. 55). We can now turn to his chapters on Rousseau, some two hundred pages of densely argued commentary which make up by far the most impressive example of Derrida's 'applied grammatology'.

5. Rousseau: Writing as Necessary Evil

There are many good reasons why Rousseau should figure so centrally in Derrida's argument. For one thing, he had much to say about writing, most often by way of deploring its influence and regretting his own enslavement to it as a necessary means of spreading his ideas. Writing for Rousseau was a 'dangerous supplement', an addition to the natural resources of speech that always threatened to poison the springs of authentic human understanding. It belonged to that stage of cultural development where the living community of face-to-face contact had given way to a vast, impersonal network of social relations, a degenerate state of existence which Rousseau never ceased to lament. Thus we find a whole series of opposed valuations which will turn out to inform every detail, every topic of enquiry in Rousseau's voluminous writings. On the one hand are ranged the positive values: speech, self-presence, origins, nature and the virtues of a small-scale 'organic' community where writing would not yet have worked its effects. On the other can be found those bad concomitants of modern mass-society: writing, inequality, structures of power, the impossibility of people simply *coming together* to talk out their differences in a communal forum.

Writing is that which invades the happy sphere of one-to-one familiar address, setting individuals at a distance from each other and imposing an alien order of social existence. And in this, Derrida argues, Rousseau is repeating that same logocentric gesture which has characterized the entire discourse of Western metaphysical thought. 'Self-presence, transparent proximity in the face-to-face of countenance and the immediate range of the voice, this determination of social authenticity is therefore classic: Rousseauistic but already the inheritor of Platonism . . .'

(*Of Grammatology*, p. 138). The organic community of Rousseau's imagining is simply the equivalent, in socio-political terms, of that pervasive 'metaphysics of presence' which requires the absolute subordination of writing to authentic (spoken) language. Our modern, complicated order of social existence is a bad necessity that somehow *supervenes* upon nature and forces us into all manner of violent, corrupt or inhuman relations. Writing is likewise the 'dangerous supplement' which opens the way to manifold abuses of nature. Certainly it has allowed us to extend the communicative reach of language far beyond the limits of 'face-to-face' contact. But it also brings along with it a whole neglected range of harmful, distorting effects. Writing is *par excellence* the instrument of social control, since those who possess it are the lawgivers, priests and wielders of ultimate power. Without writing – so Rousseau believes – we might yet exist in a state of communal grace, untouched by the evils of social inequality and class division. Rousseau's ideal is thus based on the model of 'a small community with a "crystalline" structure, completely self-present, assembled in its own neighbourhood' (p. 137).

Now Derrida will argue that this dream is simply unsustainable; that writing is 'always already' there in Rousseau's reflections on society and language, even as he tries to conjure up that idyllic state of nature *before* the advent of a feared and tyrannical writing. As with Plato and Saussure, so here: there emerges a 'logic of the supplement', an order of subliminal constraints that operate within Rousseau's text to twist its meaning against all his overt or express intentions. 'Such is the gesture of [this] arche-writing: arche-violence, loss of the proper, of absolute proximity, of self-presence, in truth the loss of what has never taken place, [what] has never been given but only dreamed of and always already split, repeated, incapable of appearing to itself except in its own disappearance' (p. 112). This effect can be observed at every stage and in every dimension of Rousseau's manifold writing activities. On the one hand it marks his reflections on the experience of authorship, on what it is to be a writer and the dangers of that self-engrossed, solitary trade. On the other it affects Rousseau's cultural anthropology, his various theories of language, society and the history of human institutions. What emerges in the course of Derrida's reading is *not* just a series of associated 'themes' in Rousseau but a singular logic of reversal and displacement which governs the entirety of his literary output.

In the *Confessions,* Rousseau has some hard things to say about the consequences of writing, about the bad effect of reading too many books and the vices attendant on an overly literate civilization. Writing is on the side of decadence, artifice and everything opposed to a healthy state of social existence. Writing is a 'supplement' that tends to pervert our sense of the natural priority belonging to speech. And yet, of course, Rousseau was himself a writer, an exceptionally prolix and dedicated writer, one whose every thought and experience seemed to find a place in his written work. So what can be this strange compunction that operates everywhere in Rousseau's text, leading him to denounce the very means by which his own life-history is set down for others to read? An answer begins to emerge as Derrida fastens on the various metaphors which attach themselves to the idea of writing in Rousseau's *Confessions.* To commit one's memories to print is to risk losing that vital sense of continuity which links past events to present (living) recollection. It is a dangerous practice because writing always tends to take over from the business of straightforward, authentic self-revelation. There is a narrative interest that develops to the point where Rousseau feels himself at times more involved in the process of inventing elaborate *fictions* than of simply telling the truth about himself. He is caught between the desire to narrate past experience in a writing that others may read and the knowledge that, in doing so, his experience may be falsified beyond all hope of accurate recall. And this predicament is peculiarly painful since Rousseau sets out in the *Confessions* to write with unprecedented candour, addressing himself to topics of an intimate (often a sexual) nature which had hitherto been treated very obliquely, if at all. So there is a special, acutely paradoxical force to Rousseau's reflections on the inherent duplicity of writing and the various temptations it puts in the way of any genuine truth-telling enterprise.

Derrida describes this situation of Rousseau's writing in terms of a classic double-bind predicament. 'Rousseau condemns writing as destruction of presence and as disease of speech. He rehabilitates it to the extent that it promises the reappropriation of that of which speech allowed itself to be dispossessed. But by what, if not already a writing older than speech and already installed in that place?' (p. 142). It is not just that Rousseau is occasionally struck by his tendency to elaborate intriguing episodes beyond the strict call of autobiographical truth. Rather, he is involved in a conflict of priorities — between writing his *Confessions* for others to judge and keeping faith with his own deep mistrust of all writing — which cannot be resolved either way without sacrificing Rousseau's entire project. For it is also the case that Rousseau finds himself unable to envisage a truly representative version of his own experience that would *not* have passed by way of this 'dangerous supplement' involved in the practice of writing. It is only by recounting his confessions — exposing them to all the dangers of narrative treatment — that these memories take on a semblance of living recollection. Otherwise they exist in a limbo of private, incommunicable meaning which no one except Rousseau himself could possibly hope to comprehend. Writing them down is not just a matter of convenience, a handy means of preserving his thoughts for readers outside the privileged circle of Rousseau's intimate friends. Those thoughts would have no reality *even for Rousseau* were it not for the fact that they could be thus inscribed in a form accessible to others.

Derrida cites some remarkable passages from the *Confessions* which bring out this dependence on writing as the means by which Rousseau seeks to guarantee the reality of his own past experience. 'I would love society like others, if I were not sure of showing myself not only at a disadvantage, but as completely different from what I am. The part that I have taken of writing and hiding myself is precisely the one that suits me. If I were present, one would never know what I was worth' (quoted in *Of Grammatology,* p. 142). Rousseau often confesses to this sense of present unreality, of somehow existing at a strange remove from his own immediate thoughts and feelings. He fails to come across, to make his presence felt in company or in conversation, since there is always that curious feeling of detachment which prevents him from talking or behaving naturally. And so it comes about that *writing* – the act of confessional narration – takes on for Rousseau a special kind of 'supplementary' power, an ability to make his experiences real by setting them down for others to read. Then it is always possible to explain his own motives, to do himself justice by revealing just how complex and elusive were his thoughts on any given occasion. The *Confessions* will stand as a tribute to Rousseau's very special kind of authenticity, his refusal to accept the kinds of role-playing compromise forced upon lesser mortals by their need to maintain social appearances. Writing is the act of belated self-vindication by which Rousseau will at last show up in a favourable light, freed from the irksome constraints of everyday behaviour.

But there is a danger which goes along with this calculated *deferment* of present satisfaction for the sake of future benefits. It means that nothing one does or says will ever be wholly authentic, since the very fact of saving things up for the written record will involve an element of bad faith, a habit of social reserve which can always be seen as mere hypocrisy, artifice or cunning. And writing is precisely the mechanism which allows Rousseau to practise this art of concealment. It gives him the advantage of perpetually having the last word, making up for his moral lapses or defects by treating them on the principle 'tout comprendre, c'est tout pardonner'. But this treatment runs the risk of presenting Rousseau in such a uniformly favourable light as to deprive the *Confessions* of any real claim to honest self-reckoning. Rousseau is always ready to catch himself out in these moments of hypocrisy, to make a clean breast of it by admitting that he, like everyone else, prefers to think well of his own character. But even then there is the awkward suspicion that all this obsessive laying-bare of motives might be just another kind of self-promoting ruse designed to make Rousseau more *interesting* to the reader. So the whole elaborate show of self-recrimination would amount to a brilliant (if involuntary) subterfuge on Rousseau's part, a means of distracting attention

from the bad faith involved in narrating one's life for others to
read.

Paul de Man has pursued these ironies to the limit in his own
deconstructive reading of the *Confessions*.[1] Rousseau is caught
up in a curious textual predicament whereby his every attempt to
acknowledge some weakness or fault of character becomes
twisted into a kind of self-justifying narrative logic. By calling
himself to account so strictly, Rousseau can always rely on the
reader giving him the benefit of the doubt, since the result makes
such a singular, intriguing piece of first-person narrative discourse. In which case the *Confessions* would be far from
honouring its declared ideal: to tell the plain truth of Jean--
Jacques' experience without the least regard for niceties of social
convention. It would have to be read as a series of rhetorical
gambits designed to head off the ultimate question as to whether
Rousseau presently and genuinely *means what he says,* or
whether he is using the confessional mode as a means of evading
this ethical injunction. Thus, according to de Man, there is
always the risk that such intimate revelations will 'indeed
exculpate the confessor, making the confession (and the confessional text) redundant as it originates'. At this point the desire
for honest self-reckoning will have given way to a different
desire, one that places the interests of narrative complexity and
intrigue above the requirement of straightforward truth-telling
virtue. In the end, 'Rousseau's text . . . prefers being suspected of
lie and slander rather than of innocently lacking sense.' And this
because the act of writing his *Confessions* is one that inevitably
leaves its mark on the various episodes that Rousseau hopes to
summon from the reserves of living memory. Writing and
narrative are different names for this self-alienating process at
work within language, a process that makes it strictly impossible
for thought to achieve the authentic condition of self-present,
living recall.

So Rousseau *must* resort to writing, whatever its unwelcome
effects and liabilities. The need to communicate leaves him bereft
of any real choice in the matter. And the marks of this enforced
subjection to the written are everywhere apparent in Rousseau's
texts. 'To recognize writing in speech . . . is to begin to think the

lure. There is no ethics without the presence of the *other* but also, and consequently, without absence, dissimulation, detour, writing' (*Of Grammatology,* p. 140). Derrida will trace the effects of this guilty recognition not only in Rousseau's more 'personal' writings but also in his generalized reflections on language, music, sexual morality and the politics of culture. In each case Rousseau wants to say one thing but ends up, if one reads his text closely, saying quite another, or effectively countering the gist of his own express argument. And this comes about *not* through some local oversight, some accidental failure to put the case clearly or perceive its problematical drift. In fact Derrida gives Rousseau every credit for posing these questions with a clarity and force which lend his writings an exemplary status for the purposes of deconstruction. What they bring out is the logic of 'supplementarity' which marks all attempts to think the origin of language or to ground that origin in a moment of primordial, self-present speech.

Rousseau is preeminently the philosopher of origins, one who sought by every possible means to restore language to a natural state of simplicity, innocence and grace. And this desire carried across into Rousseau's politics, his ethics and his notions of historical development. Always it is a matter of setting up some cardinal opposition between *nature* and *culture,* with everything authentic and original on the one side and everything false, modern or degenerate on the other. Nature for Rousseau is the source of all goodness and virtue, while culture represents an inherently corrupting influence, a perpetual fall into error and bad faith. But this fall has always already occurred, so that the signs of it are there to be read even in those passages where Rousseau describes — or attempts to describe — what life would be like had culture not intruded its alien, artificial values. Rousseau is constrained against his own deepest wish to give evidence that nature — or the *concept* of nature — is a product of cultural representation; that there is no thinking back beyond the point where thought was first inscribed in this strangely aboriginal 'logic of the supplement'. And it is Rousseau's great virtue — as Derrida reads him — that his writings hold firmly to logocentric values even while subjecting them to a kind of involuntary autocritque.

Myths of origin: music and speech

We can see this process very strikingly at work in Rousseau's theory of the origins of language.[2] What must have come first, he argues, was a language of the passions or of primitive instinct, one that had not yet evolved those complex grammatical structures required to articulate abstract thoughts. This was a *natural* language, an authentic means of expression which properly avoided the dangers attendant on other, more sophisticated speech-forms. Which is also to say that it existed at the furthest possible remove from writing, if by writing we understand the highly developed set of cultural conventions by which language contrives to communicate at a distance, without the advantages of face-to-face contact. It is only when language breaks with this original ethos of speech and self-presence that it needs to fall back on the 'dangerous supplement' of writing. And the same applies to music, where Rousseau detects a gradual weakening of the expressive impulse as *melody* – the pure, spontaneous element of song – gives way to *harmony,* or the skilful arrangement of multiple voices in consort. The more sophisticated harmony becomes, the more completely it depends on graphic notation, on the existence of scores which make it possible to read and perform such difficult music. Rousseau thinks of this as an absolute loss, as a falling-away from that happy condition when music and speech were perfectly united in the natural medium of song. For they both took rise – so Rousseau would have us believe – in the expression of those genuine, passionate feelings which once exerted a universal human appeal. But then there came about the decline into writing or harmony, the process by which speech-song lost its original communicative power and resorted to increasingly abstract conventions. 'To the degree that the language improved,' Rousseau writes, 'melody, being governed by new rules, imperceptibly lost its former energy, and the calculus of intervals was substituted for nicety of inflection' (quoted in *Of Gramma-*

tology, p. 199). Such is Rousseau's considered diagnosis of what has gone wrong with present-day music, especially the elaborate contrapuntal style preferred by French composers such as Rameau. Unlike the Italians, who still had the vigour and passion of a pure singing line, these decadent Frenchmen resorted to complex harmonies merely to cover their want of genuine inspiration.

The same thing happens when spoken language avails itself of the various benefits supposedly obtained by refining and extending its basic resources. At some stage (Rousseau suggests) there must have occurred a decisive change in the character of human social existence. This change came about when the primitive community of persons on speaking terms with each other gave way to a division between those who possessed the skill of writing and those who lacked that skill. The former would then be well placed to dictate their will through access to the law and to various means of enforcing or exploiting its provisions. The latter would be faced with a simple choice: either obey those provisions or be classed as criminals, social misfits, scapegoat figures cast out from the community of law-abiding citizens. So the question of writing, or the 'proper' relationship between writing and speech, opens up a whole series of associated questions in Rousseau's discourse on the nature and origins of social institutions. Writing is whatever threatens to invade the utopian community of free and equal discourse which exists among primitive peoples. It gives rise to injustice, to political oppression and to all those evils that attend the birth of modern 'civilized' society. Rousseau can only account for these effects by evoking some primal catastrophe, some accident that has befallen mankind through the perverse addiction to false ideas of social and intellectual progress. What Rousseau *cannot* think – expressly at least – is the notion of these evils having always existed as far back as the origins of human society.

But this is precisely Derrida's claim: that the blindspots in Rousseau's discourse are produced by the workings of a 'supplementary' logic which effectively suspends and disqualifies all recourse to the idea of origin. There is no thinking about the character of language, of history, culture or social relations which would not already have presupposed the fall into writing, difference and other such articulated forms of communal life. Rousseau '*declares* what he *wishes to say*, that is to say that articulation and writing are a post-originary malady of language; he says or *describes* that which he *does not wish to say*: articulation and therefore the space of writing operates at the origin of language' (*Of Grammatology,* p. 229; Derrida's italics). He wants to think of all these bad, supplementary effects as having 'come upon the origin unexpectedly', overtaken the innocent community of speech through no possible fault of its own. But even as Rousseau presents this case his text begins to tell a very different story, one which locates the unfortunate swerve at a point anterior to all articulations of origin. 'The becoming-writing of language is the becoming-language of language' (p. 229). For Rousseau is unable to conceive of language and society except in terms of difference, structure and unequal distribution of power. To this extent Rousseau is a structuralist *malgré lui*, one who doesn't want to think in such terms but who is constrained to do so by the logic of his own arguments. How was it that language ever got started, or that words took on some determinate sense, if not through the existence of signifying codes and conventions that must have been *always already* in place? When Rousseau thinks (albeit unwillingly) that 'articulation' is the essence of language, and not a mere symptom of its latter-day decline, he is broaching the single most important principle of modern (post-Saussurean) structural linguistics. And when he hits upon the same awkward fact about culture — that its origins are not to be thought of except in its specific *difference* from some real or imagined state of nature — then Rousseau is already far along the road to a structuralist anthropology. That is to say, he is obliged to treat all the signs of human cultural emergence, even at the most 'primitive' level, as pointing to a kind of aboriginal swerve from nature. His refusal to acknowledge this predicament expressly is the cause of all those complicating tensions in Rousseau's text which lend themselves so readily to the purposes of deconstruction.

'Before all determinations of a natural law, there is, effectively constraining the discourse, a law of the concept of nature' (p. 233). This 'law' takes effect in various ways, some of which seem quite specific to the reading of Rousseau's text, while others are more in the nature of *a priori* limits and constraints on the project of human understanding. That 'language is born out of the process of its own degeneration' (p. 242) is a claim on Derrida's part which asks to be applied in both senses. It certainly has to do with some structural characteristics (not 'themes') that figure prominently in Rousseau's discourse and provide the materials for a deconstructive reading. But it is also a 'law' which will seem to govern every possible thought about the origins of language, the history of social institutions and the emergence of culture from a state of necessarily *pre-human* nature. Rousseau wants to think that there is (or once was) a perfect adjustment between man's social and his natural needs, such that this distinction could scarcely yet have made sense. It would then be nothing more than man's proper nature to live in peace with his fellow beings; to respect their equal claims before an unwritten (natural) law; and to speak always from the heart, since there could be no motive, as yet, for his resorting to strategies and intrigues. Rousseau undoubtedly *wants* to think this. But his thought no sooner touches on the question of origins than it finds itself up against the stark impossibility of conceptualizing 'human nature' in these terms. What is human (or defined as such by every discourse in the sciences of man) is precisely what cannot be reduced to some order of natural, pre-social origins. The distinction between 'nature' and 'culture' is prerequisite to any kind of anthropological theory. So there is always already a *concept* of nature, a particular way of drawing that distinction which carries along with it a whole tacit system of cultural values and presuppositions. Such is the 'law' which operates not only in Rousseau's text but whenever thinking tries to hark back to some authentic (preconceptual) state of nature.[3]

So Derrida is advancing something more than a new 'interpretation' of Rousseau when he describes this logic of supplementarity and its various unsettling effects. What is in question is a powerful mythology of human nature which can only be asserted (as Rousseau asserts it) by forgetting or effacing the signs of its cultural production. To acknowledge these signs would be to set in train a series of disruptive shifts and reversals

107

whose effect would reach back to the putative origins of man, language and society. And Rousseau cannot help but acknowledge them, despite his set purpose of maintaining the 'natural' (logocentric) order of values. Always there is a moment of *différance* at the source, a falling-away from nature, identity and origins which makes it impossible for Rousseau to say what he evidently means to say. And so, Derrida writes, 'this property (*propre*) of man is not a property of man: it is the very dislocation of the proper in general . . . the impossibility − and therefore the desire − of self-proximity, of pure presence' (p. 244). This pattern is repeated over and again in Rousseau's texts, not only when he deals expressly with linguistic or anthropological themes, but also in his treatment of music, sexuality and other connected topics.

Music is especially important to Rousseau because − as we have seen − he links it directly to the passional origins of speech, and finds in it the same symptoms of latter-day cultural decline. The harmonic elaborations of the modern French style are a 'gothic and barbarous' development, a path which, according to Rousseau, 'we should never have followed if we had been more sensible of the true beauties of art, and of music truly natural' (quoted in *Of Grammatology*, p. 345n). Harmony is the merest of artificial supplements, the mark of a public taste corrupted by the prevalence of novelty and fashion. But Rousseau runs into a characteristic problem when he tries to think the essence of a musical style as yet unaffected by this vicious craving. Melody, he writes, 'has its principle in harmony, since it is an harmonic analysis which gives the degrees of the scale, the chords of the mode, and the laws of the modulation, the only elements of singing' (quoted p. 212). Thus it proves impossible to conceptualize the nature of music without perforce admitting that harmony has been there from the outset, as a part of music's natural resources. There is always a harmony *within* melody, no matter how carefully Rousseau attempts to keep the two principles apart.

It should be emphasized here that Derrida is *not* simply latching on to isolated turns of metaphor in Rousseau's text, ignoring its logical structure of argument for the sake of some ingenious new interpretation. What he seeks to bring out is a different logic, one that Rousseau does not wish to entertain but that nonetheless determines every detail of his argument. The 'supplement' of harmony is insistently there in his text, '*named even though it is never (as it nowhere is) expounded*' (p. 213). And this is the point at which a deconstructive reading breaks with all traditional, normative ideas of textual commentary and critique. It is not so much interested in what the text says – what it is 'about' at the express thematic level – as in the organization of its logical resources *despite or against* its manifest drift. In the case of Rousseau on the origins of music, it is (Derrida writes) 'this difference between implication, nominal presence, and thematic exposition that interests us here' (p. 213). Opponents may choose to regard deconstruction as a mere licence for interpretative games which exploit every chance of perverse misreading thrown up by some casual metaphor. But this vulgarized account bears not the least resemblance to what Derrida actually performs in his reading of Rousseau. Here it is a question of locating very precisely the divergence between logic and rhetoric which twists Rousseau's meaning against his avowed intentions. And this requires a rigour and a scrupulous adherence to the letter of the text which could scarcely be further removed from that popular idea of what 'deconstruction' is all about.

Rousseau will attempt to save the situation by distinguishing between 'good' and 'bad' kinds of melody, the one as close as possible to a pure singing line, the other already too far gone down the road to harmonic decadence. But if song is *essentially*, as Rousseau says, 'a kind of modification of the human voice', then it cannot be conceived as having come to birth in some golden age of authentic expression when speech and song shared a common point of origin. Melody is already the result of a difference, a falling-away from the self-sufficient plenitude of speech. Just as harmony substitutes a calculus of intervals for the natural resources of song, so melody – itself unthinkable except in relation to harmony – cannot be equated with a pure, unmodified speech. In Rousseau's philosophy of music 'the interval is a part of the definition of song. It is therefore, so to

Derrida

speak, an originary accessory and an essential accident. Like
writing' (p. 200). Rousseau *wants* to think that such accidents
are in no way essential; that they befall language and music
always from outside, through some malign agency wholly
unrelated to the origins of speech or song. If his texts say
otherwise, it is not because they are simply illogical, or because
Rousseau is writing about subjects he doesn't fully understand. On the contrary, Derrida claims: there is a 'logic proper to
Rousseau's discourse', though not on the level at which his texts
explicitly ask to be read. Deconstruction may seem to uncover a
series of root contradictions or disabling non-sequiturs at the
heart of Rousseau's philosophy. But this is to suppose that his
writings must properly fall in with a classical logic whose axioms
include precisely those assumptions about language and reason
which are called into question by the logic of supplementarity.
That Rousseau embraced those assumptions — that they are
indeed basic to his whole argumentative strategy — is not to say
that they are *actually* or *necessarily* borne out in the reading of
Rousseau's texts.

After all, the word 'supplement' itself creates problems of
conceptual grasp as soon as one attempts to define it. Take for
instance the supplementary volumes that are brought out
periodically by the publishers of a standard reference work like
the *Oxford English Dictionary*. In a sense these are just a kind of
optional extra, an appendix to the original set. So one could
always claim to possess the 'complete' *OED* without needing to
buy the supplementary volumes as and when they appeared. On
the other hand there is a sense in which the work is *not* complete
unless it includes all the supplements published to date. In this
case, each addition to the ongoing sequence would form an
integral part of the work, thus bringing about a revised notion of
what exactly constitutes the *OED*.[4] There is a curious double
logic that inhabits this word and prevents its sense from ever
quite being captured by a stable (dictionary) definition. 'Supplement' and its various cognates figure with remarkable persistence in Rousseau's writings. And this should alert us — so
Derrida argues — to the presence of a logic whose workings may
well be resistant to all kinds of straightforward conceptual

110

definition, including those that Rousseau himself purports to provide.

So what exactly *is* this 'logic of the supplement' which apparently operates outside all the laws laid down by classical reason? To speak of it in this way is again to suggest, like Rousseau, that 'inside' and 'outside' are terms which exist in some fixed order of priority, such that the supplement would always supervene upon some natural, self-present origin. 'This conforms to the logic of identity and to the principle of classical ontology (the outside is outside, being is, etc.) but not to the logic of supplementarity, which would have it that the outside be inside . . . that what adds itself to something takes the place of a default in the thing, that the default, as the outside of the inside, should be already within the inside, etc.' (p. 215). Rousseau's language constantly admits this disturbing suggestion, even when he strives by all possible means to hold it at bay. Most revealing are the logical twists and roundabout locutions that he is forced to adopt in face of these intractable problems. Derrida attends very closely to the tenses and moods of Rousseau's verbs, in particular his use of subjunctive forms to describe what *should* have been the case had things not fared so badly with language and the history of civilization. These subjunctives go along with a shuttling movement between past, pluperfect and future-perfect tenses, to conjure up a realm of deferred possibility where language would not yet have suffered its calamitous decline into writing. All the evils of present-day advanced Western culture can thus be blamed upon an accident (or series of accidents) which need not have happened had wisdom or common sense only prevailed. But things went otherwise, not only as a matter of historical record but also within the very logic and conceptual resources of Rousseau's argument. Writing 'wrenches language from its condition of origin, from its conditional or its future of origin, from that which it must (ought to) have been and what it has never been; it could only have been born by suspending its relation to all origin' (p. 243). Rousseau cannot bring himself expressly to conceive this possibility, since of course it would undermine his entire philosophy of nature, origins and presence. But what Rousseau wants to think and

111

what his texts actually say are two very different matters. And this difference is there to be read in the play of grammatical moods and tenses ('would have', 'might yet be', 'would always have been' and so forth) which mark Rousseau's discourse at certain crucial points in his argument.

Modern philosophers have developed techniques for dealing with varieties of logical entailment which don't fall under the classic (Aristotelian) terms of analysis.[5] For clearly it is the case that propositions *can* have a truth-value without necessarily holding good for all conceivable situations or at all (past and future) points in time. Aristotle's logic of deductive inference fails to account for such instances since it covers only the sorts of statement that are timelessly or unconditionally valid by virtue of their analytic form. So there is now quite a range of alternative systems (tense-logic, modal logic, the logic of so-called 'possible worlds') that seek to make good this deficiency. Nevertheless it is hard to imagine how any such system could possibly cope with the extreme complexities of mood and tense encountered in the reading of Rousseau's texts. His arguments are always already caught up in the movement away from some imaginary source which would surely have served to arrest this slippage if only Rousseau could manage to describe it adequately. 'The question', Derrida writes, 'is of an originary supplement, if this absurd expression may be risked, totally unacceptable as it is within classical logic' (p. 313). But such remarks should not be taken to suggest that deconstruction is just a kind of irrationalist licence to dispense with all the protocols of rigorous, consequent thinking. Only by plucking them out of context for polemical purposes can his opponents ignore the meticulously argued character of Derrida's readings.

Nor is it the case that deconstruction entails a complete disregard for questions of authorial intention. Certainly Derrida imputes a significance to Rousseau's texts which flies in the face of their express meaning and which, on all the evidence, Rousseau himself could scarcely have been brought to entertain. But this is not so much to discount intentions as to argue for a different, more nuanced understanding of what it is for a text to *mean what it says* or — conversely — to say something other than its specified intent. 'Rousseau's discourse lets itself be constrained by a complexity which always has the form of a supplement of or from the origin. His declared intention is not annulled by this but rather *inscribed* within a system which it no longer dominates' (p. 243). Thus Derrida declines to go along with that fashionable strain of post-structuralist libertarian talk which celebrates the 'death of the author' and the vertiginous prospects henceforth opened up for inventive reading.[6] Such ideas ignore the very real constraints that are placed upon criticism by its need to make intelligible *sense* of texts which undeniably ask to be read in certain ways. What is at issue is not the intentionality of language – the precondition of all understanding – but the belief that texts must always point back to their source in a moment of pure, self-authorized meaning. 'The security with which the commentary considers the self-identity of the text . . . goes hand in hand with the tranquil assurance that leaps over the text toward its presumed content, in the direction of the pure signified' (p. 159). Language is intentional through and through, but not in the sense that its meaning either could or should be confined to what the author (supposedly) intended.

Psychoanalysis and the 'logic of the supplement'

This suggests that deconstruction is closely allied to certain present-day forms of psychoanalytical criticism. And indeed, there are points of resemblance between Derrida's project and the highly influential post-structuralist reading of Freud propounded by Jacques Lacan.[7] This reading demands that *language* be accorded the central role in defining and explaining the Freudian topology of unconscious motives and meanings. For Lacan, the unconscious is very literally 'structured like a language', its effects to be deciphered in those knots and slippages of sense which everywhere punctuate the discourse of human desire. These effects can best be understood (he argues) with the aid of some crucial terms and distinctions borrowed from the field of modern structural linguistics. Thus Lacan takes a lead from the linguist Roman Jakobson in suggesting that *metaphor* and *metonymy* are the two chief organizing principles of language, and also the figures which enable us to grasp those forces at work in the psychic economy of unconscious drives and desires.[8] Metaphor stands in for the Freudian idea of 'condensation', the way in which certain words or symbols in a patient's discourse act as a focal point for meanings that escape the logic of conscious, articulate thought. Metonymy is classically defined as the figure which substitutes part for whole, or which evokes some object by singling out a salient detail or aspect of it. ('All hands on deck' is a hackneyed but clear enough example.) And, according to Lacan, it is precisely in the workings of metonymy — in the endless substitution of signifiers, none of which restores the lost object of desire in its impossible, pristine reality — that analysis can best come to grips with the Freudian concept of 'displacement'. Desire simply *is* this differential movement perpetually at work within language, a movement which can never be brought to a halt since the relation between signifier and signified is always provisional, shifting and elusive. Hence Lacan's implacable hostility to all those perversions of Freudian analysis (especially American ego-psychology) which think to achieve the 'talking cure' by bringing about a full, lucid recognition of deep-laid motives and meanings. For Lacan, the unconscious is everywhere in language, its effects coextensive with the workings of a 'symbolic order' which permits our entry into family and social life only at the cost of instinctual repression and alienated desire. The Saussurean 'bar' between signifier and signified — that which creates the arbitrary nature of the sign — is also the law which immutably decrees the unfulfilment of desire in pursuit of its ever-changing object.

There is no room here for anything like an adequate account of Lacanian psychoanalysis. But perhaps I have said enough to bring out the marked similarities between Derrida's deconstructive reading of Rousseau and Lacan's insistence on the non-self-identical, the endlessly deferred or differential character of language in the toils of unconscious desire. However, this resemblance turns out to have sharp limits, as Derrida stresses in an essay devoted to one of Lacan's most celebrated texts, his seminar on Edgar Allan Poe's story 'The Purloined Letter'.[9] This tale has to do with matters of disguise, concealment, duplicity

114

and displaced origins. It narrates a sequence of thefts and discoveries, the object of which is a compromising love-letter stolen from the Queen by a treacherous blackmailing minister. There are two main scenes of discovery, the first when the minister detects and steals the letter in the Queen's presence, and the second when Dupin — most ingenious of detectives — recovers it from the minister's office. In each case the letter is not so much concealed as left in the most obvious location, the one place that anyone *expecting* concealment would hardly think to look.

Lacan reads this tale as a virtual allegory of psychoanalysis in its relation to language and the effects of unconscious desire. The letter is that floating signifier which circulates from one situation to the next and calls out all manner of strategic ruses and deceptions by those who would possess its secret. The precise nature of that secret is never revealed, since its existence *as* a secret is precisely what keeps the whole elaborate game in play. And yet it is not at all a well-kept secret or a genuine mystery, belonging as it does to the most banal, the most conventional of courtly intrigues. It is appropriate, therefore, that the letter is not hidden, as if it contained some deeply encrypted meaning, but casually placed where all might discover it, were their eyes not trained to seek out some dark inner recess. For such is the delusion — as Lacan would argue — encouraged by those versions of psychoanalysis which think to delve deep into the patient's psyche by uncovering truths of repressed experience *behind* or *beyond* the surface complexities of language. The analyst should rather proceed by attending closely to the logic of the *signifier,* to those detours and swerves in the discourse of patient and analyst which mark the irruption of unconscious desire. And this would apply also to the reading of Freud, both the detailed case histories and the various supposedly more abstract (or 'meta-psychological') writings. The most faithful account will be that which sticks to the *letter* of the text, which follows Freud's arguments with an ear attuned to their subliminal wordplay and twists of figural sense, rather than thinking to penetrate directly to the level of concept or theory. Only by passing through the 'defiles of the signifier' — by risking its dignity as a self-assured science — can psychoanalysis put itself in touch with the structural unconscious of language.

Derrida's chief objection to Lacan's reading of Poe is that it tends to reduce 'The Purloined Letter' to an allegory implying the ultimate *truth* of psychoanalytical discourse. Lacan may insist that the letter is caught up in an endless circulation of meanings which nowhere converge on some 'transcendental signified' or moment of authentic revelation. But if one reads his text carefully, Derrida argues, there is no denying the privileged truth-claims granted to Lacanian psychoanalysis as a key to the story's elusive theme. And in 'framing' the tale to suit his own ends, Lacan has passed over certain resistant details of its narrative logic and structure which would place sizable problems in the way of any such reading. He has assumed that letters will always (so to speak) arrive at their proper destination; that the postal metaphor in question is that of an efficient and perfectly regulated system where letters never get lost in the post or fail to turn up safely. But this is to ignore the distinct possibility — distinctly implied, that is, by the duplicitous logic of Poe's tale — that letters can *always* go astray, or texts *not* finally yield themselves up to some kind of authoritative truthful reading. In *La Carte postale* (1980) Derrida will play all manner of inventive games with this idea of the two postal 'systems', the one maintaining an efficient service (with the law and police on hand if required), while the other opens up a fabulous realm of messages and meanings that circulate beyond any assurance of authorized control. What he finds so questionable in Lacan's reading of 'The Purloined Letter' is simply the assumption that nothing ever *escapes* the privileged hermeneutical standpoint of psychoanalysis. Whereas it is the case, Derrida argues — and a case very pointedly borne out by Poe's ingenious tale — that something must *always* escape in the reading of a text, no matter how subtle or resourceful that reading. Any commentary that aims to speak the truth of a text will find itself outflanked or outwitted by a supplementary logic which defeats the best efforts of criticism. As with Poe's neat allegory of the circulating letter, there always comes a point where meaning veers off into detours unreckoned with on thematic (or indeed allegorical) terms.

Now of course this would apply equally to a deconstructive reading that claimed to have the last word by showing up the blindspots or unwitting liabilities present in other interpretations. Barbara Johnson, in her essay 'The Frame of Reference', argues that Derrida has laid himself open to exactly this kind of *tu quoque* charge.[10] That is to say, he has criticized Lacan's reliance on a privileged explanatory model, only to substitute his own preferred idea of *writing* — textuality — as the untranscendable horizon of knowledge and truth. But Derrida in a sense preempts this critique by insisting that there is no *concept* as such, no stable or self-identical idea, that attaches to the word 'writing'. Certainly it is not the 'theme' of Poe's story, any more than it figures expressly or thematically in Rousseau's discourse on the origins of language. Rather it is the name of whatever escapes, unsettles or complicates the project of a reading trained up on such commonplace assumptions. And psychoanalysis — according to Derrida — still betrays a certain lingering attachment to that ethos of thematic origins and presence. Hence his insistence that 'in spite of certain appearances, the locating of the word *supplement* is here not at all psychoanalytical, if by that we understand an interpretation that takes us outside of the writing toward a psychobiographical signified' (*Of Grammatology*, p. 159). And this would apply even to those passages in the *Confessions* where Rousseau thinks to meet his reader most honestly, on the ground of intimate self-revelation.

One last example may help to bring home the ubiquitous presence of this supplementary logic in the unfolding of Rousseau's texts. It has to do with his well-known 'secret' vice, the habit of substituting solitary pleasures for the experience of a 'natural' eroticism defined according to heterosexual norms. Rousseau is quite convinced that this is indeed a pernicious and debilitating habit. The indulgence of auto-erotic fantasy leads on to physical abuses which 'cheat nature' and 'save up for young men of my temperament many forms of excess at the expense of their health, strength, and, sometimes, their life' (quoted in *Of Grammatology*, p. 150). And this because it 'summons up absent beauties', enabling the fantasist to multiply imaginary experiences beyond all the limits of a wise, self-regulating nature. For Rousseau, childhood is the dangerous period when this habit takes hold, since the child is especially prone to 'supplement' his weakness and make up for the absence of a real object of desire by discovering all manner of substitute figures. It may be the mother or (as in Rousseau's case) the foster-mother who first attracts this libidinal investment. But even here there is a dangerous supplementarity at work, since she is placed beyond reach of those very desires by the grim law of paternal and social constraint. Thus the child embarks upon an endless quest for alternative fantasy-objects, a quest that increasingly alienates desire from its proper fulfilment in mature, adult sexuality. And insofar as the mother is herself a substitute – a figure who can only stand in temporarily for the child's confused erotic feelings – she is already caught up in this same bad logic of supplementary swerves from nature.

Once again, Rousseau is unwilling to admit that the supplement may be there at the source, or that such undoubted 'perversions' of nature may infect every order of natural morality. The only way that he can reckon with these dangerous facts (masturbation, sexual fantasy, all forms of auto-erotic desire) is to treat them as accidental defects due to some fault in the child's upbringing or perhaps some wider, distinctively modern cultural malaise. 'Rousseau neither wishes to think nor can think that this alteration does not simply happen to the self, that it is the self's very origin. He must consider it a contingent evil coming from without to affect the integrity of the subject' (p. 153). But the *Confessions* everywhere tell a different story, one which has Rousseau inescapably dependent upon fantasy – as indeed upon writing – to compensate for a lack which was always there, which existed and exists at the heart of sexual desire. For it is Rousseau's complaint (in both senses of the word) that his experience with women has never lived up to those images of passionate fulfilment that thronged his sleeping and waking fantasy-life. Always the reality comes to represent a certain falling-short, a failure of desire in the very act of attaining its wished-for object. Is enjoyment made for man, Rousseau asks, or man for enjoyment in anything like its natural, real-life heterosexual form? 'Ah! If I had ever in my life tasted the delights of love even once in their plenitude, I do not imagine that my frail existence would have been sufficient for them, I would have been dead in the act' (quoted in *Of Grammatology*, p. 155). Thus Rousseau will explain how he has resorted to the pleasures of a guilty, unnatural practice only on account of his extreme susceptibility to women, his fear that nature might be overwhelmed by such potential excess of passion. And this is to imply that what is 'natural' for Rousseau — what obeys the dictates of prudence, good sense and measure — is a principled avoidance of that sexual activity which others (those enjoying a normal, healthy constitution) can presumably indulge without fear. But Rousseau cannot explain this defect in himself without suggesting that its effects reach beyond his own (as he would have it) peculiar case history to the nature of sexual relationships in general.

So it is not just Rousseau's 'frail existence', or his psycho-pathology of aberrant desire, that leaves him a prey to such perilous overstimulation. As Derrida writes of the above and kindred passages from the *Confessions*: 'if one abides by the universal evidence, by the necessary and *a priori* value of this proposition in the form of a sigh, one must immediately recognize that "cohabitation with women", hetero-eroticism, can be lived . . . only through the ability to reserve within itself its own supplementary protection' (p. 155). Rousseau may wish the reader to conclude that this weakness is accounted for by accidental features of his own upbringing, his maternal fixation and — worst of all — his compulsion to *write* as a substitute for genuine, lived experience. But in the process of describing this (supposedly untypical) series of accidents, Rousseau's text cannot help but imply that human sexuality is always and every-where a kind of 'supplementary' experience, one that can never be traced back to source in a moment of pure, natural fulfilment. It is not just the fact that Rousseau is self-evidently writing these memories down, but beyond that the more disturbing suggestion that they only 'come alive' in the act of narrative imagining, the very process which — according to Rousseau's declared belief — should set them at odds with living experience. What is natural *ought* to be the encounter of man and woman in the passionate communion of heterosexual love. Such an act would have no need of imaginary supplements, of erotic fantasy or other such sources of heightened (and perverse) pleasure. It would thus resemble speech — authentic, self-present speech — in its power to express the most intense emotions with a perfect assurance of reciprocated feeling. But this ideal is too much for Rousseau's imagining, or — more precisely — it can *only* be imagined as already caught up in a chain of endless supplementary inscriptions. Erotic fantasy is for Rousseau the precondition of enjoying sexual experience. And writing is the means by which this fantasy protects itself from the 'mortal expenditure' that would surely overwhelm him if Rousseau should ever yield himself up to the living reality.

So there is more at stake here than a curious twist of psychopathological origin that leads Rousseau to associate writing with the perils of auto-eroticism. The latter is just one of the guises assumed by a supplementary logic which seems to preempt his every move in the process of argument or narrative. Rousseau is quite unable to give up these bad habits, whether of sexual fantasy in the absence of any living partner or — even worse — of conjuring up imaginary partners ('absent beauties') while actually, presently making love. For it has become a necessity with Rousseau to compensate for his own weak powers of present satisfaction by calling up a whole repertoire of substitute pleasures. And this habit cannot be separated from his activity as a writer, an activity that Rousseau is equally unable to give up. 'Between myself and the most passionate lover there was only one, but that an essential, point of distinction, which makes my condition almost unintelligible and inconceivable' (quoted in *Of Grammatology,* p. 149). This distinction — the fact of his enslavement to auto-eroticism — is what impels him to write so obsessively on the topic of his own sexual character. But it is precisely in *writing* that Rousseau's sexuality turns out to exert such a strange and unsettling effect. The more he seeks to explain or excuse his 'almost inconceivable' predicament, the more it comes to seem a universal condition, borne out by all the signs of a supplementary logic everywhere at work within language and sexual desire. So that finally Rousseau is con-

strained to imply — without at any point expressly acknowledging — the perverse unnaturalness of nature itself. Auto-eroticism
'neither begins nor ends with what one thinks can be circum-
scribed by the name of masturbation. The supplement has not
only the power of *procuring* an absent presence through its
image, procuring it for us through the proxy (*procuration*) of the
sign; it holds it at a distance and masters it' (p. 155). And this
need for conserving one's present energies — for mastering
experience 'at a distance' of imaginary desire — cannot be
confined (as Rousseau would confine it) to the case history of
one man's sexual aberrations. It connects too readily at every
point with Rousseau's reflections on the origin of language, the
dangers of a supplementary writing and the evils attendant upon
modern, sophisticated social life. What is in question here is that
primordial metaphysics of presence which dreams of a happy
human condition where speech would suffice for all the proper
purposes of human exchange. It is writing, classically the 'sign of
a sign', forever bereft of such authentic self-presence, that brings
home the absolute *impossibility* of language ever living up to this
ideal.

In which case, Derrida argues, we shall have to revise the
conventional idea which insists that writing is a *representation*
of speech, reality or lived experience. We have seen already (in
Chapter 3) how Derrida reads Mallarmé alongside Plato by way
of deconstructing this classical order of mimetic assumptions. In
Rousseau a similar effect is produced by following out the
supplementary logic of a writing which refuses to occupy its
proper, subordinate place in the economy of language and
desire. And it is here, in the context of Rousseau's life-history,
that Derrida comes up with his notorious pronouncement: 'il n'y
a pas de hors-texte' ('there is no "outside" to the text'; *Of
Grammatology,* p. 158). It is *not,* he continues, simply a matter
of our having no access to Rousseau's experience except through
the writings that have come down to us. This would indeed be
reason enough to mistrust any straightforward biographical
appeal to the 'facts' of the case, independent of their written or
narrative form. But in the end there is simply no distinguishing
between the facts of Rousseau's life and the multiplied effects of

121

a supplementarity which determines that life in its every last detail. That Rousseau in some sense *lived* these effects – that they were intimately bound up with his experience as a sexual, social and political being – is an idea which Derrida is certainly prepared to entertain. In fact he quotes a good many striking observations from Rousseau which suggest that the author was far from 'unconscious' of this strange link between his writing activity and the various symptoms of thwarted or displaced desire which marked his passage through life. For 'writing', as Derrida employs the word here, is *not* just synonymous with written or printed marks on a page. Nor is it opposed to a real world existing outside or beyond the text, at least in the sense that one might draw a clear demarcation between the two realms. This is what Derrida terms *arche-writing,* that which exceeds the traditional (restricted) sense of the word in order to release all those hitherto repressed significations which have always haunted the discourse of logocentric reason. To perceive how this repression still operates in Rousseau's text – seeking to maintain the classical economy, to subjugate writing to a self-present speech – is also to perceive how writing breaks the bounds of its standard, restricted definition. And this should be enough to discountenance those resolutely partial readings of Derrida that accuse him of driving an 'idealist' wedge between literature and its social, political or worldly dimensions.

Nature, culture and the politics of writing

For there are certainly some real political issues bound up with the Rousseauist mystique of origins and presence. These have to do with the supposed evils of a modern 'civilized' existence cut off from the primitive state of communal grace. Such evils accrue more than anything from the workings of a selective 'representation' that allows democracy to function only at the cost of delegating power to a privileged few individuals. And what enables them to exert this power is precisely their access to *writing* as the means by which authority is encoded and legitimized. 'In opposition to the autarchic cities of Antiquity, which were their own centres and conversed in the living voice, the modern capital is always a monopoly of writing. It commands by written laws, decrees, and literature' (*Of Grammatology*, p. 302). Rousseau is profoundly disenchanted with the way that democracy has worked out in practice. In the name of giving power back to the people through their elected representatives, it has in fact produced a whole bad order of 'supplementary' powers and privileges vested in the various delegate bodies. 'Political decentralization, dispersion, and decentring of sovereignty calls, paradoxically, for the existence of a capital, a centre of usurpation and of substitution' (p. 302).

There is a by now familiar kind of reasoning at work in Rousseau's thoughts about democracy and the ills that it is heir to. For what are these abuses if not the outcome of a supplementary process that infects democracy *at source*, that springs not so much from the decline of political institutions as from their very nature and origins? Ideally the parliament should be coextensive with the people, each man or woman their own 'representative' in the face-to-face exchange of ideas and opinions. But such a concept of representation no more bears thinking through to its logical conclusions than the idea of language (socialized language) as a pure, self-present speech. In each case the ideal is a limit-point of nostalgic imagining which eludes any adequate conceptualization in social or political terms. Thus Rousseau, like Plato and Hegel, can propose nothing better than a 'writing of the voice', one that will at least acknowledge its derived, supplementary character and respect the absolute priority of speech. Such writing may even promote 'a more efficient civil order', enabling the mechanisms of representation to produce certain genuine benefits. 'In so far as it effaces itself better before the possible presence of the voice, it represents it better and permits it to be absent with the smallest loss' (*Of Grammatology*, p. 301). Nevertheless, according to Rousseau, the dangers of writing must always outrun its various incidental advantages. For writing is the origin, the essential precondition of all those forces which attack the state of nature and precipitate the long decline into modern mass-civilization. Democracy is compromised from the outset since it must involve some form of *representation*, a process by which individual voices or members of the body politic surrender their moral autonomy and consent to take laws from elected citizens set up to govern them. No matter how 'efficient' its workings – and no matter how desirable, in relative terms, as a means of present-day government – this delegation of powers can only strike Rousseau as an insult to man's natural dignity. At best it is a necessary evil, like the 'good' (phonetic-alphabetical) writing which *represents* the sounds of spoken language as faithfully as possible, and thus maintains a residual sense of nature, propriety and truth.

There are some large political questions raised by this deconstructive reading of Rousseau on the origins of civil society. On the one hand Rousseau's was the single most influential voice in challenging that deep-laid conservative ideology which held that man – natural man – was a creature born in sin, incapable of achieving any kind of civilized existence without the sanctions of law, custom and a disciplined religious and political life. On the contrary, Rousseau declared: 'man was born free, but is everywhere in chains', the victim of an alienated social existence which corrupts and distorts his good native instincts. The effect of this teaching was undoubtedly to produce a powerful sense of political injustice and a drive toward creating some new political order which would properly enshrine the principles of natural justice. So much is a matter of historical record, of Rousseau's well-documented influence on social reformers and apostles of revolution in France and elsewhere. Nor can this influence be separated from Rousseau's leading philosophical ideas, his harking back to a state of nature and grace that must have existed *before* all these past and present abuses. In short, it might appear that Derrida is out to deconstruct precisely those motifs in the Rousseauist mythology that exerted the most powerful progressive or emancipating force in real political terms.

But this is to ignore the very different uses to which that mythology has been put by other, more reactionary creeds. Certainly there grew up a counter-tradition of expressly conservative political thinking which pinned its faith to those same organicist metaphors of man and nature. This tradition found its first and major spokesman in Edmund Burke, and is still very prominent among right-wing ideologues. It was always attractive to literary intellectuals and cultural theorists, especially those (like the later Wordsworth and Coleridge) who had travelled the well-worn path from a youthful phase of revolutionary zeal to a mood of political disenchantment and quietism. In its more embattled form, this philosophy insists on the evils of enlightened critique or ideas about 'social progress'; on the virtues of a simple, traditional lifestyle, unaffected by the winds of political change; and on the need for a disciplined acceptance of authority as the only means of preserving social order.[11] This organicist ethos finds an echo in the thinking of cultural critics from the later Coleridge to Eliot and F.R. Leavis. Here again, there is the persistent nostalgia for some long-lost state of communal grace, a society where class divisions might exist but not in any conscious, articulate or threatening form. Eliot's idea of a 'dissociation of sensibility', a misfortune that overtook English culture at just about the time of the Civil War, is one version of this homespun mythology that has exerted a very potent latter-day appeal.[12]

   In Eliot's case – and, more ambiguously, that of Leavis – the conservative implications are clear enough. But even with Wordsworth, in his Preface to the *Lyrical Ballads,* the radical thrust of a Rousseauist cultural politics – the insistence on a poetry written in the 'ordinary language of men', as against the stilted class-conventions of eighteenth-century style – is compromised by its recourse to that same mythology of nature, origins and presence. Wordsworth's drastically simplified pronouncements on the subject of 'poetic diction' are closely bound up with his nostalgic ideal of a small, tightly knit, 'organic' community where there would be no need for mere conventions of social address. Poetry could thrive only when rooted in the authentic, everyday language of a culture where face-to-face *speech* was the normal currency of exchange. And indeed it was the quest for such enabling conditions that impelled Wordsworth and Coleridge to seek out their own kinds of favoured pastoral retreat. Of course this is to simplify the complicated history of cultural politics at work within English romanticism. But it has been argued persuasively that the withdrawal from active political engagement on the part of poets like Wordsworth and Coleridge — a withdrawal brought about very largely by the pressures of British counter-revolutionary sentiment — went along with their turn toward forms of increasingly self-occupied, contemplative nature-mysticism.[13] And Rousseau was as potent an influence here as he had been in the earlier, radical phase. The holiness of the heart's affections was a doctrine that adapted easily enough to an ethos of political quietism once the prospects for actually changing the world receded beyond present hope.

This sketch of an historical episode may provide at least the beginnings of an answer to our question: what are the *political* interests at stake in Derrida's reading of Rousseau? Why should he deploy such elaborate textual resources to show up the blindspots, the self-contradictory or aporetic moments in Rousseau's various projects? We can start by posing the question as Derrida poses it in a passage that effectively turns this challenge around. 'Why is the origin of civil man, the origin of languages, etc., the origin, in a word, of the supplementary structure and . . . of writing also, catastrophic? Why does it follow an upheaval in the form of a reversal, of return, of revolution, of a progressive movement in the form of a regression?' (*Of Grammatology*, p. 255). Derrida's response might be taken to run as follows. The Rousseauist mythology of origins and presence is one that appeals to a human nature which would somehow preexist all conceivable forms of organized civil society. Though harnessed initially to a progressive current of ideas, it proved in the long run a very useful support for those conservative philosophies which held out against the disruptive effects of modern (enlightened) thinking. Rousseau's perpetual harking back to origins was a denial of everything that belonged on the side of reason, progress and history itself. 'The expression "primitive times", and all the evidence which will be used to describe them, refer to no date, no event, no chronology' (p. 252). And this because it is literally *impossible* to think one's way back — as Rousseau would have us think — to the pre-social origins of society, the pre-linguistic origins of language, etc. All that remains is a pure mythology devoid of any reasoned or historical substance.

This mythology operates everywhere in Rousseau's writing. It is, so to speak, the conceptual deep grammar which articulates his manifold themes and interests. And this could only be a grammar *without tenses,* existing in a timeless and illusory realm of mythical oppositions. 'One can vary the facts without modifying the structural invariant. It is a time before time . . . Dispersion, absolute solitude, mutism, experience irrevocably destined to a prereflexive sensation, immediate, without memory, without anticipation, without the power of reason or comparison, such would be the virgin soil of any social, historic, or linguistic adventure' (p. 252). History is immobilized, turned back toward a non-existent point of origin which suspends all dealing with change, difference or political circumstance. And this is why writing has to be repressed as the absolute precondition of Rousseau's maintaining his mythology of man and nature. Writing is that which opens the possibility of history, knowledge, representation and articulate thought in general. 'Writing', that is to say, as *archi-écriture,* as the system of cultural signs and inscriptions that will always — perversely — preexist the moment of natural, self-present speech. For it is only through writing and its cultural effects that Rousseau can think the origins of language, society and civil institutions. Logocentrism — or the Rousseauist 'metaphysics of presence' — is the desire *not to recognize* this order of necessity inscribed in the texts of Western tradition from Plato to the structuralist sciences of man. It is a desire that would finally erase all the traces of historical, social and sexual difference in order to dream a presence beyond their bad, disruptive effects. And this is why Rousseau's arguments can always be recaptured by a certain conservative mystique of nature and origins. Only by reading his texts deconstructively — by showing how they are haunted by writing in the form of a generalized 'political unconscious' — can criticism hope to resist this powerful and still very active mystique.

Dreams of origin: 'The Writing Lesson'

Derrida finds this Rousseauist mythology of origins and presence still very much at work in the modern sciences of man. And nowhere more so, he argues, than in structuralist thinking about language, society and cultural history. We have seen how the speech/writing opposition continues to haunt the text of Saussurean linguistics. Speech is here conceived as the natural, authentic condition of language and writing as a poor derivative, one that the linguist must perforce take into account but only as a bad necessity or a methodological convenience. Derrida refers in passing to Saussure as 'the linguist from Geneva', a reference that is clearly meant to point up this connection. Geneva as Rousseau's home and refuge, but also as the birthplace (according to a certain mythology) of modern democratic ideals and institutions. What animates this myth is the idea of a self-enclosed community of citizens where writing, politics and social difference will not yet have come to exert their corrupting effects. But those effects − so Derrida argues − were always already there, inscribed in that same utopian discourse which runs through the texts of Western tradition from Plato to Rousseau and his present-day heirs. It is precisely the *repression* of writing in its various institutional forms and guises which governs the workings of this logocentric discourse and produces the nostalgia for lost origins and presence.

One striking example is to be found in 'The Writing Lesson', a chapter from Lévi-Strauss's book *Tristes Tropiques*.[14] Derrida reads this text by way of introducing his chapter on Rousseau in *Of Grammatology*. What Lévi-Strauss represents − to perfection, one might say, for Derrida's purpose − is the Rousseauist moment in modern structural anthropology, the moment of harking back to a 'natural' state of mankind and society before the fateful advent of writing. The chapter recounts one particular episode which stands out in Lévi-Strauss's recollection as a vivid expression of his own ambivalent feelings *vis-à-vis* the business of anthropological study. For there is, he believes, a dark side to this discipline, a sense in which the anthropologist comes first as a guilty spectator, and then as the alien who exploits and destroys the lifestyle of 'primitive' cultures. Lévi-Strauss makes no secret of where his sympathies lie in this mythical encounter between two worlds. He dislikes modern civilization for its narrowly rationalist ethos, its 'enlightened' obsession with history and progress, and (most of all) its deep-grained ethnocentric belief in the superiority of European culture. Conversely, what he admires about those other, less 'advanced' peoples is their closeness to nature, their way of thinking in mythological (as opposed to enlightened, scientific) categories, and their seeming indifference to the whole bad notion of historical progress. These are 'cool' cultures in the sense that they exist in a kind of perpetual present, at ease with their surroundings and therefore not impelled — like the 'hot' civilizations of the West — to push always onward in the vain pursuit of technological and political change.[15] In short, Lévi-Strauss sides avowedly with those whose culture is most threatened by the presumptuous, expansionist designs of European man. And this attitude is carried over into his treatment of their myths, customs, kinship-systems and other such products of collective representation. He will seek to understand these phenomena from the viewpoint of one who is himself engaged in the same kind of thought, in providing (that is to say) interpretative 'theories' which can only take the form of further variations on a range of mythical themes. For it is merely a sign of the prevailing ethnocentric bias in Western anthropology that it tends so often to adopt a stance of superior enlightened wisdom. There is no way of analysing myths — no scientific or 'meta-narrative' position — which could ever justify such hubris. Only by acknowledging the mythical status of his own project, his need to make sense of other people's experience in much the same way that they make sense of it themselves, can the anthropologist escape this condition of chronic bad faith.

In 'The Writing Lesson', as Derrida reads it, these convictions are pushed up against their limits of intelligibility. Lévi-Strauss describes his encounter with an Amerindian tribe (the Nambikwara) whose existence up to then — if we are to believe his account — was an idyll of undisturbed primitive peace. More specifically, they lacked all knowledge of writing, and therefore all acquaintance with the social evils that writing inevitably brings in its train. According to this guilty scenario it is the anthropologist who introduces writing, who unthinkingly takes notes in the presence of these people and so draws catastrophe down upon the tribe. Lévi-Strauss was most struck by the way that they appeared instantly to grasp the fact and significance of writing, without (of course) yet being able to write or read in anything like the customary sense. And it was their leader who saw the implications most clearly, who perceived – as Lévi-Strauss interprets his reaction – how writing could be used in the interests of maintaining an unequal distribution of knowledge and power. It is for this reason that the incident comes to figure in *Tristes Tropiques* as an allegory of everything that plagues the anthropologist's professional bad conscience. It is tempting, Derrida says, to read this story 'as a parable in which each element, each semanteme, refers to a recognized function of writing: hierarchization, the economic function of mediation and of capitalization, participation in a quasi-religious secret; all this . . . is here assembled, concentrated, organized in the structure of an exemplary event' (*Of Grammatology*, p. 126). The anthropologist would then arrive on the scene, like writing itself, as representative of all that threatens to violate the pure simplicity of origins. The writing lesson can only be recounted in tones of self-recrimination, with Lévi-Strauss effectively shouldering the blame for Western civilization and its bad hegemony. What is lost at the moment of access to writing is the Rousseauist dream of a communal existence which once required only the face-to-face contact of authentic (spoken) language.

But there was never such a moment, Derrida declares, or never the means of describing it in terms that would make any kind of consistent, intelligible sense. What Lévi-Strauss actually *writes* and what he would have us believe are two very different things. The real lesson to be drawn from this scene of instruction is that writing was already there, that its effects were clearly marked across a great range of tribal customs and activities long before the emissaries of culture arrived to destroy the idyll. Lévi-Strauss himself provides copious evidence that this was indeed the case, although – like Rousseau – he is constrained to deny it in accordance with his own deep convictions. The Nambikwara were *already* caught up in an order of 'civilized' relations where social inequality and differences of rank were facts of everyday experience. Otherwise what could possibly account for their leader's exceptional quickness in grasping the powers and implications of writing? Lévi-Strauss here resorts to what Derrida calls a kind of 'epigeneticism', the idea that writing suddenly appeared on the scene as if by some power of spontaneous invention linked to its essentially bad, contagious character. But this account only holds up if one takes the whole episode at face value. On a different (diagnostic or deconstructive) reading it will appear that Lévi-Strauss has effectively exposed the inadequacy of his own interpretation; that 'writing' in this context cannot be restricted to its narrow or literal definition (marks on a page); and that all those effects denounced by Lévi-Strauss under the guise of an evil, intrusive writing were *in fact* and *of necessity* there at work from the outset. These effects would include property-relations, the laws governing kinship and marriage, all forms of communal taboo and the myths, customs and legitimizing rituals whose function is to perpetuate their rule. What is in question, therefore, is 'arche-writing' as Derrida uses that term: everything that escapes the ethos of nature, origins and presence and is thus metaphorically or covertly placed on the side of a bad, unnatural writing. To question this whole economy of discourse is to see how *Tristes Tropiques* effectively rehearses its own deconstruction by providing all the evidence that things were never − could never have been, on any possible analysis − as Lévi-Strauss wishfully describes them.

One example must serve to bring out the force of Derrida's argument here. Lévi-Strauss mentions a game played by some of the Nambikwara children, one that involved the deliberate infringement of a certain social taboo. This was the ban on revealing proper names to anyone outside the close-knit family or tribal group. Lévi-Strauss describes how little girls would approach him with an air of conspiratorial guilt and proceed to wreak revenge upon some rival by telling him, a stranger, that rival's name. As Lévi-Strauss reads it, this game is a further sign of the breakdown in communal trust brought about by his own arrival on the scene. It was not hard, he writes, to 'egg the children on', one against another, until he had learned not only their names but those of many adults as well. Thus the anthropologist finds himself siding guiltily with everything that threatens to disrupt or destabilize the Nambikwara way of life. But Derrida once again reads a different lesson in this episode, and one – as he would claim – more faithful to the letter of Lévi-Strauss's own account. For after all there could have been no game, no pleasure taken in the act of illicit transgression, had there not already existed a powerful set of communal constraints regarding the use of proper names. In fact the word 'proper' is misleading here, Derrida thinks, since it suggests a peculiarly intimate bond between name and bearer, such that the children's act of revenge (and his own role in encouraging their game) would indeed appear to violate some authentic condition of mutual trust. And yet, Derrida says, the very existence of names is a sign that individuals are subject to a social order within which they are no longer treated as autonomous selves. Thus 'the lifting of the interdict, the great game of denunciation and the great exhibition of the "proper" . . . does not consist in revealing proper names, but in tearing the veil hiding a classification and an appurtenance, the inscription within a system of linguistico-social differences' (*Of Grammatology*, p. 111). The originary violence lies not in the mischievous naming of names but in the system which makes such mischief possible, so to speak, 'in the first place'.

This system is what Lévi-Strauss cannot (expressly) acknowledge, determined as he is to portray the Nambikwara as having once lived – before he came among them – in a state of natural innocence and grace. And so it is that *writing* takes on all the attributes of an evil that must always arrive from outside to destroy this idyllic way of life. Writing comes to stand metonymically, in Lévi-Strauss's discourse, for everything that threatens the self-same (*propre*) within speech, consciousness and communal existence at large. Its effects include 'the loss of the proper, of absolute proximity, of self-presence, in truth the loss of what has never taken place, of a self-presence . . . only dreamed of and always already split, repeated, incapable of appearing to itself except in its own disappearance' (p. 112). The sense of 'writing' is overdetermined to the point where its manifold meanings and surrogates can only be handled – their threat warded off – by the classical appeal to a logocentric myth of origins. On the one hand Lévi-Strauss does everything in his power to pin writing down to a restricted definition which opposes it to speech, self-presence etc., and thus gives it a derivative or strictly 'supplementary' sense. On the other he is constrained by the logic of his argument to confess the preconditional necessity of writing (taken in the extended, Derridean sense) over everything that supposedly would antecede writing and keep it firmly in its place. Again, the point is *not* simply to invert this binary opposition, so that writing would henceforth take absolute priority over speech. This gesture would still be inscribed within the same logocentric order of thought. Rather, what Derrida is asking us to conceive is the radical instability, the strictly *undecidable* character, of any such loaded metaphysical opposition. Writing in the restricted (conventional) sense may indeed be the poor relation of speech, since it is defined as the phonetic-alphabetical transcript of a preexisting spoken language. But once we see how 'writing' is metonymically deployed – how it assumes the full burden of Lévi-Strauss's case against 'civilized', enlightened reason – then this opposition begins to break down and its terms enter upon a series of bewildering substitutions and swerves from origin. What Derrida brings out is the strict *impossibility* of maintaining the mythical value-system that confines writing to any such restricted definition. Thus: 'if writing is no longer understood in the narrow sense of linear and phonetic notation, it should be possible to say that all societies capable of producing, that is to say of obliterating their proper names, and of bringing classificatory difference into play, practise writing in general' (p.109).

This reading of Lévi-Strauss provides a useful point of entry for considering Derrida's relationship to structuralism and the modern 'sciences of man' as conceived in structuralist terms. What he fastens on in Lévi-Strauss's project is the central opposition between 'nature' and 'culture', the starting-point for all such attempts to theorize the emergence of human institutions (language, myth, kinship-systems) from a realm of imaginary pre-social existence. Lévi-Strauss thinks to keep his analyses on the side of a 'primitive' thinking that would seek to interpret these phenomena on their own proper terms, that is to say, by respecting mythological thought and not trying to explain it from a standpoint of enlightened reason. He uses the word *bricolage* − roughly speaking, 'the ad hoc assemblage of miscellaneous materials and signifying structures' − to describe how mythologies make sense of the world in a way quite remote from our own, more logical and regimented habits of thought.[16] The *bricoleur* is a kind of Heath Robinson figure, happy to exploit the most diverse assortment of mythemes − or random combinatory elements − in order to create a working hypothesis about this or that feature of social life. The opposite approach is that of the typecast 'engineer', one who starts out with a well-defined concept of the machine (or explanatory theory) he wants to construct, and who follows this blueprint through to its logical conclusion. Lévi-Strauss claims that his own work in structural anthropology belongs to the realm of *bricolage*, that it offers no more (or no less) than the bringing together of numerous meanings and myths in a quest to make sense of materials already to hand. 'Mythical thought', he writes, 'builds ideological castles out of the debris of what was once a social discourse' (quoted in *Of Grammatology*, p. 139). And this would apply equally to the analyst of myths, one whose claim to theoretical rigour would always come up against the awkward fact of his or her involvement with the same sense-making strategies, and the same kinds of 'found' material. Such thinking could only be deluded if it set itself up as a form of metanarrative or scientific discourse having nothing in common with the first-order business of mythical *bricolage*.

Derrida seizes on this dichotomy (*bricoleur* versus 'engineer') as yet another of those binary oppositions which are only held in place by a failure to pursue their logic wherever it may lead. Perhaps it is the case, as Lévi-Strauss argues, that 'the most radical discourse, the most inventive and systematic engineer are surprised and circumvented by a history, a language, etc., a *world* . . . from which they must borrow their tools' (p. 139). But if so, what becomes of that crucial distinction between the two kinds of knowledge, the one devoted to system and method, the other given up to pure *bricolage*? Lévi-Strauss would appear to have deconstructed the basis of his own working method, that method which thinks to align itself squarely with the processes of mythical thought. Derrida pursues this argument yet further in his essay 'Structure, Sign and Play in the Discourse of the Human Sciences'.[17] Here it is the structuralist project at large that he questions on account of its various contradictory commitments. On the one hand structuralism (following Saussure) rejects the idea of a language of mythology that would issue from some ultimate, self-authorized source of meaning beyond the play of linguistic and cultural difference. It is this delusion that is captured in Lévi-Strauss's image of the engineer, he who 'supposedly [is] the absolute origin of his own discourse', and who 'constructs the totality of his language, syntax and lexicon' (*Writing and Difference*, p. 285). In which case undoubtedly the engineer is a myth, a 'theological idea', and one which could only have been invented by a kind of mytho-poetic *bricolage*. But this reversal of priorities, while demoting the engineer from his falsely assumed status, also has the effect of thoroughly undermining the claims of structural anthropology. 'As soon as we admit that every finite discourse is bound by a certain *bricolage*, and that the engineer and the scientist are also species of *bricoleurs*, then the very idea of *bricolage* is menaced and the difference in which it took on its meaning breaks down' (p. 285). Thus Lévi-Strauss is left without a cogent rationale for his practice of mythical interpretation. Any thinking that seeks to go beyond the categories of reason itself will always, it appears, come up against this inbuilt aporia. *Bricolage* affirms 'the necessity of borrowing one's concepts from the text of a heritage which is more or less coherent or ruined' (p. 285). But at this point there would seem to be no tenable distinction between concept and myth, coherence and ruin, theory and the ways of an all-embracing *bricolage*.

There is another opposition which plays a vital role in Lévi-Strauss's thinking and which points back even more clearly to Rousseau as a strong precursor. For it is in terms of nature versus culture — on the basis of that most rooted binary distinction — that Lévi-Strauss erects his entire project of structural anthropology. On the one side are those 'universal and spontaneous' conditions of life which obey no laws of human devising and so belong firmly to the realm of natural phenomena. On the other are the various myths, conventions, kinship-systems etc. which regulate social behaviour and thus fall squarely within the cultural domain. But there is one crucial instance which appears to defy classification according to this clear-cut binary logic. This is the incest taboo, a law whose effects are everywhere at work in the complex permutations of system and structure that Lévi-Strauss sets out to analyse. And it is precisely this ubiquitous character of the incest taboo that makes it such a problematic case for any discourse, like that of Lévi-Strauss, erected on the *difference* between nature and culture. 'The incest prohibition is universal; in this sense one could call it natural. But it is also a prohibition, a system of norms and interdicts; in this sense one could call it cultural' (p. 282). This is not just a technical problem which could always be resolved by adjusting the terms of analysis, so that 'culture' would henceforth be taken to include such universal facts of human experience. Empirical fieldwork might establish their universality and thus — from a purely descriptive standpoint — collapse the distinction between nature and culture. But there would still be the 'scandal', as Derrida describes it — the moment of aporia or deadlocked reasoning — where thought comes up against the stark impossibility of grasping this ultimate paradox. For what is at stake is not some regional problem peculiar to a certain kind of anthropological thinking. On the contrary, Derrida writes: 'it could perhaps be said that the whole of philosophical conceptualization, which is systematic with the nature/culture opposition, is designed to leave in the domain of the unthinkable the very thing that makes this conceptualization possible: the origin of the prohibition of incest' (pp. 283-4). Like Rousseau when he attempts to think the origin of language, Lévi-Strauss is caught up in a shuttling exchange of priorities which resists any form of coherent theoretical grasp.

To be sure, Lévi-Strauss might respond that his project is a species of applied *bricolage*; that it makes good sense at the 'mytho-poetic' level, and therefore has no need to claim a systematic or 'totalizing' power. But this is to beg the obvious question as to how structural anthropology can operate without some cogent rationale for its massively ambitious undertaking. The very notion of *bricolage* depends, as we have seen, on the opposite idea: that of a discourse whose workings would be governed by the strictest order of logical necessity and rigour. That idea may be delusive, an impossible dream, as Lévi-Strauss argues in rejecting the demand for a comprehensive 'theory' of myth. But it cannot be simply given up, least of all by the structural anthropologist whose aim is to articulate the deep logic or grammar which underlies the surface relativities of culture. What is at issue here is the status of explanatory theories in general, the question how far — or by what conceptual right — reason can exercise its sovereign claims. Lévi-Strauss may be justified in arguing that no theory can escape the effects of *bricolage*; that the 'heritage' of concepts must at some point fall prey to an improvised piecing-together of ideas whose logic is beyond the grasp of pure reason. But this is not to say that thinking can dispense with that heritage, or abandon the labours of conceptual critique by embracing an alternative, 'mytho-poetic' mode of thought. For it remains the case that Lévi-Strauss inherits a discourse whose crucial terms and distinctions have been endlessly debated, refined and worked over by thinkers in the Western philosophical tradition, from Plato to the present-day structuralists. And preeminent among the themes of that discourse is the nature/culture opposition, the starting-point of all theoretical reflection on the powers and limits of reason.

So the main question about Lévi-Strauss's project, as Derrida reads it, is essentially the *philosophic* question: 'shall we have to abandon any epistemological requirement which permits us to distinguish between several qualities of discourse on the myth?' (pp. 287-8). Or, to put it another way: are all kinds of knowledge to be treated simply as alternative mythologies, forms of *bricolage*, none of them possessing any particular claim to theoretical consistency or truth? Derrida argues that this question cannot even be raised 'for as long as the problem of the relations between the philosopheme or the theorem, on the one hand, and the mytheme or the mythopoem, on the other, has not been posed explicitly' (p. 288). Hence the blindspots in Lévi-Strauss's writing, the points at which a Rousseauist mystique of origins (the appeal to *bricolage* and mytho-poetics) comes into conflict with a highly sophisticated structuralist *theory* of myth.

Such is the burden of Derrida's argument in his reading of Lévi-Strauss. 'The quality and fecundity of a discourse are perhaps measured by the critical rigour with which this relation to the history of metaphysics and to inherited concepts is thought' (p. 282). Up to a point, deconstruction goes along with the strategy that undermines 'totalizing' theories of knowledge in the name of a general *bricolage* that would admit no logic except the strange logic of chance and random (anomalous) occurrence. But it also insists that the path to this conclusion is a *critical* path; that it cannot be pursued without the most rigorous attention to those concepts that are shaken up along the way. 'We have no language — no syntax and no lexicon — which is foreign to this history; we can pronounce not a single destructive proposition which has not already had to slip into the form, the logic, and the implicit postulations of precisely what it seeks to contest' (p. 280). Which is to say that deconstruction is not so much a passage 'beyond' philosophy — or beyond the resources of logocentric reason — as a testing of the language, the concepts and categories, which make up that same ubiquitous tradition.

I have argued that 'Structure, Sign and Play' is a rigorous *philosophical* account of certain unlooked-for liabilities and blindspots in the discourse of structural anthropology. But this is not how the essay has most often been read, at least by the proponents of so-called 'American deconstruction'. It was first delivered at a conference organized by Johns Hopkins University in 1966. The occasion was intended as a gathering-point for continental and American scholars, the speakers making up a distinguished company of French philosophers, literary critics, anthropologists and other representatives of the 'sciences of man'.[18] Clearly it was hoped that French structuralism would establish a beachhead in American universities and begin to break down the cultural barriers existing between the two traditions. In the event it was Derrida who literally had the last

138

word, and who offered a critique of Lévi-Strauss — and implicitly of the whole structuralist enterprise — which exerted the most
widespread influence. In fact this text became the principal
source for that (mainly American) view of deconstruction which
regards it as a kind of hermeneutic free-for-all, a joyous release
from all the rules and constraints of normative critical understanding.

This seems to me a mistaken view and one that derives from a
certain institutional rivalry between philosophers and literary
critics. Yet there are, undeniably, passages in 'Structure, Sign
and Play' which appear to support such a reading. They have to
do with the choice that Derrida poses at the end of his essay, a
choice between two interpretations of 'structure' and two incompatible projects of interpretation. The one would venture
only a limited way toward conceiving of language, myth and the
sciences of man in radically structuralist terms. That is to say, it
would accept (like Saussure or Lévi-Strauss) the idea that our
signifying practices only make sense insofar as they enter into a
play of relationships and differences which cannot be reduced to
'positive terms' or pure, self-identical meanings. But it would
still be turned back toward a myth of origins that located the
source of this differential play in a moment of authentic nature
or speech. Such thinking, as Derrida describes it, 'dreams of
deciphering a truth or an origin which escapes play and the order
of the sign, and . . . lives the necessity of interpretation as an
exile' (*Writing and Difference*, p. 292).

The other possibility is that of abandoning such nostalgic
ways of thought and accepting that there can henceforth be no
limit to the range of strong-willed interpretative options. Such
would be the Nietzschean 'transvaluation of values' as applied
(belatedly) to all those present-day structuralist theories which
are still in the grip of a lingering 'metaphysics of presence'. To
register the force of this critique would be to re-think the notion
of 'structure', no longer seeking to limit the play of its differential elements by always referring them back, in the last instance,
to some organizing 'centre' or thematic point of origin. 'This
affirmation then determines the noncentre otherwise than as loss
of the centre' (p. 292). It renounces the quest for a determinate

structure of meaning, since 'structure' in this sense is a concept that serves preemptively to close off the infinitized 'freeplay' of language. What it proposes is rather 'the joyous affirmation of the play of the world and of the innocence of becoming, the affirmation of a world of signs without fault, without truth, and without origin which is offered to an active interpretation' (p. 292).

It is not hard to see why 'Structure, Sign and Play' is cited so frequently by Derrida's disciples and opponents alike. To the former (most of them literary critics) it signals an end to that repressive regime that has so far governed the practice of interpretation. For the latter, it goes to confirm their worst (or their readiest) suspicions: that Derrida is merely an ingenious player of sophisticated word-games that need not concern the 'serious' philosopher or anyone responsibly engaged with such issues. What is ignored by *both* parties to this debate is the intricate process of argumentation − the detailed critique of Lévi-Straussian anthropology − by which Derrida leads up to his Nietzschean conclusion. Turn back a few pages and one finds him asserting that 'the passage beyond philosophy does not consist in turning the page of philosophy (which usually amounts to philosophizing badly), but in continuing to read philosophers *in a certain way*' (p. 288).

This statement has a kind of uncanny prescience, given the fate of 'Structure, Sign and Play' at the hands of less careful exegetes. At least it should remind us of three main points. First, that Derrida cannot be read by selecting statements to suit one's polemical purpose, and thereby ignoring their specific context of argument. Secondly, that deconstruction is *not* the antithesis of philosophic reason, but engages with it on terms that are always and inevitably marked by their own philosophical provenance. And thirdly − I would concede − that 'Structure, Sign and Play' is a text which, at least in its closing paragraphs, falls below the highest standards of Derridean argumentative rigour. Thus the essay winds up with a glance toward that which is 'proclaiming itself [through this Nietzschean mutation of discourse] only under the species of the nonspecies, in the formless, mute, infant, and terrifying form of monstrosity' (p. 293). Such writing could hardly fail to get deconstruction a bad name among those concerned (very properly concerned) to make cogent sense of its arguments. I shall have more to say about Derrida's adoption of a certain 'apocalyptic tone' as a means of drawing out the inbuilt antinomies of classical ('enlightened') reason. But in the next two chapters I want to look more closely at his relation to what might be called the 'mainstream' line of intellectual descent, from Kant to the proponents of modern analytical and 'ordinary language' philosophy. We will then be better placed to understand where Derrida specifically departs from that tradition.

6. Derrida and Kant: the Enlightenment Tradition

There is no excuse for the sloppy misreading of Derrida that represents him as some kind of transcendental solipsist who believes that nothing 'real' exists outside the written text. It is a notion he has often been at pains to rebut, most explicitly in a passage from *Positions* (1972) where Derrida responds to a series of questions on precisely this topic. It is necessary, he says, to interrogate those various naive or pre-critical ideas of reference that envisage a straightforward matching-up between language and the world 'outside'. Deconstruction must work to problematize such habits of thought by showing how strictly impossible it is to draw a firm line between reality and representation. That is to say, it must fasten on those blindspots in the discourse of commonsense empiricism which betray its naive ontological commitments and its failure to think through the issues raised by a rigorous epistemological critique. To this extent, certainly, deconstruction can be seen as suspending or subverting the most commonplace ideas of referential truth. But Derrida is quick to point out that this suspension is by no means incompatible with a strictly *materialist* approach to questions of language and representation. What has chiefly characterized such thinking − from ancient philosophers like Democritus to Marx and his present-day exponents − has been its resistance to premature concepts (or metaphors) that masquerade as timeless, immutable truths. And among these concepts, Derrida would argue, is precisely that form of *metaphysical* 'materialism' which takes for granted a drastic opposition between the real world of empirical self-evidence and the secondary meanings that are placed upon it by thought, language or textual representation.

So Derrida responds to his Marxist interlocutors by turning their argument round and asking them to specify more exactly what would *count* as a materialist 'position'. Would it not necessarily involve a radical re-thinking of that whole metaphysical tradition that shuttles between a dogmatic empiricism on the one hand and various kinds of idealist metaphysics on the other? And if this is the case then deconstruction should be seen as closely and productively involved with the project of materialist critique. What is in question here (Derrida argues) is *not* the mere retreat into a realm of infinitized textual 'freeplay' or dissemination where reality no longer obtrudes. Rather, it is the need to resist (or deconstruct) those antinomies of classical reason that have always posed the issue in these or related metaphysical terms. 'In effect, we must avoid having the indispensable critique of a certain naive relationship to the signified or the referent, to sense or meaning, remain fixed in a suspension, that is, a pure and simple suppression, of meaning or reference.'[1] And this will involve a sustained and rigorous attention to the ways in which a certain *idea* of referential language − or indeed a certain materialist metaphysics − has managed to deflect such thinking from its proper aim.

Elsewhere (notably in his book-length essay on Condillac)[2] Derrida shows more precisely how the break with metaphysics in its traditional, idealist form can always go along with a kind of pre-critical positivist ontology that remains largely captive to the same dominant motifs. It will take more than a simple inversion or exchange of priorities − an insistence on the 'real', as against mere 'writing' or representation − to achieve any kind of effective materialist critique. And it is here, Derrida argues, that deconstruction has its work cut out, since it has to avoid both a premature metaphysics of 'the real' and − what may follow from that very resistance − a fetishized notion of 'the text' which would then fall prey to all manner of idealist delusions. It should thus be possible to generalize the concept of writing ('its extension with no simple exterior limit') while not winding up, as Derrida says, with 'a new self-interiority, a new idealism . . . of the text'.[3] And at this point, presumably, there would no longer exist any grounds for the quarrel between Marxism and deconstruction. That quarrel has come about because the discourse of Marxism still tends to preserve such loaded ('metaphysical') distinctions as that which sets a firm, categorical limit between world and text. If it could only conceive its own project differently – as involving, in Derrida's words, 'the insistence on matter as the absolute exterior of opposition' – then materialism might find itself making common cause with deconstruction.

These arguments are ingenious but finally unconvincing. As a matter of record they have not done much to dispel the idea among Derrida's opponents that deconstruction is just an update of idealist metaphysics in 'textual' guise. Thus one finds Derrida in a more recent interview (1981) deploring the widespread misunderstanding that reads in his work 'a declaration that there is nothing beyond language, that we are imprisoned in language . . . and other stupidities of that sort'. And then, rather wearily, he goes on to explain once more that his object has *not* been to deny any connection between language and the real, but to show how 'the question of reference' is far more complex than traditional theories allow. 'To distance oneself from the habitual structure of reference, to challenge or complicate our common assumptions about it, does not amount to saying that there is *nothing* beyond language.'[4] But the fact that Derrida has so often been read as saying just that – and not only by blinkered polemicists with very stubborn preconceptions – suggests that this whole debate has run into a familiar kind of epistemological dead-end. What I want to do in the rest of this chapter is attempt to sort out at least some aspects of this confusion and then argue that Derrida's more recent texts have shifted the debate on to different ground. I shall also suggest that present arguments about the politics of deconstruction have often got off on the wrong foot by strategically misreading what Derrida has to say.

Philosophical scepticism: claims and counter-claims

G. E. Moore came up with what he thought an obvious solution to the problems of philosophical scepticism. In the course of a lecture (published under the title 'Proof of an External World') Moore held out his two hands and used the left to indicate the right and vice versa.[5] Here at least was 'proof' that his two hands existed, from which small beginning one might then proceed to a general vindication of the commonsense-realist view. Now it is widely felt — among philosophers at any rate — that Moore missed the point about epistemological scepticism; that his proof was good for all practical purposes but failed to address the deeper problem of how we can *know* that such perceptions correspond to anything in the external world. Barry Stroud gives voice to precisely this doubt in his recent, exceptionally clear-headed survey of the modern (post-Cartesian) sceptical tradition. 'We feel that he [Moore] construes the epistemologist's words only in a non-"philosophical", everyday, and therefore completely uninteresting way.'[6] It is an open question, Stroud thinks, whether Moore deliberately missed the point or whether perhaps he just couldn't see what the sceptic was getting at. On either account one would have to conclude that philosophy was no better off for Moore's 'solution', even if common sense appeared to have won the day.

Stroud sees Kant as the thinker who raised this problem of knowledge in its most pressing (and henceforth inescapable) form. On the one hand Kant thought it a 'scandal' that philosophy had as yet provided no satisfactory *proof* for the existence of an external world. Empiricists like Hume had made knowledge dependent on the manifold sensations and impressions by which we come to know (or to *think* we know) what goes on outside our heads. But this had played straight into the hands of those idealists, like Berkeley, who concluded that the real world might just as well be a private construction out of those same internal sensations and impressions. Kant considered this an affront to reason and a good cause to suspect that philosophy had got things completely inside out. He therefore denied that the reality of an 'outside' world could ever depend on our inferring its existence from the facts of our own 'inner sense'. That could only lead *via* Humean scepticism to a full-blown idealist conclusion in Berkeley's manner. So Kant insisted that we *must* have knowledge of external reality; that such knowledge cannot be construed as deriving solely from our own sense-impressions; and that only by avoiding this latter doctrine (the epistemic priority of inward experience) can philosophy escape the toils of sceptical doubt.

But Kant also had arguments in plenty against what he called 'transcendental realism', the idea that things exist just as they are quite apart from our ways of perceiving or knowing them. 'If we treat outer objects as things in themselves, it is quite impossible to understand how we could arrive at a knowledge of their reality outside us, since we have to rely merely on the representation that is in us.'[7] Kant was therefore very far from endorsing the kind of knock-down empiricist riposte that Moore thought sufficient to refute the claims of philosophical scepticism. Indeed, it was Kant who preempted such responses by raising the epistemological stakes and thus effectively drawing a line between Moore's style of everyday, commonsense realism and issues of a different, 'philosophical' order. Kant's 'transcendental idealism' was intended to provide exactly those further *a priori* grounds of assurance that couldn't be supplied by a straightforward appeal to empirical self-evidence. It would serve to convince all rational enquirers that knowledge of the external world was not (or not simply) to be taken on faith, but that it figured as part of the basic conceptual framework defining the very powers and limits of human reason. Only by grasping its own knowledge-constitutive interests could reason avoid the twin perils of 'transcendental realism' on the one hand and 'empirical idealism' on the other. And indeed these amounted to the same root delusion, since both philosophies drove a wedge between 'things in themselves' and the way those things are perceived and known by the human mind. Scepticism required something more by way of answer than a bluff commonsensical statement of the facts.

But if Kant raised these questions to a point of conceptual refinement far beyond anything dreamed of in Moore's philosophy, he still left room for those same sceptical doubts which he had started by expressly ruling out of court. After all, the very basis of Kant's 'transcendental idealism' was the argument that we *couldn't* have direct or unmediated knowledge of the world, since this would reduce our cognitive capacities to a state of reflex passivity (and thus leave us prey to scepticism once again).

But as Stroud points out, Kant's 'solution' to this problem is really no solution at all, or not the kind of answer that could possibly convince either a thoroughgoing sceptic or a common-sense realist like Moore. 'The thought that we can have no knowledge of things as they are independent of us is what makes scepticism so distressing. Why is that thought any less distressing when entertained in the transcendental mode rather than in the empirical mode?'[8] If Kant brought about a revolution in philosophy, it wasn't on account of his realist convictions or his once-and-for-all silencing of epistemological doubt. What Kant bequeathed to later philosophers was a new and more refined set of problems, such that Moore's attempted 'solution' could only seem wilfully uncomprehending.

This is some of the background history that needs to be borne in mind when interpreting Derrida's various statements on the question of referentiality. He is not, any more than Kant, denying that there exists a world 'out there', or that language can engage with that world in a variety of practical ways. What he does most emphatically deny is the notion (Kant's 'transcendental realism') that imposes a certain reified *concept* of reference, and so closes off these dimensions of productive exchange between the world and the text. There is a passage from *Dissemination* (p. 43) which makes this point with particular force. 'Every time that, in order to hook writing precipitously up with some reassuring outside or in order to make a hasty break with idealism, one might be brought to ignore certain recent theoretical attainments' − [and here Derrida outlines some salient strategies of deconstructive reading] − each time this occurs 'one would all the more surely regress into idealism, with all of what . . . cannot but link up with it, singularly in the figures of empiricism and formalism.' Like Kant, Derrida sees how easily these classical 'positions' become mixed up, to the point where a form of metaphysical empiricism can hardly be distinguished from its typecast 'idealist' counterpart. And again like Kant, he insists that such confusions can only be avoided by a scrupulous attention to the problems involved in arriving at 'the real' through our representations of it.

Now Derrida clearly has a different approach to this whole

problematics of knowledge and perception. For him, it is not by way of *conceptual* critique (in the Kantian sense) that these issues are best brought to light, but by a sedulous reading of the philosophic texts where such 'concepts' are ceaselessly reworked and placed in question. 'Once inserted into another network, the "same" philosopheme is no longer the same . . ./Simultaneously, "unique and original" philosophemes, if there are any, as they enter into articulated composition . . . are affected by that composition over the whole of their surface and under every angle. We are nowhere near disposing of rigorous criteria for judging philosophical specificity, the precise limits framing a corpus or what properly belongs to a system.'[9] These remarks are taken from Derrida's 'Economimesis', an essay which latches on to those blindspots or moments of rhetorical excess where the whole imposing edifice of Kantian thought seems threatened by a radical instability. More precisely, Derrida argues that aesthetics (as conceived in the *Critique of Judgement*[10]) is absolutely central to Kant's epistemology; that the interrelated questions of mimesis, of artistic disinterest and the 'framing' of aesthetic experience are involved in a play of figural substitutions which resists any form of *de jure* conceptual closure. Representation in general — which includes that most classical of 'philosophemes', the notion of linguistic reference — becomes caught up in this functioning of a text that must perforce remain strategically blind to its own most crucial turns of argument. And these 'turns' are precisely rhetorical *tropes,* passages in the discourse of Kantian reason where it seems that every concept, every element of system and method is subject to a certain dislocating force that can always reinscribe it in a different, a radically alien economy of sense.

So it would clearly be wrong — a determinate misreading — to represent Derrida as carrying on the Kantian tradition of conceptual critique. Too many passages in his writing refuse to settle down and rejoin that tradition on anything like its own categorical terms. But the analogy with Kant does provide a useful corrective to those other, equally myopic misreadings which treat Derrida as some kind of transcendental solipsist, labouring under the absurd delusion that there is nothing 'real'

outside the play of textual inscription. Certainly Derrida maintains (like Kant) a vigilant mistrust of materialist philosophies
that think to place themselves 'beyond' metaphysics at a stroke
by declaring for the ontological primacy of matter over mind, or
world over word. But this is in order to demonstrate the
complicity, the reciprocal dependence that has always existed
between idealism in its various guises and a certain naive or
unreconstructed realist philosophy. Thus Derrida turns back the
arguments of Houdebine and Scarpetta by calling their attention
to those elements of Marxist dialectic that remain partly captive
to Hegelian concepts and categories. 'I do not believe that there
is any "fact" which permits us to say: in *the* Marxist text,
contradiction *itself,* dialectics *itself* escapes from *the* dominance
of metaphysics.'[11] His point is not merely to head off an
awkward encounter by adopting a no-win sceptical position
which has the last word by insisting that words are in any case
all that we can have. Rather, he is arguing that debates like this
are essentially misconceived; that the whole long history of
baffled encounters between 'idealist' and 'realist' positions has
served to dissimulate their deeper collusion in the same metaphysical enterprise.

What is therefore needed, he suggests, is a vigilant reading of
all those texts, from the ancient materialists to Marx and Lenin,
where an effort is made to re-think the categories of mind and
matter from a standpoint outside such received conceptual
oppositions. When Lucretius writes of the 'corporal nature of
the soul or spirit', or Lenin refers to matter as possessing the
'unique property . . . of being an *objective reality,* of existing
outside our consciousness', they are each (as Derrida reads them)
making this attempt to break with metaphysics in its multiform
varieties.[12] That the break can never be adequately achieved in
language — least of all in the language of philosophy — is evident
enough, since to theorize its nature is perforce to adopt, in
however circumspect a fashion, those same metaphysical terms
of debate. Certainly Derrida is far from claiming that deconstruction has come out on the far side, or pushed such a distance
'beyond' metaphysics as to leave Marxism way behind. On the
contrary: his point in thus engaging with dialectical materialism

is to draw out the sense of common purpose beneath this apparently sharp divergence of views. But there is no question here of resolving differences (as Houdebine and Scarpetta strive to suggest) through a kind of conceptual *Aufhebung* which would finally transcend all the old antinomies. What Marxism and deconstruction each have to bear steadily in mind is the heterogeneity of matter, the fact that it 'exceeds metaphysical discourse (not being thoroughly caught in it)'.[13] And this should be enough to rebut those polemical misreadings of Derrida that wrench his statements out of context so as to give them an idealist or (in the non-Kantian sense) a 'transcendental' slant. Such arguments can only be mounted from the standpoint of a naive or metaphysical realism, one that lines up squarely on the ground of G.E. Moore's riposte to the claims of philosophical scepticism.

Against pragmatism: Derrida, Rorty, Lyotard

So we won't understand what Derrida is doing unless we take stock of the problems created by Kant and his successors in the modern tradition of epistemological critique. That is to say, when we read some of Derrida's more 'outrageous' pronounce-ments — like his denial that perception, or anything like it, really exists — we will be missing the point if we think to refute such claims by a straightforward appeal to commonsense knowledge. But this is *not* to conclude (with pragmatists like Richard Rorty) that Derrida is one of those undeceived modern thinkers who are at last learning to live with the non-availability of knowledge, truth or cognitive 'foundations' of any kind. Rorty has no time for Derrida's more detailed or complex passages of textual argumentation./On his view these are just regrettable lapses into the kind of pointless activity which has characterized philosophy ever since it picked up the mistaken idea — mainly from Descartes and Kant — that truth-claims could be either asserted or criticized in any decisive way. What Rorty likes about Derrida is the way that he debunks such claims, showing (as Rorty would have it) the bankruptcy of all epistemology and the need for philosophers to give up imagining that they might have special truths to impart. So Derrida becomes a kind of half-way honorary pragmatist, having deconstructed a great deal of surplus ontological baggage but then fallen victim to the lure of his own negative metaphysics or systematized anti-philosophy.[14] On his 'good' side Derrida has come up with some useful devices for reminding us that philosophy is just another 'kind of writing', with no privileged access to knowledge or truth. On his 'bad' side he has shown an unfortunate tendency to keep harping on about (say) Kant or Husserl as if there were still some *point* in returning to the age-old problems of epistemological critique.

For Rorty those problems are of interest only insofar as they figure in the unfolding narrative of Western philosophy to date. What we have learned — or what we should have learned by now, after so much argument and so few solutions — is the lesson that philosophy is really best treated as a kind of edifying narrative, a history which hangs together in various interesting ways but no longer seriously claims to deliver any kind of ultimate or authentic *truth*. If philosophers would only accept this scaled-down version of their intellectual role, then they would find themselves usefully in touch with a whole range of adjacent cultural activities, from literary theory to the pragmatist turn in 'post-modern' thinking about science, technology and social concern. It is only the old, deluded hankering for absolute *truth* — the idea that knowledge can ultimately 'cut nature at the joints' — which prevents philosophers from seeing all this./If they did come to accept it, then philosophy would suffer some loss of prestige, at least in terms of the high mystique that has traditionally attached to its name. Quite simply, it would figure as one voice only in an ongoing dialogue of cultural interests, no longer aimed toward 'truth' as such but concerned to keep up the conversation and preserve a flourishing intellectual life. And to Rorty it seems that the best conditions to encourage such a flourishing are those that prevail in the advanced ('North Atlantic bourgeois liberal') modern democracies.[15]

Thus it is no coincidence that pragmatism — the most distinctively 'American' of homegrown philosophic outlooks — figures as the upshot, the wished-for *dénouement* of Rorty's historical tale. Pragmatists accept that there is no truth apart from what suits our present practical needs. According to William James, truth must be defined as that which is 'good in the way of belief', good (that is to say) insofar as it promotes the interests of a given community or culture. And those interests are best served by a new self-image of philosophy, one that gives up its old high truth-claims – including the claim to criticize consensual systems of belief – and which henceforth accepts its role as one voice only in the ongoing dialogue. If it rejects this decently unambitious role and tries to hang on to its privileged truth-telling status, then philosophy is condemned to play an increasingly marginal and specialized role *vis-à-vis* society and the 'human sciences' at large.

On Rorty's diagnosis there would seem to be two main forms of this recurrent and still very active delusion./One is the 'technical' style of philosophy which seeks (and always fails to come up with) ultimate answers to such misconceived questions as the meaning of truth, the structure of objective knowledge or the limits and capacities of *a priori* reason. Rorty thinks that modern analytical philosophy has often – too often – taken over these problems from Descartes, Kant and others in the 'mainstream' epistemological tradition. It has merely given them an up-to-date linguistic twist, appearing to shed the surplus baggage of idealist metaphysics, but in fact reproducing all the old antinomies in a different rhetorical guise. And this despite the fact, as Rorty argues, that linguistic philosophy (at least in its 'stronger', more pragmatic forms) has plainly undermined the whole project of epistemology by showing what contradictions emerge from the effort to interpret its central claims./So philosophers who want to revive that tradition are misreading not only the multiplied evidence of past failures but also the signs of a new, more worthwhile activity presently to hand./And this applies whatever their particular 'technical' interest, be it a theory of ethical rights and obligations, a new account of sense and reference or a refinement on the theme of truth-conditional semantics. To such questions as these there are no *answers* to be had, at least if the requirement of a 'genuine' answer is that it hold good not only for present (agreed-upon) purposes but arguably for all time and against all conceivable objections. So what Rorty calls the 'realist backlash' in current ideas about language and representation is merely one instance of an unfortunate — but, he hopes, a short-lived — reversion to bad old Kantian habits of thought

The other form of retrograde thinking, according to Rorty, is that which pins its faith to political progress through enlightened critique of existing institutions and ideas. For this is to imagine that there exists some ideal vantage-point, accessible to reason, which stands outside all the prevalent norms of consensual knowledge, and thus enables the theorist to expose all their blindspots of ideological misrecognition. Rorty believes that no such standpoint is attainable, since every kind of knowledge must ultimately appeal to the validating context of cultural assumptions from which it takes rise and within which its truth-claims are judged. There could be no way to *make sense* of any theory that issued such a radical challenge to prevailing ideas. And from this Rorty draws the implicitly conservative lesson that revolutions in thought must be either ineffectual (since meaningless according to the dominant consensus), or really not 'revolutions' at all, since the consensus does in the end find room for them without the kind of drastic upheaval they envisage. Again, Rorty's position is that of the sturdy common-sense pragmatist, mistrusting all those grand theories (of knowledge, history, class-consciousness or whatever) that claim to know more and see further than current beliefs would allow. Marxism is clearly the main target here, though his objections would also apply to the Kantian tradition of enlightened thinking on matters of ethics and political theory. When Rorty calls himself a 'post-modern bourgeois liberal', it is precisely in order to distance *his* kind of 'liberalism' from the claims implicit in the Kantian sense of that word. No longer is it a question of adjudicating moral and political issues in light of those purportedly self-evident truths whose universality must yet be tested in the critical tribunal of autonomous individual conscience. 'Post-modern' liberalism conceives itself more on the American model, as a generalized consensus of ideas and interests that works to guarantee the flourishing and continuance of a certain communal self-image. The *quaestio quid juris* of Kantian ethics

– or the questions of political justice raised by Kant's more revolutionary successors – would be simply beside the point according to this 'post-modern' notion of how philosophy should properly serve the interests of society at large.[16]

It is Jean-François Lyotard who provides Rorty with a usage of the word 'post-modern' that includes all these large implications. For Lyotard, we have moved into an era ('we' being the inhabitants of the wealthy, technologically advanced Western societies) when it is no longer possible to believe in those grand 'metanarrative' accounts of human progress or emancipation.[17] Partly this is a matter of history having eluded their masterly projections by taking so many unforeseeable ('illogical') turns. Partly it has to do with the emergence of a new technology, that of the computer and information networks, whose complexity and potential for creating new modes of social interaction are far beyond the powers of present-day 'rational' control. Old ways of calculating consequences, of reckoning up cause and effect, begin to seem largely obsolescent where so much depends on the constant exchange of endlessly interpretable meanings and messages. Perhaps this is indeed a 'revolution' like nothing in previous history, an upheaval in the structures of knowledge and power which must needs bring about corresponding changes in the social and state apparatus. Possibly – as Lyotard inclines to believe – those changes may exert an emancipating force, a tendency toward the decentralization of power and political initiative. But there is no way of knowing or of rationally predicting that this will be the case. Any attempt to *theorize* the outcome, to extrapolate from present trends to future results, falls back of necessity into old, teleological or 'totalizing' habits of thought. And it is precisely such explanatory systems – historical 'metanarratives', as Lyotard calls them – that have shown themselves inadequate to cope with this new situation. Thus it might turn out that the information network became the most oppressive, because most diffuse and far-reaching, instrument of social control. The very absence of legitimizing authority could make it into something like a dream-machine of surveillance, with everyone plugged into the system and unable to perceive or resist its effects.

Lyotard is unwilling to predict which way things will go because the nature of this current ('post-modern') condition is such as to effectively disqualify specific forecasts. In the absence of metanarrative theories we can only take our bearings from the various piecemeal myths of information which make up the currency of present-day exchange. Rorty agrees with this, arguing that 'first-order natural narratives' are really all we possess, so that any new attempt to tell the story of stories — perhaps in Hegelian or Marxist terms — is a species of grandiose delusion.[18] All that is left of the grand metanarrative tradition is what Rorty calls 'naturalized Hegelianism', or the story-telling interest minus the idea that everything makes sense from the viewpoint of Absolute Reason or historical progress. Thus pragmatism is firmly installed as the one philosophy that takes full account of this current situation in the discourse of post-modern culture. For Rorty, as for Lyotard, the only justification that truth-claims can have is their persuasive efficacy, their power to convince in the context of existing belief-systems. Lyotard distinguishes in speech-act terms between the old, 'constative' criteria of truth and falsehood and the present-day stress on 'performativity' as a measure of practical effect. 'The performativity of an utterance, be it denotative or prescriptive, increases proportionally according to the amount of information about its referent one has at one's disposal. Thus the growth of power, and its self-legitimation, are now taking the route of data-storage and accessibility, and the operativity of information.'[19] Rorty is making much the same point when he argues that philosophy had better set out to be interesting and relevant, rather than 'true' in some ultimate, epistemological sense. And Derrida — as Rorty reads him — would appear to be headed toward the same pragmatist conclusion, though held up along the way by some unfortunate tangles with Kant, Husserl and other old-fashioned seekers after truth.

Politics and the principle of reason

In the first part of this chapter I argued that Derrida was in fact very much involved with that whole post-Kantian problematics of reason and representation. It is simply not the case – as Rorty would suggest – that Derrida (on his 'good' side) rejects all forms of epistemological critique and treats philosophy as just one 'kind of writing' among others, with no specific interest in questions of knowledge and truth. He may indeed regard such questions as beyond hope of definitive answers, at least on the terms laid down by traditional (logocentric) reason. Undeniably he thinks that these issues have been posed in a form that evades certain crucial problems in the textual or written constitution of philosophic arguments. And in order to make this point the more forcibly he has insisted that philosophy *is* a 'kind of writing', one that requires meticulous close-reading in a manner to which philosophers are perhaps less accustomed than literary critics. But this is not to say that Derrida has emerged into some 'post-philosophical' realm of pure textuality where truth and falsehood are mere words and the principle of reason no longer applies.

Rorty wants to praise Derrida for *not* worrying about all those Kantian problems, like the business of discovering *a priori* grounds for our belief in the reality of external phenomena. So he finds no difficulty with Derrida's more extreme 'textualist' pronouncements, regarding them (in almost Wittgensteinian terms) as therapeutic devices for discouraging a pointless obsession with insoluble questions. There is no genuine 'problem' of linguistic reference – whether conceived in Kantian or modern analytical terms – so long as we accept that things just *do* make sense, for all practical purposes, according to current conventions. So Derrida would simply be making the point once again that epistemology, or the quest for cognitive foundations, is a fruitless enterprise that need not engage us any longer. But this is to ignore the awkward fact that Derrida has devoted the bulk of his writings to a patient working-through (albeit on his own, very different terms) of precisely those problems that have occupied philosophers in the 'mainstream' tradition, from Kant to Husserl and Frege. And this because those problems are indubitably *there,* installed within philosophy and reaching beyond it into every department of modern institutionalized knowledge.

Thoroughgoing pragmatists like Rorty and Lyotard reject the principle of reason and argue that knowledge can only be assessed according to its practical or 'performative' effects. But this denial ends up in Rorty's case by producing a consensus-view of truth which simply reaffirms the current self-image of 'North Atlantic bourgeois liberal' culture. There are two things wrong — intellectually and politically wrong — with a pragmatist position like this. It ignores the extent to which reason, in its various practical or technocratic forms, has shaped every aspect of Western experience and so — inescapably — set the main terms for debate. And it also fails to see that this experience can only be grasped by a critique that upholds the values of enlightened reason, even while seeking to diagnose their present repressive or distorting effects. For Derrida, those effects are very precisely located in the discourse of legitimizing power and knowledge whose history is to be read in the texts of a philosophical tradition extending from Plato to Husserl and beyond. Simply to *reject* that tradition — thinking to occupy a whole new domain of 'post-modern' cultural debate — is effectively to give up any hope of informed rational critique.

Derrida addresses these questions most directly in his essay 'The Principle of Reason: the University in the Eyes of its Pupils'.[20] His theme in this inaugural lecture at Cornell was the intimate relation between reason itself and a certain idea of the modern university. It is an idea that goes back to Kant and his effort to define philosophy's place in relation to the other intellectual disciplines. For Kant, philosophy was one of the 'lower' faculties, in the sense that it exerted no direct influence on law, government or the other branches of state executive power. Its privileged status *within* the university was in fact guaranteed by its willingness to abstain from such meddling outside its proper limits of competence. Philosophy was recognized as 'a place of pure rational knowledge, a place where truth has to be spoken without controls and without concern for "utility", a place where the very meaning and the autonomy of the university meet' (p. 18). And this division of intellectual labour corresponds very closely — as Derrida remarks — to that arrangement in the Kantian theory of mind that places pure reason 'outside and above' the faculties of technical or practical grasp. There is a trade-off here between philosophy's claim to pursue its own interests without fear of state repression, and the state's equally 'reasonable' demand that philosophy confine itself to pure speculation and not become involved with practical affairs. Such is the implicit contractual agreement that under-writes not only Kant's blueprint for a liberal university system, but also his account of those other 'faculties' that guarantee the scope and the limits of human knowledge.

'One cannot think the possibility of the modern university, the one that is re-structured in the nineteenth century in all the Western countries, without inquiring into that event, that in-stitution of the principle of reason' (p. 8). It is by means of this inaugural gesture, this parcelling-out of knowledge into 'pure' and 'practical' kinds, that there develops a discourse of the faculties with large implications for present-day teaching and research. It was always a fiction, Derrida maintains, this belief in keeping philosophy pure and preventing it from any admixture of practico-political interests. And never has the pretence been more transparently obvious than nowadays, when just about every programme of research can turn out to have technical (and very often military) uses. In this situation the United States Navy can 'very rationally' subsidize academic work in semiotics, linguistics and interpretation theory. To think of such disciplines as Kant once thought of philosophy — as being answerable only to the 'disinterested exercise of reason' — is to show a very marked degree of ivory-tower idealism. And this pervasive intrusion of practical interests extends even to the most ad-vanced work in the current 'theoretical' sciences of man. 'At the service of war, of national and international security, research programs have to encompass the entire field of information, the stockpiling of knowledge, the workings of all semiotic systems, translation, coding and decoding, the play of presence and absence, hermeneutics, semantics, structural and generative lin-guistics, pragmatics, rhetoric' (p. 13). In short, there is no way of drawing a line, in Kant's confident *de jure* style, between the proper concerns of theoretical reason and the various fields (legal, administrative, military-industrial) where such knowledge may be put to use. Those who continue to debate such questions are taking over an 'enlightened' doctrine of the faculties whose origin lies in that same root division of intellectual labour which marked the emergence of modern technocratic reason. We are deluded if we think that what goes on inside the university — whether in departments of philosophy, literature or 'pure' science — can ever be kept separate from what happens in the world outside.

But this raises the obvious problem: how can deconstruction claim any warrant to criticize existing structures of power/ knowledge if it operates, of necessity, within that same space of deeply compromised academic discourse? One possible response is to take Lyotard's line: to announce that we have entered a 'post-modern' era where the old forms of legitimizing reason no longer exert any genuine critical force. But this leads on to a consensus-view of truth which tends, as we have seen, to endorse the political-discursive status quo and preempt any form of rational critique. Derrida firmly rejects this way of thinking (and along with it, implicitly, much of what passes for 'deconstruction' among American literary intellectuals). Those who adopt a critical stance on these questions 'need not set themselves up in opposition to the principle of reason, nor need they give way to "irrationalism" '. Continuing to work within the university, they can still properly assume, 'along with its memory and tradition, the imperatives of professional rigor and competence' (p. 17). And this by reason of the need for any 'competent' critique to think through its own position with a scrupulous regard to those concepts of scope and method which define the limits of a 'discipline', a faculty or field of enquiry.

Of course there is the option of rejecting such merely institutional subject-boundaries, and deciding (like Rorty) to treat 'philosophy' as just one voice in the post-modern liberal consensus. But this amounts to a form of 'irrationalism' in precisely Derrida's sense of the word: a retreat from the principle of reason which renders theory incapable of grasping or indeed resisting its effects. It is significant in this connection that Rorty holds William James and John Dewey to be the strongest, most consequent of pragmatist thinkers in the native American tradition. He is less enthusiastic about C.S. Peirce, mainly on account of Peirce's belief that every intellectual discipline requires some ultimate cognitive faith, some idea (as Peirce expressed it) of 'truth at the end of enquiry'. To Rorty this seems a regrettable instance of the pragmatist breaking faith with the perfectly adequate standards of relevance or interest provided by his own cultural time and place. Peirce is depicted, with a certain pitying fondness, as having fallen back into bad ('epistemological') habits of mind, habits which his stronger contemporaries – Dewey especially – managed to renounce once and for all. That Derrida takes a very different view is evident from a passage that he quotes from Peirce in 'The Principle of Reason'. Here Peirce acknowledges the straightforward pragmatist doctrine of his own early writings, his belief that 'the meaning and essence of every conception lies in the application that is to be made of it'. But he goes on to qualify this doctrine in terms that Derrida cites with approval. 'Subsequent experience in life [Peirce writes] has taught me that the only thing that is really desirable without a reason for being so, is to render ideas and things reasonable. One cannot well demand a reason for reasonableness itself.'[21]

Now Derrida's project in these recent texts *is*, quite literally, to 'demand a reason for reasonableness itself'. Unlike Peirce, he regards rationality in its current (technological and other) forms as a highly specific historical formation which cannot be appealed to as some kind of ultimate ground. To this extent he is carrying on the critique of Western instrumental reason which Heidegger saw as the essential task of any authentic modern philosophy. But Derrida has insisted, from his earliest writings, that there is no possibility of thinking back beyond the origins of this 'false' enlightenment, of returning (as Heidegger wished) to some primordial state of Being when language was in touch with the ultimate truths of experience. Such a project is too deeply implicated in all those logocentric assumptions (of origin, teleology, speech as self-presence) that Derrida detects at every stage of the Western philosophical enterprise. What he *does* undoubtedly inherit from Heidegger is the stress on actively re-thinking the 'origin' of reason, or demanding (what Peirce believes cannot be demanded) an answer to the question: 'Is the reason for reason rational?'

Thus Derrida describes it as his purpose in this essay 'to bring about a dialogue between Peirce and Heidegger', a dialogue that would question the principle of reason without thereby giving way to an irrationalism devoid of critical force. Picking up a series of pertinent distinctions in the passage from Peirce, Derrida suggests what this project might amount to in deconstructionist terms. 'We would have to go beyond the conceptual opposition between "conception" and "act", between "conception" and "application", theoretical view and praxis, theory and technique' (p. 9). And this *not* in order to draw the pragmatist conclusion that reason is bankrupt, or theorizing pointless, insofar as it departs from the self-understanding of a given society and its needs. What is required is the kind of immanent critique which interrogates the principle of reason precisely in terms of those founding oppositions whose logic is inscribed in Kant's doctrine of the faculties. For it is here — and in the modern university, that site of recurrent crises in the relation between 'pure' and 'practical' knowledge — that these issues are posed with maximum force. 'From now on,' Derrida writes, 'so long as it has the means, a military budget can invest in anything at all, in view of deferred profits: "basic" scientific theory, the humanities, literary theory and philosophy' (p. 13). That is to say, it can 'rationally' invest in such programmes, since no calculation — no reckoning based on traditional ideas of means–end rationality — can possibly rule out their future utility. To this extent Derrida agrees with Lyotard. There has indeed occurred a momentous shift in the relations of knowledge and power, such that the operative truth-conditions (or 'performativity') of any given programme will be subject to all manner of delayed effects and unlooked-for incidental 'profits'. But Derrida more crucially differs from Lyotard in arguing that this process — for all its random, 'aleatory' character — still has to be reckoned with on terms that derive what *critical* force they possess from the principle of reason. And it is here, specifically, that deconstruction parts company with 'post-modern' pragmatism in its various forms.

Logic and rhetoric: 'nuclear criticism'

I have argued (and understood Derrida as arguing) that deconstruction is a rigorous attempt to *think the limits* of that
principle of reason which has shaped the emergence of Western
philosophy, science and technology at large. It is rigorous insofar
as it acknowledges the need to engage with that principle in all
its effects and discursive manifestations. Thus the activity of
deconstruction is strictly inconceivable outside the tradition of
enlightened rational critique whose classic formulations are still
to found in Kant. 'Even the principle of uncertainty (and . . . a
certain interpretation of undecidability) continues to operate
within the problematics of representation and of the subject-
object relation' (p. 14). That 'certain interpretation of undecidability' is of course another name for deconstruction, for a mode
of thinking that can best exert its critical leverage at those points
where rational discourse comes up against the limits of calcula-
bility. And this is precisely where Derrida locates the sources of
resistance to an otherwise ubiquitous diffusion of power/
knowledge through the channels of present-day instrumental
reason. It may be the case — as he readily concedes — that *any*
kind of research, even in 'marginal' disciplines like literary
theory, is liable to find itself somehow coopted to the purpose of
extending or refining that system. But insofar as it has to make
constant allowance for such wholly unpredictable benefits, the
system suspends any power of *deciding* in advance what shall
count as useful (strategically exploitable) research. And this
margin of undecidability is where deconstruction finds a hold for
exhibiting the aporias and the swerves from 'rational' aim that
characterize modern technocratic reason.

Thus Derrida can argue that those same marginal disciplines
are in fact well placed to perceive the contradictions of a system
that has far outrun its own self-regulating principles. 'If the
analysts end up for example working on the structures of the
simulacrum or of literary fiction, on a poetic rather than an
informative model of language, on the effects of undecidability,
and so on, by that very token they are interested in possibilities
that arise at the outer limits of the authority and the power of the

principle of reason' (p. 14). To gain some idea of what this might mean in practice I want to look briefly at the text of a paper that Derrida delivered at a 1983 conference on so-called 'nuclear criticism'.[22] Here he puts forward a number of seemingly extravagant claims for the pertinence of deconstruction as a strategy for thinking *within* and *against* the 'logic' of nuclear deterrence. There is, Derrida argues, a sense in which deconstruction is peculiarly fitted to press these questions beyond the present stalemate, the paralysis of reason, engendered by the nuclear threat. For one thing, 'deterrence' is a word for which there exists no adequate *concept,* no place within a system of coherent or intelligible thinking that would make proper sense of it in any given context. Of course this predicament is one which, according to Derrida, extends to every form of discourse whose rhetorical complexity exceeds its own powers of presumptive control over language. (Which is indeed to say, quite simply, *every* form of discourse.) Deconstruction points to those blind-spots of argument where a text generates aberrant meanings or chains of disruptive implication that work to undermine its manifest 'logical' sense. It would hardly be surprising if the claims and counter-claims of current nuclear doublethink turned out to exemplify such blindness in a specially striking form. But Derrida is suggesting much more than this. If deconstruction in some sense belongs to the nuclear epoch – if it possesses, as Derrida would argue, some particular 'competence' in the matter of nuclear critique – then this is *not* on account of its supposed irrationalism or its natural kinship with the sophistries of deterrence. On the contrary: deconstruction insists on thinking through those paradoxes in the nature of reason ('pure' and 'applied') whose effects are most starkly and urgently visible in nuclear-strategic debate.

The question of 'competence' is crucial here, and it receives at least the outline of an answer in Derrida's text. Competence is no longer exclusively vested in those experts – whether nuclear scientists or strategic analysts – whose knowledge becomes increasingly obsolete, given the exorbitant complexity of the issues involved. There is no kind or measure of expertise that could possibly grasp these issues, or hope to come up with 'rational' solutions in the way of weapons design or deterrent strategy. In this area, Derrida writes, 'there is a multiplicity of dissociated, heterogeneous competencies. Such knowledge is neither coherent nor totalizable' (p. 22). And this means that the exercise of 'competent' reason in these matters may *not*, after all, be restricted to the experts, those whose knowledge embodies the powers and the limits of classical (means—end) rationality. In fact their very training in the logistics of calculated response may prevent them from seeing just how far the current situation has left such reasoning behind. It is wrong — and extremely dangerous besides — to suppose that the experts must have the last word since they alone grasp the full complexity of the nuclear issue. Their knowledge is based on the self-deluding premise that strategies of deterrence (or nuclear war-fighting plans) are matters of applied expertise and rational prevision. But this is to ignore the *rhetorical* dimension of nuclear thinking, the fact that every new weapons system, every shift in the prevailing policy of 'defence', will entail some largely unpredictable change in the way such moves are construed by the 'other side'. There is simply no reckoning with the multiplied chances of error and misinterpretation that are opened up by each new gambit in the nuclear game. So those 'experts' who decisively influence such far-reaching changes of policy are nonetheless incompetent to grasp what is at stake or to calculate the likely outcome. Their knowledge is an obsolete knowledge, failing to recognize the extent to which nuclear 'reality' has entered the realm of apocalyptic fantasy. What *counts* in strategic or deterrent terms is not so much the destructive capacity of weapons or the superior logic of tactical reasoning on either side. Rather, it is the power to raise the fantasy stakes to a point where rival interpretations are effectively played off the field.

So the question of competence is not to be decided on grounds of either technical know-how or strategic expertise. Such grounds scarcely exist in this current, unnerving situation where nuclear bluff — the exchange of unthinkable threats and counter-threats — has reached such fantastic proportions. 'The dividing line between *doxa* and *episteme* ["mere opinion" and "knowledge"] starts to blur as soon as there is no longer any such thing as an absolutely legitimizable competence for a phenomenon which is no longer strictly techno-scientific but techno-militaro-politico-diplomatic through and through, and which brings into play the *doxa* or incompetence even in its calculations' (p. 24). And this is where deconstruction can bring its critical strategies to bear upon the discourse of nuclear power-politics. It can point out, first, the rhetorical (or performative) status of those claims that are advanced on behalf of this or that strategic position. Such claims have no basis in fact, logic or the existing reality of armed confrontation. They are a species of elaborate fiction, but a kind that can bring about escalating sequences of bluff and double-bluff which are just as 'real', in their potential effects, as any startling new development in weaponry. 'We can therefore consider ourselves competent,' Derrida writes, 'because the sophistication of the nuclear strategy can never do without a sophistry of belief and the rhetorical simulation of a text' (p. 24). Here he is applying what amounts to a reverse lesson from Clausewitz: that war (and the strategic build-up to war) is the continuation of diplomacy by alternative means. But he is also arguing that diplomacy is and always has been a *rhetorical* phenomenon; that '"diplomatic power" would not exist without the structure of a text' (p. 26). And it is the nuclear issue that brings this point home with particular force by creating a plethora of discourses whose meaning and logic are entirely bound up with their power to simulate the (as yet) unthinkable event of terminal catastrophe.

Other philosophers — including some in the Anglo-American analytical tradition — have likewise pointed to the paradoxes and the manifest illogicalities involved in the 'concept' of nuclear deterrence.[23] This concept rests on the primary assumption that no country would actually launch an attack on any rival nuclear power in the full knowledge that its own population would suffer the inevitable consequences. But from this it would follow that neither side — supposing them to possess this degree of self-preserving rationality — could possibly have any *serious* intention of using nuclear weapons in defence of its national interests. To make strategic plans for their actual use in some given situation is to admit that deterrence may not work, or at least that one has to act tough — show the readiness to use them — if the weapons are to have any genuine deterrent effect. But again, this reduces the concept to logical incoherence, since if one succeeds in getting the other side to *believe* that one is in fact prepared to use them, then the only 'rational' response on their part is to launch an early attack in times of crisis and so preempt a similar first strike on the adversary's part. Any hint on either side that their use is inconceivable — whether on moral or strategic grounds — would undermine the credibility of deterrence itself, and open the way to all kinds of (none the less dangerous) nuclear bluff. And in any case it is impossible to believe that such an elaborate pretence could ever be kept up, given all the complex chains of command and the unlikelihood of this whole machinery *not* going into action as soon as war seemed imminent. And yet the very concept of deterrence — insofar as it is a *working* concept — implies that both sides must still be subject to the principle of reason, which in turn should ensure that its supposed rationality will never be put to the ultimate test.

These paradoxes can be analysed in various ways. From one point of view they belong to the domain of motivational psychology, at least when that domain is taken to include such forms of ultimate paranoid delusion. From another ('analytical') standpoint they are perhaps best treated in terms of a logical critique that would bring out the determinate contradictions involved in present-day nuclear strategy. Then again there is the tradition of Critical Theory as developed by thinkers like T.W. Adorno and Jürgen Habermas, concerned to preserve the values of enlightened critique but also to diagnose the specific *distortions* of that principle brought about by modern (repressive or instrumental) reason.[24] These are all possible ways in which philosophy can work to sharpen the insights and strengthen the arguments of those who engage with the nuclear issue at the level of reasoned debate. But the question remains as to why deconstruction should claim any particular 'competence' here. For an answer — one answer — I would cite Derrida's statement that 'if there are wars and a nuclear threat, it is because "deterrence" has neither "original meaning" nor measure. Its "logic" is the

166

logic of deviation and transgression, it is rhetorical-strategic escalation or it is nothing at all' ('No Apocalypse', p. 29). This might be taken as simply a different, a 'Continental' way of making the familiar point: that deterrence is founded upon premises and principles that won't stand up to logical analysis. But Derrida wants to argue a much closer, more vital and productive link between 'nuclear criticism' and the strategies of deconstruction. If the latter possesses any special competence – any powers of analysis developed to a unique degree – then this has to do with precisely that absence of 'original meaning', the 'logic' of alogical transgression and the effects of 'rhetorical escalation' as against the 'measure' of enlightened reason.

Of course these statements are open to misreading in the usual way. To call nuclear war a 'fabulous or fictive referent', to deny its reality both in the sense that it has not yet happened and that all our conceptions of it are based on strictly *inconceivable* fantasies and projections – this, it will be argued, is the crazy but predictable outcome of Derrida's well-known solipsistic tendencies. It is no great step, after all, from the generalized conviction that 'there is nothing outside the text' to the more specific form of lunacy that thinks nuclear weapons a figment of our collective rhetorical devising. But this is to ignore – as I have already argued – not only the detailed context of Derrida's statements but also the entire post-Kantian history of epistemological critique. And nowhere is Derrida more insistently engaged with that history than here, in his reflections on the nuclear issue. ' "Nuclear criticism", like Kantian criticism, is thought about the limits of experience as a thought of finitude . . . As for the history of humanity, that example of finite rationality, it presupposes the possibility of an infinite progress governed according to an Idea of Reason, in Kant's sense, and through a treatise on Perpetual Peace' ('No Apocalypse', p. 30). Despite its fairly evident irony, this statement is not to be interpreted as a gesture of outright repudiation, a total break with the Kantian ideas of enlightenment, progress and rational critique. Rather it pronounces the necessity of re-thinking those ideas with the utmost rigour, since nowadays crucial decisions are still being made *as if* in compliance with the principle of reason, but actually in accordance with an escalating logic of rhetorical overkill which possesses neither 'measure' nor reason.

It is this situation that has undermined the 'competence' of those who invent nuclear strategies or who ultimately decide – as the myth would have it – whether war shall take place. 'All of them, that is, very few, are in the position of inventing, inaugurating, improvising procedures and giving orders where no model . . . can help them at all' (p. 22). So great is the range of rhetorical gambits (promises, threats, bluffs, double-bluffs, simulated moves and counter-moves) that no reckoning-up of likely outcomes will serve to determine a rational course of action. It is on the basis of *this* predicament, Derrida argues – one in which 'the limit itself is suspended', where 'crisis, decision, and choice are being subtracted from us' – that we need to re-think the conditions and possibility of rational critique. This new assessment will have to take account of all those conflicting modalities of discourse that go to create such an utter confusion of strategic means and ends. It must therefore include 'the relations between knowing and acting, between constative speech-acts and performative speech-acts, between the invention that finds what was already there and the one that produces new mechanisms or new spaces' (p. 23). And it will need to work with a critical awareness of how these distinctions have taken effect, not only insofar as they have produced the very paradigms of modern 'technocratic' reason, but also in the sense that they offer the only means of enlightened resistance and critique. From the standpoint of current nuclear protest this attitude translates very directly into practical terms. Disarmers must do more than confront these issues with a passionate moral conviction and a rhetoric as powerful as that brought to bear by the advocates of peace through nuclear strength. They have to show that such arguments are totally misconceived; that deterrence is a notion whose 'logic', as Derrida writes, is 'either rhetorical-strategic escalation or nothing at all'. And this will involve not only a patient and detailed rebuttal of opposing claims, but also – indispensably – an appeal to critical reason by way of bringing out the contradictions and aporias present in the discourse of nuclear power-politics.

My reading of Derrida is of course sharply at odds with that prevalent idea of deconstruction as a species of last-ditch irrationalism which denies both the principle of reason and the existence of any reality 'outside' the text. I have argued that this is a gross misunderstanding of Derrida's project; that the issues he raises belong within the tradition of Kantian enlightened critique, even while pressing that tradition to the limits (and beyond) of its own self-legitimizing claims. Indeed I would go further and suggest that his thinking in these recent texts shows distinct signs of convergence with the project of a critical theorist like Habermas.[25] That is to say, it seeks new grounds for the exercise of enlightened critique through an idea of communicative competence which allows for specific *distortions* in present-day discourse, but which also holds out the possibility of grasping and transcending these irrational blocks. From the 'post-modern' standpoint, as analysed by Lyotard, such a project is disqualified at the outset by appealing to some higher, 'metanarrative' level of explanation which is simply no longer available. Habermas would then appear as one more deluded spokesman for that same 'dialectic of enlightenment' whose latter-day turn toward repressive rationality he (like Adorno and Horkheimer before him) had originally set out to diagnose. This quarrel between Habermas and French post-modernism has been the topic of intense discussion recently, so I shall do no more than summarize the main issues here.[26] What is most important is Habermas's line of counter-argument: that post-modernists like Lyotard are giving themselves over to a form of unprincipled pragmatism which renounces the very possibility of reasoned critique. And in doing so they are effectively depriving thought of any power to engage with social and political realities on other than passively conformist terms.

Of course it would be absurd to suggest any simple equivalence of method or aim between Habermas's project of rational reconstruction and Derrida's ceaseless problematization of the principle of reason. Nevertheless I would argue that we err more grievously by assimilating Derrida to a strain of post-modern irrationalism whose effects he has done nothing to endorse. Certainly it has been a main object of Derrida's texts to show

169

how philosophers, from Plato to Husserl, have striven and failed to suppress the signs of rhetorical disruption in the discourse of philosophic reason. But he has also been careful to repudiate that facile misreading of deconstruction – prevalent among literary critics – which thinks to turn the tables on philosophy by proclaiming that 'all concepts are metaphors', or that philosophic truth-claims are really metaphorical through and through. As Derrida points out in his essay 'White Mythology', this argument ignores a very crucial problem, namely that all our working definitions of metaphor – from Aristotle down – have been couched in terms that ultimately derive from the language and conceptual resources of philosophy.[27] It is impossible to break with that tradition simply by reversing one's priorities, declaring the omnipresence of metaphor and hence the bankruptcy of philosophic reason. Such moves represent the first stage only in a deconstructive strategy which must then go on to re-think the whole structure of opposing valuations attached to the ideas of 'metaphor' and 'concept'. For it is only insofar as we have inherited certain ways of *conceptualizing* metaphor – techniques, that is to say, for distinguishing between 'literal' and 'figurative' language – that we can get any kind of argumentative hold for discussing these questions.

So it is idle to maintain that philosophy comes down to a handful of disguised or occluded metaphors *unless* one makes this further concession: that metaphor itself is unthinkable outside a certain genealogy of philosophic concepts. And this argument extends to the wider issue of priority between language and thought. One cannot simply say (in a gesture common to structuralism and post-structuralism alike) that language determines the very concepts and categories by which different cultures or philosophic systems interpret the world. For it is precisely *from* philosophy – from the terms and distinctions made available by analytic reason – that linguists have adopted their various ways of arguing this relativist case. 'Whoever alleges that philosophical discourse belongs to the closure of a language must still proceed within this language and with the oppositions it furnishes. According to a law that can be formalized, philosophy always reappropriates for itself the discourse that de-limits it.'[28] And this applies equally to the Kantian tradition of enlightened critique as Derrida essays its structural genealogy, its limits and effects. There is no possible leap 'beyond' philosophy except on terms that philosophy will always turn out to have conceived or somehow determined in advance.

7. Letters Home: Derrida, Austin and the Oxford Connection

There is no philosophical school or tradition that doesn't carry along with it a background narrative linking up present interests with past concerns. Most often this selective prehistory involves not only an approving treatment of ideas that fit in with the current picture but also an effort to repress or to marginalize anything that doesn't so fit. Bertrand Russell's *History of Western Philosophy* is one fairly blatant example of this strategy at work. The story it tells is a Whiggish account of how thinkers managed – against all the odds of metaphysical delusion – to come out at last (with Russell and his peers) on the high plateau of logical consistency and truth. On the way to this *dénouement* Russell avails himself of various techniques for pointing up the narrative drift. His book takes in all the accredited 'major' figures, some of whose opinions Russell is hard put even to summarize without remarking how nonsensical they appear from a modern (logical) point of view. Elsewhere – as with Leibniz or Kant – he takes the more accommodating line of winnowing out the structures of valid argument and consigning what remains to the history of dead metaphysical ideas. It is this latter technique that has characterized the approach of analytical philosophers to the history of their discipline. The question is not so much what those earlier thinkers arguably meant to say as what techniques now exist for translating their concerns into a modern (most often a linguistic-analytical) register.

The same selective process goes to construct that typecast narrative which treats the 'British' and the 'Continental' styles of philosophizing as two completely separate, indeed antagonistic lines of descent. Thus it is taken for granted that the two sides are so far apart, with so little in the way of shared methods and assumptions, that any kind of dialogue is certain to produce mere bafflement or cross-purpose talk. British philosophers with an interest in 'Continental' theory feel themselves forced into a marginal role by the highly professionalized ethos that prevails within their discipline. This feeling is only strengthened by their more or less accepting the background mythology that explains how the two 'traditions' grew up in a state of hostility often amounting to downright mutual contempt. There are several different versions of this story at present, but they all serve equally to reinforce the sense of incommensurable aims and languages. One (the 'ordinary-language' version) takes its lead from the later Wittgenstein in arguing that most of the problems that have long vexed philosophers — and continue to vex these 'Continental' thinkers — result from their use of a pointless metaphysical jargon which puts them at odds with the common-sense wisdom of everyday usage. On this account, such thinkers have failed to learn the lesson bequeathed by a long tradition of misguided speculative thought. They have persisted in errors and delusions of their own creating, hooked on a kind of malign verbal magic — 'bewitchment by language', as Wittgenstein described it — which prevents them from seeing the plain sense of things. The other exemplary narrative is that which takes not 'ordinary language' but logic (or the modern refinements of logic introduced by philosophers like Frege) as its reference-point for deciding which episodes of previous or subsequent thought are to count as 'serious' philosophy. Of course there are deep disagreements between this and the 'ordinary-language' view, since linguistic philosophy in the Fregean mode holds out for a formalized logic beyond the powers of unaided self-description vested in natural language. But these two points of view come together in regarding large tracts of philosophical country as simply too remote and treacherous to warrant further exploration. Only by avoiding the metaphysical swamps and the high terrain of speculative thought can philosophers hope to make progress through a sense of shared rational goals. And those others, like Derrida, who question this enterprise — who think to 'deconstruct' its most basic working assumptions — can always be written off as 'literary' thinkers incapable of serious philosophic argument.

173

Not that this sense of being excluded from the mainstream applies only to British thinkers of a broadly 'Continental' mind. An essay by Jacques Bouveresse ('Why I Am So Very UnFrench') describes what amounts to the same experience from an opposite but equally embattled standpoint. Here we have a French philosopher whose interests lie mainly with the Anglo-American 'analytical' tradition; who shows small patience with Foucault, Derrida and other purveyors of intellectual 'fashion'; and who lines up squarely with those across the Channel who would identify 'philosophy' with the raising of questions capable of clear and definitive answers. Bouveresse has a list of specific complaints against the way that philosophy is carried on in present-day France. He speaks of 'the disastrous weakening of the critical sense, the progressive transformation of the know-ledgeable (or presumed-to-be-knowledgeable) public into a sort of religious community dedicated to the cult of a few con-secrated stars'.[1] Hence – as Bouveresse explains – his own reaction in favour of an utterly different philosophical style, one that prizes the close twin virtues of lucidity and problem-solving power. Hence also his aversion to the habit of thought that treats philosophical questions, in Hegelian fashion, as so many stages in a grand dialectic whose progress and significance can only be grasped in historical terms. Bouveresse admits that analytical philosophy sometimes gives rise to a distorted view of past achievements which wrenches them out of their historical con-text in order to lend them an up-to-date appearance. But this tendency seems to him 'less scandalous, all things considered, than the tendency to make the historical understanding of authors and doctrines . . . a philosophical aim in itself rather than an indispensable means or preliminary step'.[2] And this for the reason that *genuine* problems – as conceived by *serious* philosophers – have a lasting significance and power to perplex that transcends all mere relativities of time and place.

From his position as a kind of internal exile, Bouveresse reproduces exactly the image of 'Continental' philosophy that one finds among Anglo-American champions of the mainstream analytical tradition. In particular, he seizes on the blurring of distinctions between philosophy and other contiguous disciplines, the fact that they all become 'kinds of writing' with no especial privilege attaching to the truth-claims of philosophic reason. This development he associates with the tendency, among French thinkers, 'systematically to absolve errors of reasoning and method (to the extent that these are still actually perceived) in order to retain only what is essential, namely the literary qualities'.[3] It is against this levelling or relativized notion of the human sciences — with philosophy not even *primus inter pares* — that Bouveresse takes his stand. In this present situation, he writes, 'the mere fact that it continues to conceive of philosophy as an *argumentative* discipline already constitutes by itself a weighty argument in favour of analytic philosophy.' What Bouveresse seeks above all is to make philosophers aware of their own distinct vocation and the fact that genuine philosophical problems cannot be reduced to the fashionable emphasis on matters of 'literary' style. The two main threats to 'serious' philosophy come about through confusing it with the *history of ideas* on the one hand and *rhetoric* (or some version of textual critique) on the other.

'Keeping philosophy pure' is how Richard Rorty describes this perennial urge to beat disciplinary bounds and fence the subject off from adjacent terrain.[4] After all, philosophy has had to give up a good many of its own territorial claims as its various sub-disciplines either matured into self-respecting sciences or tended to split off (like psychology) with different ends in view. So it is perhaps understandable that philosophers — especially those in the analytic camp — should now take care to frame very precisely the rules that determine what shall count as philosophic argument. Despite all their differences, there exists at least a tacit consensus between those who accept the authority of 'ordinary language' and those who look beyond it to various kinds of formalized logical account. On both sides it is assumed that philosophy is a disciplined effort to elucidate the conditions of meaningful utterance — the 'conceptual grammar', as some would have it — which enable us to make sense of language. And on both sides, similarly, much of what passes for current Continental 'philosophy' can only seem a species of heady rhetorical delusion that belongs (if it really belongs anywhere) in departments of comparative literature.

Bouveresse doesn't mention Derrida by name, but it takes no very sagacious reader to guess that he is the main target of all these criticisms. What Bouveresse has to say about the 'literary' turn in recent French philosophy – the foregrounding of style and the lack of concern with 'serious', substantive questions – finds an echo in the many attacks on Derrida mounted by mainstream Anglo-American thinkers. Basic to these is the charge that Derrida has erased the distinction between 'philosophy' and 'literature', treating the former as a purely textual phenomenon and thus effectively subjugating *reason* to *rhetoric*. And of course – as Derrida repeatedly shows – this move has been unthinkable in philosophic terms at least since those exemplary scenes of instruction when Socrates deployed his dialectical skills against the sophists and other such mere rhetoricians. This inaugural gesture was henceforth repeated whenever philosophers came to suspect that language, through its unruly figural powers, was threatening to get the upper hand of reason and so undermine their whole enterprise. Occasionally there would spring up temperance movements – like the famous Royal Society programme – devoted to weaning language away from its unseemly dependence on such dangerous devices. But mostly philosophers got along well enough on the standard assumption that rhetoric was anyway just an ornament to logic, so that metaphors might be a passing distraction but scarcely a threat to the business of rational argument. For Derrida, on the contrary, it is only the strength of philosophical prejudice – sustained by a persistent refusal properly to *read* its own texts – that holds this assumption in place. What philosophy declines to think through with any rigour is the salient fact of its textual constitution, its dependence on the figural resources of a language that opens up strange and unsettling possibilities of sense. Bouveresse sees exactly what is at stake when he equates the current emphasis on 'literary' style with the tendency to question or suspend those rules of philosophic reason that have always ensured the predominance of logic over rhetoric. His response – as a lone voice of sanity and truth among the apostles of fashion – is to declare flatly that the rules still hold and that nothing can come of this rhetorical turn except 'errors of reasoning and method'.

John Searle adopts a similar tone when he takes Derrida to task for his flagrant 'misreading' of Austin on the topic of speech-act theory.[5] On one level this exchange can be read as just another example (albeit an extravagant case) of Anglo-American 'commonsense' logic up against the high gyrations of French post-structuralist theory. Derrida himself concludes by voicing doubts as to whether this presumed 'encounter' of traditions can really have taken place, given the extraordinary gaps of understanding that emerge along the way. But if there is − as one can hardly deny − a breakdown of communications here, it is not just a case of Derrida perversely refusing to recognize Searle's plain intentions and clear-headed argument. A careful re-reading of 'Limited Inc' − Derrida's response to Searle's critique of his (Derrida's) text on Austin − should be enough to question the idea that analytical philosophy has all the 'rigour' and deconstruction nothing more than an over-developed taste for elaborate verbal games.

There already exist several fairly detailed accounts of the Searle/Derrida exchange.[6] My purpose here is not so much to rehearse the arguments and differences as to reflect on what they mean − or what they have so far standardly been *taken* to mean − against the background of Anglo-French cultural debate. In Searle's view, and that of his supporters in the 'analytic' camp, the main points at issue can be summarized readily enough. Derrida has misread Austin's text in the obvious sense that he has resolved *not* to take it as a matter of faith that Austin has succeeded in saying what he means or meaning what he says. Derrida assumes, on the contrary, that the most revealing passages of Austin's argument are those where his choice of metaphors, parables or casual locutions is such as to create real problems for any close reading of his text. To Searle, these problems simply don't exist, being a product of Derrida's perverse determination to ignore the plain drift of Austin's intentions while seizing on minor points of textual detail that philosophy − 'serious' philosophy − can afford to pass over. Surely Derrida cannot be serious when he questions the idea that language is properly and essentially a means of communication? Or when he actually suggests that fictive or imaginary speech-acts (excluded by Austin from 'serious' consideration) may in fact be the model and type-case of performative utterance in general? Or again, when he problematizes the idea of 'context' to the point of denying that it could ever serve as the ground of appeal for deciding what speech-acts properly mean in any given situation? That Derrida indeed puts his name to such arguments can only strike Searle as sufficient evidence that he is not engaged in the business of 'serious' philosophical argument. That he makes yet further elaborate play with the notion of 'putting one's name' to a text — of claiming, like Searle, some proprietory hold over future interpretations — merely goes to confirm this impression. For Searle, it is just a fact that speech-acts *do* have certain conventional (but nonetheless real and binding) conditions attached to their proper use. To find this situation — as Derrida does — a cause of philosophical perplexity is not only to misread Austin at several crucial points but to misconceive the very nature of language.

Such — briefly summarized — is Searle's response to what he sees as a wholesale disregard for the elementary protocols of philosophic argument. Like Bouveresse, he assumes that thinking can only be led astray by attending too closely to matters of 'literary' style, or by allowing an interest in rhetoric to get in the way of straightforward logical consistency. Yet Derrida's text has a rigour of its own, a quality too easily ignored if one reads it simply with a mind to enjoying its exuberant games at Searle's expense. Admittedly there is much in 'Limited Inc' that can hardly be interpreted as anything but a species of elaborate textual play designed to trap Searle in the typecast role of literal-minded innocent dupe. Thus Derrida quotes whole chunks of Searle's argument, but quotes them shrewdly out of context, or in such a way as to lay them open to readings totally at odds with their (presumed) intent. And this by way of reinforcing the point: that language is subject to a generalized 'iterability' — or readiness to be grafted into new and unforeseeable contexts — such that no appeal to performative intent can serve to delimit the range of possible meaning. From Searle's

178

point of view this is just another case of Derrida wilfully grasping the wrong end of the stick. The 'iterable' character of speech-acts is nothing more nor less than the precondition of their functioning at all as bearers of communicable meaning. Otherwise every form of words would be tied so completely to its unique original context that only the speaker could possibly know what it meant. So surely it is absurd of Derrida (Searle thinks) to seize upon this plainly *indispensable* feature of language and use it as a pretext for raising yet further misconceived problems about speech-act theory.

But Derrida is able to demonstrate quite easily that Searle has missed the point, here as elsewhere; that he has failed to grasp what is essentially at stake in this questioning of ideas like 'context' and 'intention'. If Derrida were 'seriously' claiming that all communication is impossible − that we can't, in practice, know what any piece of language *means* because the relevant codes and conventions are radically underdetermined − then Searle's rejoinder would certainly hit the mark. But this is precisely *not* the point of Derrida's critique. What he calls into question is the right of philosophy to erect a wholesale theory of mind and language on the basis of commonsense notions that work well enough for all practical purposes but take on a different, more doctrinaire aspect when applied as a matter of philosophic principle. This is why Derrida goes to such lengths to demonstrate the ways in which Searle's text can be turned back against its own governing suppositions. He is not denying that language possesses an 'intentional' aspect that allows us − again, for all practical purposes − to interpret various kinds of performative utterance in keeping with the relevant conventions. But he *is,* most emphatically, denying the idea that philosophy can lay down the rules of this procedure by explaining how language *should or must* work if its workings are to make good sense. 'What is limited by iterability is not intentionality but its character of being conscious or present to itself' ('Limited Inc', p. 249). Searle adopts the same proprietory stance in relation to both his own and Austin's texts. That is to say, he assumes absolute control over the way those texts should 'properly' be read, a power that passes by lineal descent from Austin to Searle.

And of course the central arguments of speech-act theory are closely bound up with this claim that it is possible — indeed imperative — to get Austin's meaning right. After all, it would create some awkward problems for Searle if Austin's text could be shown to elude the best efforts of so 'serious' and responsible a commentator.

But this is precisely what Derrida sets out to show, first in his reading of Austin and then — at quite extravagant length — in his follow-up 'response' to Searle. It is a question of uncovering what Derrida calls 'a type of "structural unconscious"' . . . which seems alien, if not incompatible with speech-act theory given its current axiomatics' (p. 213). The theory, that is to say, seems constructed with a view to excluding the effects of that textual 'unconscious', insofar as they disrupt the kind of hermeneutic mastery envisaged by a reader like Searle. Again, Derrida is far from denying that we do require at least some *presumed* general grasp of an author's purpose in order to read any text whatsoever. Interpretation, as he puts it, 'operates *a fortiori* within the hypothesis that I fully understand what the author meant to say, providing he said what he meant' (p. 199). But this is an empirical fact about the psychology of reader-response and *not* any kind of guarantee — such as speech-act theory would claim to provide — that understanding must indeed have taken place. Hence Derrida's insistence that the 'iterability' of speech-acts is a function necessarily freed from all dependence on the truth of our intentionalist hypotheses. Any *theory* will have to get along in the end 'without in itself implying either that I fully understand what the other says, writes, meant to say or write, or even that he intended to say or write *in full* what remains to be read, or above all that any adequation need obtain between what he consciously intended, what he did, and what I do while "reading"' (p. 199). And such are the misunderstandings engendered in the course of this exchange between Derrida and Searle that the point is brought home with considerable force.

It might seem from all this that Searle stands squarely on the side of commonsense reason while Derrida pursues the usual 'French' line of high metaphysical abstraction. But in fact the exchange brings out an odd reversal of these stereotyped cultural

roles. It is *Searle* who effectively translates the Cartesian requirement of 'clear and distinct ideas' into a speech-act theory
founded on the notion of privileged access to self-present
meanings and intentions. Derrida even goes so far as to claim
that Searle's 'premises and methods' are 'derived from continental philosophy, and in one form or another . . . are very present
in France' (p. 173). They derive, that is, from a tradition of
hermeneutic thinking whose influence extends well beyond the
movement that currently goes by that name. It is this tradition
that underwrites Searle's belief in the recoverability of intentions
and the power of a text like Austin's to reveal its true meaning in
the presence of an 'authorized' interpreter like Searle.

As a self-conscious discipline, hermeneutics took rise with the
nineteenth-century speculative turn in Biblical commentary and
language study. It was then refined and developed — often to
very different ends — by thinkers like Heidegger, Gadamer and
Ricoeur. But it is not this modern, specialized discipline that
Derrida has chiefly in mind when he associates speech-act theory
with the 'hermeneutic' tradition. He is suggesting that philosophy has *always* been marked by this drive to appropriate
meaning and truth in the name of a sovereign reason. And,
furthermore, that local distinctions (as between Anglo-American
'empiricism' and French or German 'metaphysics') are of little
account compared with this encompassing heritage. Austin may
have believed — like Searle after him — that philosophy in its
'ordinary-language' mode was on the way to renouncing a long
history of fruitless metaphysical toils. Yet he set about this task
of demystification by claiming an authority — supposedly vested
in common forms of speech — that infallibly rejoined that same
logocentric tradition. 'Metaphysics in its most traditional form
reigns over the Austinian heritage: over his legacy and over those
who have taken charge of it as his heirs apparent' (p. 236).
Where this covert metaphysics appears most insistently is in
Searle's need to establish a series of enabling preconditions for
speech-act theory. These require (1) the authority of Austin as
original source of these ideas; (2) that Austin's texts make their
meaning fully available to 'serious', authorized interpreters; and
(3) that understanding can thus be rendered proof against

Derrida's style of perverse 'misreading'. On the contrary, says Derrida: there is nothing in his own account of Austin that is not provoked by the odd turns of metaphor, the fictive examples and self-deconstructing arguments that Austin himself so frequently produces. In this sense Derrida can stake a fair claim to having *read* Austin more attentively — more 'rigorously', even — than a faithful exponent like Searle.

For there are two kinds of 'rigour' in question here, and not (as Searle would have it) a straight choice between argument on the one hand and mere verbal games on the other. Searle's is the kind of analytical rigour that knows *in advance of reading* precisely what protocols a text must obey if it is to count as 'serious' philosophy. Thus Derrida cites a passage from Searle where he states the conditions that are sure to obtain 'once one has a general theory of speech-acts'. This 'once', Derrida notes, has a curious double function, serving in effect both to map out a future programme for research and determine its conclusions in accordance with a present ideal. 'Floating as it does between the logical and the chronological,' Searle's casual phrase 'organizes the suspense among all the presumptive heirs' (p. 237). What it chiefly suggests is that the work of achieving this 'general theory' has been programmed in advance by Austin (who unfortunately died too soon to carry it through), and now falls to those — like Searle — who are fully in possession of Austin's intentions. So this is the one kind of 'rigour': an assurance of right-minded grasp that always already shares the purposes of those whose ideas are worth 'serious' attention. It is a form of preemptive self-authorization that Derrida finds neatly figured in Searle's use of the word 'develop'. 'Searle might be considered to have "developed" the theory: to have produced it, elaborated, and formulated it, *and* at the same time to have merely extended it in detail, guided it to adulthood by unfolding its potential' (p. 236). By such means can 'theory' place itself in full command of a still 'developing' but henceforth safely institutionalized field.

The other kind of 'rigour' is that which Searle refuses to recognize in Derrida's text, touching as it does at many points upon the 'structural unconscious' of his own and Austin's writing, while also contriving to escape the closed circle of

182

self-authorized discourse. It is a rigour invisible to those who read in the assured expectation that texts will reproduce their own tidy notions of logical consistency. But this is not to say that Derrida's text is unconcerned with 'logic' or with the kinds of counter-argument that must rise against it from the standpoint of analytic reason. What is in question here, Derrida writes, is the power of logical concepts (or preconceptions) to determine in advance what shall *count* as an adequate reading of philo-sophical texts. 'The law and the effects with which we have been dealing . . . govern the possibility of every logical proposition, whether considered as a speech-act or not' (p. 235). And this means in turn that there cannot exist any protocol of method, reason or law that would ultimately 'provide a decision' or 'impose its norms upon these prelogical possibilities of logic'. Which suggests that Derrida is broaching something like a Kantian transcendental deduction, an argument to demonstrate ('perversely' enough) that *a priori* notions of logical truth are *a priori* ruled out of court by a rigorous reflection on the powers and limits of textual critique. To think the 'prelogical possibili-ties of logic' is, for Derrida, to open up a region of enquiry beyond all the certitudes of method and reason that have organized traditional philosophic discourse. Here as in his other works, it involves a reflection on *writing* (or textuality in general) as that which everywhere precedes and articulates the 'laws' of logical thought. His response to Searle may give the impression of totally rejecting reasoned argument in favour of elaborate verbal chicanery designed to head off serious debate. In fact, as I have argued, it should rather be seen as possessing a fugitive but nonetheless highly consequent logic of its own, a technique for drawing out those ruses of 'unconscious' significa-tion that haunt the language of speech-act theory.

'A Socrates who writes . . .'

Derrida ranks Searle among the 'self-made, auto-authorized heirs of Austin'. His point is to expose that habitual presumption which enables philosophers to go (as they think) straight to the conceptual heart of a text without wasting time over matters of resistant or (to them) unrewarding detail. Hence Derrida's contrary insistence: that it is often in the margins or obscure minor passages of a text — in the footnotes, perhaps, or a casual parenthesis — that its strains and contradictions stand most clearly revealed. Such passages are the starting-point for many of Derrida's most powerful deconstructive readings. The very fact that they bear a problematical relation to the rest of an author's work — or, beyond that, to the ruling assumptions of philosophic discourse — may have caused them to be tucked away out of sight in a footnote or simply passed over by commentators in search of more enduring truths. It is precisely by seizing on such uncanonical texts, passages or details that deconstruction seeks to resist the homogenizing pressure of received ideas.

I have suggested that it is wrong to view the Derrida-Searle 'debate' as simply a ritual exchange of hostilities between two utterly different philosophic cultures. Wrong because, first, the issues involved transcend such localized differences and take in — according to Derrida — everything at stake in the philosophic enterprise. Wrong again, because Derrida's deconstructive strategies are not just a kind of irresponsible playing with words, but a rigorous and consequent thinking-through of the problems thrown up by philosophy's forgetfulness of its own written or textual character. And the picture is misleading for a third reason, since Derrida is responding to something in Austin's text that he finds characteristic of 'English' philosophy, insofar as such national distinctions make any sense. The three-sided encounter (Austin-Derrida-Searle) takes on a strange topographical dimension where boundaries are constantly crossed and confused in the shuttling exchange of 'traditions'. Thus Derrida can ask: 'Isn't Searle ultimately more continental and Parisian than I am?' (p. 173). And claim, furthermore, that what eludes Searle's grasp in the reading of Austin's text is precisely what invites — even requires — a deconstructive account. This series of transactions, as Derrida describes it, 'seems to be occurring — to take geographical bearings in an area that disrupts all cartography — midway between California and Europe, a bit like the Channel, midway between Oxford and Paris' (p. 173).

On a simplified reading this intellectual landscape can be mapped out clearly enough. 'California' (Searle) is one point of the triangle, representing a certain kind of American analytical philosophy, trained up on plain realism, commonsense logic and a principled mistrust of 'Continental' thinking. Oxford stands in for Austin's style of linguistic speculation, a style unconcerned with matters of 'theory' and happy to pursue problematic cases even where they lead — as frequently happens — to a breakdown of speech-act classifications. It is this ludic propensity in Austin's writing — call it his 'literary' style — that Derrida can shrewdly play off against Searle's authoritarian discourse. As for Paris, it occupies an ambivalent place in this complex topography, on the one hand a home-base for Derrida's excursions, on the other a seat of that 'hermeneutic' enterprise that he finds oddly carica- tured in Searle's performance. And this whole situation is further confused by the fact that Derrida is here writing for American readers who will have a quite separate fix on these issues of cultural difference. Thus he writes: 'I have read it [Searle's text] in English but I am trying to respond in French, although my French will be marked in advance by English and destined in advance for a translation that will doubtless present certain difficulties' (p. 173). In fact these 'difficulties' serve Derrida as pretext for an intermittent running address to the translator, raising (among other things) the question of where *he* — Sam Weber — stands in relation to this shifting multiplicity of cultural contexts.

So Derrida by no means identifies with the 'French' as opposed to some (equally notional) 'British' tradition of philos- ophy. In fact his recent texts — especially *La Carte postale*[7] — have shown a growing interest in the Oxford connection and the deconstructive uses of certain ideas broached by thinkers like Austin and Ryle. What Derrida finds so congenial about 'Ox- ford' philosophy is partly the absence of an American-style professionalized ethos; partly its openness to seductive metaphors and fictive turns of argument; and partly, no doubt, its interest in topics — like the difference between *using* and merely *citing* or *mentioning* certain forms of words — that figure importantly in his own texts. The place takes on a utopian appeal insofar as it represents a mode of philosophizing that shrewdly subverts all established orthodoxies (including that of 'linguistic philosophy', as conceived by proponents like Searle). So it is no coincidence that Oxford is the setting (or textual *mise-en-scène*) for the first 'chapter' of *La Carte postale,* presented as a sequence of anecdotal 'postcards' addressed by Derrida to various – real or imaginary – correspondents. The occasion was a visit to Britain during 1977, when Derrida spent several weeks in Oxford attending seminars and reading haphazardly in the Bodleian Library. To the 'serious' philosopher this might all seem irrelevant and just another instance of perverse self-indulgence on Derrida's part. But the point is precisely to challenge that traditional image of philosophy as a discourse of ultimate truth-telling power whose function is to rise above mere contingencies of time and place.

The postcard motif serves Derrida's purpose as a means of strategically reversing this age-old prejudice. It allows him to keep philosophical issues in play, but also to prevent them from settling down into a fixed agenda for debate. Above all, it suggests that communication is not (or not always) what philosophers – and speech-act theorists especially – imagine it to be: a closed circuit of exchange where intentions are never mistaken and messages always arrive on time at the appointed place. Derrida described writing (in *Of Grammatology*) as the 'wandering outcast' of Western logocentric tradition, denounced by philosophers from Plato to Husserl for its proneness to misinterpretation, its lack of that self-authorizing power or presence vested in spoken language. Writing exerts a 'disseminating' influence on language, such as to multiply the possibilities of meaning and prevent any assurance that 'true' communication has in fact taken place. And it is here that the postcard comes to signify, for Derrida, the existence of a writing at the utmost remove from traditional ideas of meaning and communicative truth. The postcard is indeed a 'wandering exile', a message most often casually inscribed and promiscuously open for all to read. At the same time it is a writing that can only make sense to one person (the presumed addressee) whose knowledge of the sender enables him or her to figure out its otherwise impossibly cryptic message. The postcard thus exemplifies the twofold sense in which language eludes the sovereignty of philosophic reason. On the one hand textuality exceeds all the limiting specifications placed upon language by the need to maintain a strictly controlled economy of concepts. On the other, the postcard may be seen to insist that meaning is indeed *irreducibly* specific, but tied down to local particulars of time and place that likewise escape the universalizing drift of reason. In both respects it serves as an emblem of everything that is forgotten or repressed on the way to philosophic truth.

What Derrida is suggesting − in short − is that we read the great texts of Western tradition ('from Socrates to Freud and beyond') as so many messages that circulate without any absolutely authorized source or destination. The particular postcard that so caught Derrida's fancy was one that he found in the Bodleian Library, reproduced from the frontispiece of a thirteenth-century English fortune-telling book.[8] The remarkable thing about this engraving was that it showed Plato standing and (apparently) *dictating his thoughts* to a seated Socrates who obediently *wrote them down*. One can see why this image should have struck Derrida with the force of an uncanny belated recognition. One of his own chief arguments or strategies of reading − in *Of Grammatology* and elsewhere − has to do with precisely this mythical relationship between Socrates, Plato and the writing of philosophy. The traditional ('logocentric') prejudice is that which equates Socratic wisdom with the authority of voice and self-presence, and writing with everything that disseminates and therefore threatens that authority. Thus Plato is the prototype of all those unfortunate philosophers who *must* resort to writing in order to communicate their thoughts, but who lay themselves open, in the process, to all manner of unauthorized reading and misinterpretation. To envisage a Socrates who *writes* is to open up a counter-tradition, however 'apocryphal', where the old logocentric myth of origins no longer holds exclusive sway. It suggests that writing is in at the source of philosophy; that there is no thinking back to an authorized voice that doesn't pass by way of certain images or metaphors derived from writing.

Such had already been Derrida's contention in his deconstructive reading of the *Phaedrus* as an allegory of logocentric reason forced up against its own self-generated textual paradoxes. There (as we have seen) it was the key-term *pharmakon* — caught in a constant oscillation of meaning between 'poison' and 'cure', oblivion and redemptive memory — that attached itself to the topos of writing and thus undermined any straightforward univocal reading of Plato's text. There is no better example of deconstruction as a form of rigorous close-reading or textual critique. But *La Carte postale* envisages an altogether different relation between writing, philosophy and its authorized self-image. Here it is a matter of mobilizing all those hitherto repressed or marginal forms of writing that exist outside the received 'authentic' tradition. Thus Derrida muses on the long-running scholarly debate that has surrounded such possibly apocryphal texts as the Letters of Plato.[9] It is not only their authorship that is at issue here but also the question of where to draw the line when deciding what counts as genuine *philosophical* writing. Tradition finds room for philosophers' letters so long as they are authentically concerned with 'serious' questions and represent a genuine dialogue of minds in pursuit of some attainable truth. What it cannot take in is the notion of a writing that is cut off completely from authorial presence and addressed to no particular (professionalized) community of interests. Hence Derrida's fascination with the postcard, at once the most ephemeral kind of writing and the kind most open to interpretative guesswork by those who lack the privileged means to crack its otherwise impenetrable codes.

That Oxford was the place where all these thoughts came together in Derrida's mind is a fact of no interest according to the dominant idea of philosophical discourse. At most they are matters of anecdotal background that belong (if anywhere) in some forthcoming volume of Derrida's autobiography. But this is precisely what Derrida denies, this pitiless divorce between essence and accident, the genuine concerns of 'philosophy' on the one hand and mere circumstantial life-history on the other. His point in deploying the postcard (of all things) as a tactical resource against the tyranny of concepts is to show how circumstance *always and everywhere* enters the discourse of philosophic reason. Philosophy is motivated by a natural desire to believe otherwise, to treat its discoveries as a matter of timeless *a priori* truth, rather than a series of interesting notions thrown up by chance encounters with ideas and events. What Derrida likes about 'Oxford' philosophy is its attachment to 'ordinary language' *not* as some repository of ultimate truth but as a means of debunking such large metaphysical pretensions. Like Austin, Derrida is fond of inventing elaborate narratives or fictional 'cases' by which to draw out some fine point of semantic presupposition. With Austin the aim — the express aim at least — is to coax philosophy down from its heights of mystified specialist jargon and lead it back to a sense of the wisdom vested in commonplace idioms. This side of his project could hold little interest for Derrida, since it merely replaces the tyranny of concepts with the equally tyrannical regime of 'ordinary language'. But there is another dimension to Austin's writing, one that has lately given rise to some highly unorthodox accounts of his work. What is emphasized here is the seductive power of Austin's language, its habit of running away with the argument to the point of collapsing all those tidy terminological distinctions that make up the currency of speech-act theory.

Shoshana Felman has written brilliantly of Austin as a kind of philosophical Don Juan, exploring the varieties of linguistic bad faith under cover of a plain diagnostic intent to distinguish the true from the false.[10] In the end Austin's metaphors and fictive examples exert such a power over his thinking that crucial distinctions are allowed to fall away and philosophy is revealed as a kind of seductive discourse always in danger of yielding to its own rhetorical devices. The 'performative' dimension of language — its capacity to persuade, cajole, seduce — proves too much for the classifying efforts of speech-act theory. Like the amorous Don, Austin is as much deceived as deceiving, taken in by the mischievous power of false promises even as he holds them up for philosophical inspection. Theory is undone by its own fascination with precisely those aspects of language that most threaten its self-assured mastery and grasp. There could only be a genuine 'theory' of speech-acts if performative language were a special case which could finally be explained on constative (theoretical) terms. In fact, as Felman shows, this distinction is undermined as the logic of Austin's argument gets into conflict with its suasive or rhetorical drift. Theory stands revealed as the dupe of its own most cherished aspirations, seduced by a dream of mastery over language that can only end up by ironically reversing those roles.

Again, it would be simplifying matters — falling back on the usual crude stereotypes — to treat this as simply a 'French' appropriation of commonsense British ideas. Certainly there is an orthodox reading of Austin, prevalent among his Anglo-American heirs, which Derrida and Felman are out to subvert. But they are also — both of them — using Austin's text as a means of contesting certain dominant trends in *French* linguistics and philosophy of language. Thus Felman takes Emile Benveniste, rather than Searle, as her main target in that other tradition of 'straight' speech-act theory which tries to extract a coherent philosophical doctrine from Austin's endlessly elusive text. And for Derrida likewise it is a virtue in 'Oxford philosophy' that it holds out against the systematizing drive that always subjugates language to concepts. Reading Austin as Derrida and Felman read him has something of the same effect that Derrida experienced when he came across the Bodleian postcard. Like the apocryphal Socrates who *writes*, this Austin represents a scandal of misplaced origins, a figure who subverts the authority claimed by his like-thinking earnest disciples. 'Psychoanalytically speaking', as Derrida puts it, these texts have much to tell about the workings of language at a level inaccessible to other, more heavily systematized forms of theory.

There might seem little enough connection between psychoanalysis and the interests of Oxford linguistic philosophy. Yet really the comparison is not so far-fetched. In both cases there are powerful institutional pressures at work that would reduce interpretation to a matter of preserving the cultural status quo. Thus psychoanalysis becomes a technique for reconciling patients to the 'normal' conditions of an alienated social existence. And linguistic philosophy is often regarded in much the same light: as a therapy designed to *talk language down* from its various 'metaphysical' bewilderments and 'lead it back', in Stanley Cavell's words, 'via the community, home'.[11] But there is another understanding — of psychoanalysis and 'ordinary language' alike — which would draw precisely the opposite lesson. Henry Staten has put the case well in his recent book on Wittgenstein and Derrida. 'Wittgenstein develops a style of writing which is radically errant, which unlids all the accidence concealed by "normal" uses of words in order to show how many different routes it would be possible to take from any given point in their discourse — routes which we had simply not thought of because we were bemused by normality.'[12] Once 'ordinary language' is shorn of its residual metaphysics — the idea that ultimate truths are somehow vested in our normal, everyday habits of usage — linguistic philosophy takes on a very different aspect. Rather than reinforce existing conventions or naturalized 'forms of life', it works to reveal the unlooked-for possibilities latent in all communication. And this brings philosophy close to psychoanalysis in just the way that Derrida suggests through the manifold intertextual tropes and devices of *La Carte postale*. The aim would no longer be that of therapeutically instructing philosophy in the ways of commonsense linguistic wisdom. It would now be a question of showing just how much philosophy had *missed* by equating its interests with those of a certain (very culture-specific) commonsense dogmatism.

This is also where Oxford linguistic philosophy impinges on Derrida's project in *La Carte postale*. It suggests — at whatever 'unconscious' level — some ways in which theory might continue to speculate on and in language without falling prey to the seductions of premature system and method. There is one recurrent topic in the British tradition, from Bertrand Russell to Gilbert Ryle, which especially engages Derrida's interest. It is the matter of *naming*, and of proper names in particular: how to distinguish the 'mention' or token reference from the genuine act of using a name. 'This is the question Fido/"Fido" . . . the question of knowing whether I name my dog or whether I mention the name of which he is the bearer, whether I *use* or cite his name. I adore these flights of theoretical fancy, so very "Oxford" in character, their extraordinary yet necessary sublety as well as their imperturbable ingenuity, psychoanalytically speaking.'[13] It is this same problematic — how to *tell the difference* between 'genuine' speech-acts and those merely cited, rehearsed or spoken in jest — that opens the way to Derrida's deconstructive readings of Austin and Searle. Oxford philosophy invites such treatment by its readiness to speculate on questions of language that often suggest deeper perplexities in the discourse of commonsense reason. It is this curious mixture of conscious and unconscious motives — what Derrida calls their 'imperturbable ingenuity' — that makes such writings a privileged zone for the psychoanalysis of philosophic texts.

And indeed, Derrida's essay on Freud in *La Carte postale* has to do with those speculative ventures of thought by which psychoanalysis both stakes its major theoretical claims and risks its own dignity as a self-respecting science of mind.[14] There emerges an uncanny pattern of transference and delayed after-effects, such that Freud's most productive hypotheses (like those explored in *Beyond the Pleasure Principle*) are caught up in a tangled intersection of 'life' and 'work', Freud's family history on the one hand and the future of the psychoanalytical movement on the other. He embarks on a quest whose beginning cannot know its end, since events and ideas will only fall into place through a pattern of belated (*nachträglich*) recognition whose 'logic' is that of the unconscious and its devious effects. It is this process that Derrida finds so aptly figured in the 'postcard' from Socrates to Freud. Authoritative language is that which obediently 'returns to the Father' in a circuit of self-assured mastery and rational control. Like the postal system in good working order, it guarantees the passage of known information from authorized sender to proper addressee. It is against this monopolistic system that Derrida proposes a different communicative model, one that would acknowledge those random, aleatory effects of meaning that philosophy has traditionally sought to repress.

Thus Derrida operates with two different metaphors of the postal system, corresponding to two different 'epochs' in the relation of language and truth. On the one hand is the legalized channel of regular exchange where messages are sent 'under

Letters Home: Derrida, Austin and the Oxford Connection

proper signature to the proper recipient'. This network is policed and maintained by the same laws that guarantee the truth of self-present meaning, the rules of correct interpretation and the 'restricted economy' of language in general. But there is another, more liberating aspect of 'the post' where the system – as Derrida puts it – appears to 'take a leap' and suggest what possibilities might be opened up if those rules were perceived as mere normative conventions.

La Carte postale is Derrida's most adventurous text to date in the effort to wrench interpretation away from its logocentric models and metaphors. But of course Derrida is not arguing – absurdly – that we should just do away with the postal system, or (as translated into philosophic terms) that we should scrap the rules and conventions forthwith and treat texts as henceforth open to any kind of wild, anachronistic reading. Rather, it suggests a loosening-up of that *particular* rule that prevents philosophy from avowing any interest – any 'serious', philosophical interest – in the circumstantial play of chance and necessity that governs its own creating. We can now look more closely at two case histories (Nietzsche and Freud) where writing and the after-effects of writing are inextricably bound up together.

8. Nietzsche, Freud, Levinas: on the Ethics of Deconstruction

In *Otobiographies* (1984) Derrida asks what is at stake when an author puts his or her name to a piece of writing. This question of names, of authorized signatures and intellectual copyright, was at the heart of his earlier exchange with John Searle on the topic of speech-act philosophy. There, as we have seen, it gave rise to some playful but nonetheless pertinent thoughts on the way that writing, once it enters the public domain, must always be subject to possible misunderstandings which cannot be ruled out of court by any straightforward appeal to context or authorial intentions. But in this case Derrida would surely have to acknowledge that his own texts were open to whatever kind of wild interpretation we might choose to place on them. He could scarcely be in a position to upbraid Searle – as he does, in fact, at several points in that essay – for ignoring the letter of his (Derrida's) text and glossing it largely in accordance with received ideas about language, meaning and communication. A simple *tu quoque* would seem to be in order, insisting that Derrida abide by the consequences of his own extreme form of epistemological scepticism. There could then be no judging – in point of fidelity or intellectual rigour – between the various ways that Derrida's texts have been taken up, applied or interpreted. Still less would it be possible to argue – as I have argued here – that deconstruction has been wrongly understood by those who regard it as a species of out-and-out hermeneutic licence, a justification for indulging all manner of interpretative games.

Otobiographies is Derrida's most explicit attempt to handle these problems thrown up in the wake of so-called 'American deconstruction'. That is to say, it is addressed very specifically to the question of how such ideas take hold in a certain institutional context; how a project can always be kidnapped, so to speak, or exploited for different political and cultural purposes. All the more appropriate that Derrida should have first delivered this text at the University of Virginia, Charlottesville, at a conference to mark the bicentenary of the American Declaration of Independence. He begins by disclaiming any competence to address such a weighty historical theme. In speech-act terms, an *excuse* is the device by which Derrida chooses to make his entry into this complex rhetorical and ideological domain. But what he goes on to say has considerable relevance to the politics of deconstruction and the question of why it has exerted such an influence on American literary criticism. One can also make out, as a kind of running sub-text, the preoccupation with proper names (for instance, the name 'Jacques Derrida'), and the way these attach to a body of writing whose fate at the hands of readers and exegetes can never be controlled or kept within bounds by any power of authorial command.

After all, Derrida asks: what exactly is or was its status, that document whose signing is conventionally taken to mark the emergence of a new national and political entity, the United States of America? Who were those first 'representative' spokesmen, those citizens and delegates who put their hand to this momentous document? More specifically: what *authorized* their signatures, given that the only constitutional source of such authority was that which they themselves were in process of creating as they signed the Declaration? And this leads on to the further question of how a representative democracy gets started, since those who had a part in its inaugural moment were strictly not empowered by any existing set of rules or procedures. These are not just frivolous problems dreamed up by a wily deconstructionist in search of some new paradoxical twist. They are widely debated in the literature of constitutional law, with various proposals for evading their more awkward consequences. Some theorists of jurisprudence — notably H.L.A. Hart — take up a version of Austin's speech-act philosophy which argues that law is essentially a species of *performative* utterance; that its rules take effect through the same kinds of tacit but binding convention that operate in the case of promises, marriage-ceremonies and so forth.[1] It would then seem merely beside the point to ask what authority can possibly attach to a law — or to texts like the American Constitution or the Declaration of Independence — whose first signatories were, at the moment of signing, not democratically authorized to play this role. To raise such questions (Hart believes) is to mistake the character of legal language. It involves a confusion of the 'constative' and 'performative' realms of discourse, a failure to see that language can signify — and carry well-defined meanings and entailments — while not obeying the strict laws of deductive inference. Their authority derives from that same understanding of operative senses and contexts which governs the practice of everyday speech-act commitment.

One way of grasping Derrida's point is to say that he rejects this commonsense 'solution' to the antinomies of law and political representation. And so he asks again: what entitled those first delegates to speak on behalf of an American people whose consent they could only assume by administrative fiat, since as yet there existed no written constitution in which it was enshrined? 'We, therefore, the representatives of the United States of America in General Congress assembled . . . do in the Name and by the Authority of the good People of these Colonies solemnly *publish* and *declare,* that these united colonies are and of right ought to be *free and independent states*' (cited in *Otobiographies,* p. 26). As Derrida remarks, there is a range of performative effects at work in this passage, including the shift from what 'is' to what 'ought to be' the basis of a free and just society. Certainly one could take the words at face value as a self-enacting statement of liberal-democratic faith. There would then be no point in asking, for instance, how the change is effected from a given (pre-constitutional) state of affairs to a new political order which would then provide the legitimizing terms of its own constitution. This is Hart's chief claim for speech-act theory as applied to the philosophy of law: that it helps to resolve all the problems that arise if one interprets legal discourse in purely constative terms. J.L. Austin was making much the same point when he suggested that a great many problems in philosophy — notably the fact/value distinction, the supposed impossibility of arguing *logically* from one domain to the other — could be seen as simply misconceived if allowance was made for the variety of performative functions in language. From this point of view, the Declaration of Independence is a document that derives its self-authorizing power from the tacit assumptions about meaning and context that enable us to recognize a well-formed ('felicitous') speech-act. The shift from 'is' to 'ought' is a perfectly familiar rhetorical move whose legitimacy requires nothing more than the established assent of freely choosing subjects before the law. To push the analysis beyond this point — as by asking what authority could possibly be claimed by those who first signed the Declaration — is merely a confusion of juridico-linguistic realms.

Derrida would hardly deny that we do get along with this commonsense idea in the majority of practical cases, from the act of promising or plighting one's troth to the acceptance of values enshrined in constitutional law. But he still makes the point that such acceptance rests on a failure — or a natural unwillingness — to admit the crucial element of 'undecidability' that attaches to speech-acts in general. 'One can understand this Declaration as a vibrant act of faith, as an hypocrisy indispensable to any political, military, or economic *coup de force*, etc., or, more simply, more economically, as the deployment of a tautology: insofar as this Declaration has a meaning *and* an effect, there must be a final, legitimizing instance' (*Otobiographies*, p. 9). And the instance in this case is God, appealing as the Declaration does to the 'Supreme Judge of the World' for an ultimate guarantee of 'the rectitude of our intentions'. Such is the recourse to a 'transcendental signified', a power that underwrites those signatures and gives them the force of an authorizing Word immune to the vagaries of historical circumstance. Questions of legitimacy are pushed out of sight by the mystique of origins that would make this document something other and more than a record of time-bound events. The 'representative' status of the signatories at the moment when they subscribed their names is no longer a question of the utmost importance. Their act becomes part of the national destiny superintended by a God whose purpose they must ultimately serve.

Clearly this analysis connects with all that Derrida has written about the 'logocentric' bias in Western thought and culture down from Plato to the modern sciences of man. But it takes on a more specific *institutional* force and pertinence in the context of his Charlottesville address. Here it is the politics of representation, the self-understanding of American liberal democracy, that Derrida has chiefly in view. This tradition rests — or so he would have us believe — on a blindness, though in some sense a necessary blindness, to problems in its own (written) constitution. We have seen how similar questions emerge in Derrida's reading of Rousseau, especially those passages from the *Social Contract* which seek to formulate political ideals in a language of pre-social nature and origins. What Derrida wants to bring out is the moment of authoritarian appeal — the recourse to an ultimate, legitimizing power — involved in all such fabulous myths of origin. And this means acknowledging the aporetic character — the root contradiction — of a liberal democracy founded on the 'representative' status of citizens who can only assume that title through a species of rhetorical imposition. 'This obscurity, this undecidability between, let us say, a performative structure and a constative structure, these are *prerequisite* for producing the oblique or necessarily obscure [*recherché*] effect' (p. 21). They are essential, Derrida argues, to the maintenance of any social order based on the assumption of collective or individual rights. Such analysis may lead to the point of conceiving them as products of 'hypocrisy, equivocation, undecidability or fiction'. Nevertheless they remain indispensable to civilized existence, as Derrida would surely concede, and not to be blithely 'deconstructed' if by this one understands — mistakenly — a mere exercise in pulling texts and ideologies apart. What is in question here is a better understanding of the ways in which civil society is maintained against the constant threat of a challenge to its founding articles.

Such recognition might have very real political consequences, especially perhaps in the American context, where a written Constitution enshrines certain supposedly 'self-evident' values and principles, but where these can be interpreted in very different ways by Supreme Court judges with a power to overturn even well-entrenched acts of state legislature. It is against this background that we need to assess Derrida's deconstructive reading of political texts. What he objects to in the standard consensus-version of speech-act theory — the version espoused by John Searle — is the idea that meanings can be simply read off by an authorized interpreter who knows full well, as by natural right, what is entailed in a true understanding. This assumption corresponds to the view of legal discourse which takes it to embody an accumulated wisdom whose 'rules' — as regards the majority of cases — may be nowhere set down in explicit (constative) form, but whose authority is nonetheless present in the force of various tacit yet ultimately binding conventions. Such a view naturally tends to predominate among those (like Hart) who base their thinking on the British system where so much is decided by common law precedent, and where judgements are reached by comparing case with case, rather than appealing to 'self-evident' principles. This difference may help to explain why deconstruction has had so much more impact in America, upon disciples and hostile commentators alike. The possession of a *written* Constitution whose principles are yet open to all manner of far-reaching judicial review — for instance, on the issues of racial equality, civil rights, abortion etc. — gives a political edge to questions of textual and interpretative theory that they do not have in the British cultural context.

Derrida goes on to consider what is at stake in the contest between canonical and non-canonical readings of texts. The subtitle of *Otobiographies* is *l'enseignement de Nietzsche et la politique du nom propre* ('Nietzsche's teaching and the politics of the proper name'). What Derrida is pointing to here is the fact that signatures do nothing to ensure the passage of an author's 'true' intentions to those who read and set themselves up as authorized heirs and interpreters. Nietzsche provides a particularly apt example since his writings have suffered the most violent series of revisionist claims and counter-claims. How far is it possible, Derrida asks, to rule out some of these readings on the ground of their having misconstrued or perverted what Nietzsche actually wrote? The most flagrant appropriation was

199

of course the enlistment of Nietzsche as a proto-Nazi ideologist, a thinker whose teachings of the *Übermensch* and the doctrine of 'eternal recurrence' were grafted on to the myth of Aryan supremacy and the sempiternal Third Reich. Derrida accepts, up to a point, the arguments commonly adduced in Nietzsche's defence: that his writings were subjected to a crude and myopic misreading, encouraged by his sister's deluded proselytizing zeal. But the question remains: *why* did Nietzsche's texts lend themselves to treatment in this manner? Can an author be held to account for his writings if their future interpretation is beyond all reckoning in terms of present intent? And if this is the case, what grounds can be shown for belief in those political or ethical values enshrined in documents, like the American Constitution, whose claim is to reveal timeless, self-evident truths? Within reach of these questions is the issue raised by Derrida's own deconstructive reading of texts in the Western cultural tradition. Is the upshot of this enterprise not (as many of its opponents have argued) to abandon every notion of determinate truth and every means of judging, in a case like Nietzsche's, on the issue of ethical responsibility?

Derrida very firmly rejects this conclusion. He insists that it cannot have been by chance — or owing to some wholly unforeseeable accident of history — that Nietzsche's texts took on their bad eminence in the Nazi period. One must ask 'why it is not enough to say that "Nietzsche didn't think this", "didn't intend that" ' or other such evasive locutions. For Nietzsche was quite resigned to the idea that his were 'untimely meditations', that the world was not yet ready for his wisdom, and that only the choice spirits of a later age would fully grasp its significance. Far from disclaiming all responsibility, this puts Nietzsche squarely in the position of taking full credit (or blame) for what was made of his fateful legacy. Indeed, his idea of 'eternal recurrence' required that the strong soul should embrace whatever strange reverses destiny imposed, and affirm them without the least sentiment of moral misgiving. Thus Nietzsche's writings, in their very appeal to what Derrida calls a *meditatio generis futuri*, effectively demand that one read them with an eye to their perversion at the hands of Nazi ideologists. It then

becomes necessary to ask 'why the only program of indoctrina-
tion [*institution d'enseignement*] which has ever been able to
take full advantage of Nietzsche's teaching has been that of the
Nazis' (p. 98). There can be no question of exonerating Nietzsche by driving a wedge between authorial intentions and the
after-effects of writing. That they served such an ideological
purpose is sufficient indication that more is involved than a gross
and stupid misreading of the Nietzschean texts.

Derrida entertains the curious hypothesis of a 'programming
machine' (*machine programmatrice*), one that would at least set
certain limits to the play of aberrant interpretations. It is a
notion related to his metaphor of 'multiple reading heads',
intended to suggest (by analogy with the record, playback and
erasing heads in a tape machine) the way that we read simul-
taneously what is there in front of us and also, in the process, a
potentially infinite range of intertextual meanings and allusions,
some of which may very well obscure or efface the immediate
sense of the 'words on the page'.[2] In texts like *Glas*, 'Living On'
and 'The Double Session', Derrida provides some graphic illus-
trations of this multiple-reading process at work. But with
Otobiographies, the emphasis shifts to a different idea of the
textual 'machine', more in the nature of a regulative system, one
that somehow programs in advance the possibilities of aberrant
reading. Here it is the question of trying to determine what it is
about the Nietzschean text that has given a hold to such diverse
interpretations. It is not that there exists some deep (perhaps
'unconscious') reserve of latent or potential meanings which are
there just waiting to be activated by contact with certain kinds of
ideological prejudice. Rather we should think (as Derrida suggests) in terms of 'mimetic perversion', of a reading that can seize
upon the text's various resources (of syntax, metaphor, structural economy) and bend them to its own purpose. And this
applies not only to Nietzsche but to Hegel, Heidegger and others
whose writings have given rise to all manner of conflicting
interpretations.

So it comes about that, in Nietzsche's case, 'the "same"
utterance [*énoncé*] can signify precisely the opposite, correspond
to its own inverted meaning, to the reactive inversion of that

201

which it mimes'. As with Derrida's readings of Plato, Rousseau and Hegel, it is a matter of enlisting the conceptual resources of a text, reading it with meticulous attention to detail, but doing so in order to challenge or subvert the received (consensual) account. Already in *Spurs* (1979) Derrida had shown how such a reading might be possible by taking up the question of Nietzsche's notorious and virulent anti-feminism. What Nietzsche *says* – and repeats with hysterical insistence – is that woman is the source of all folly and unreason, the siren figure who lures the male philosopher out of his appointed truth-seeking path. 'Progress of the idea,' Nietzsche writes: 'it becomes more subtle, insidious, incomprehensible – *it becomes female*' (*Spurs*, p. 89). But there is a kind of self-implicating irony here which Derrida is quick to point out. For Nietzsche is himself engaged in precisely that 'insidious' destruction of philosophy – the undoing of its grandiose systems and concepts, the rhetorical undermining of its truth-claims – which would seem to be woman's peculiar vice. If woman is indeed the antithesis of truth, the very principle of unreason, then she can only be counted an ally in Nietzsche's crusade against the great system-building male philosophers, from Plato to Kant and Hegel. Which means that all his anti-feminist diatribes have a double-edged character which can always be turned back, so to speak, against Nietzsche's manifest intent. There occurs, in Derrida's words, a 'regular, rhythmic blindness' in the text which marks those points where a meaning is unloosed beyond its power to acknowledge or 'consciously' grasp.

Thus woman becomes both the target of Nietzsche's misogynist scorn and – by this uncanny logic of reversal – the emblematic figure who draws him on to contest the sovereignty of reason. For 'woman' is everywhere associated with the themes of metaphor, style and writing, those same resources that Nietzsche deploys against the hegemonic truth-claims of philosophy. In this he is exploiting that age-old mistrust of 'poetic' or figural language which treats it as a mere deviation from the norm, a licence that can have no place in the 'serious', the literal or truth-seeking discourse of reason. Nietzsche (like Derrida) sets out to expose some of the ruses that have kept philosophy from examining its own constitutive figures and metaphors. Such is Derrida's argument — or at least one stage of his argument — in 'The White Mythology'. From Aristotle down, philosophers have sought to define metaphor *on their own terms*, as a figure whose workings could always be explained by reference to some other, more reliable or epistemologically privileged kind of language. 'Metaphor . . . is determined by philosophy as a provisional loss of meaning, an economy of the proper without irreparable damage, a certainly inevitable detour, but also a history with its sights set on, and within the horizon of, the circular reappropriation of literal, proper meaning' (*Margins,* p. 270). What Nietzsche does is press this critique to the point where any distinction between 'concept' and 'metaphor' must seem just a species of enabling fiction designed to keep philosophy in business.

So when Nietzsche associates metaphor with woman — with everything that beguiles, seduces or perverts the mastery of philosophic concepts — his assertions can scarcely be taken at face value. Nor is it enough, Derrida argues, merely to invert the terms of this basic opposition and declare that metaphor is henceforth the 'truth' of philosophy, or woman the name of some transcendent principle 'beyond' the reductive strategies of male reason. What opens up at this point in Nietzsche's text is the 'undecidability' of all propositions concerning metaphor and woman. 'It is impossible to dissociate the questions of art, style and truth from the question of the woman. Nevertheless the question "What is woman?" is itself suspended by the simple formulation of their common problematic . . . she is certainly not to be found in any of the familiar modes of concept or knowledge. Yet it is impossible to resist looking for her' (*Spurs,* p. 71). Thus Derrida can claim — 'perversely', one might think, but as the upshot of a close exegesis — that Nietzsche is not only ambivalent in his attitude to woman but can even be read as a crypto-feminist resisting all attempts to bypass or sublimate the question of sexual difference. When Heidegger — for one — describes Nietzsche as 'the last metaphysician', unable to think the 'ontological difference', the primacy of Being, that would finally break with that tradition, his argument ignores both the energies of Nietzsche's *style* and the scandalous hints of a *sexual* difference that escapes such hermeneutic categories.[3] Heidegger's reading merely 'idles offshore' insofar as it seeks out a truth of Nietzsche's text indifferent to these dislocating forces.

So the question of woman is 'not at all a regional question in a larger order which would subordinate it first to the domain of a general ontology, subsequently to that of a fundamental ontology and finally to the question of the truth of being itself' (*Spurs,* p. 109). Such was Heidegger's project for a genuine 'existential hermeneutics', thinking back beyond that fateful swerve from authentic truth which marked the history of 'metaphysical' thinking from Plato to the present day. But Heidegger can only maintain this reading of Nietzsche − only treat him as a failed precursor in the hermeneutic enterprise − by remaining resolutely blind to the questions of style and sexual politics. Everything that Nietzsche came to associate with woman − 'her seductive distance, her captivating inaccessibility, the ever-veiled promise of her provocative transcendence' − points to a reckoning that Heidegger must perforce ignore for the sake of maintaining his hermeneutic stance. In the end his interpretation is played off the field by a style and a rhetoric of sexual difference which thoroughly discompose the Heideggerian project. 'Here, in a manner like to that of writing, surely and safely . . . she is able to display the gifts of her seductive power, which rules over dogmatism, and disorients and routs those credulous men, the philosophers' (*Spurs,* p. 67).

So there are many competing versions of Nietzsche, none possessing any absolute claim to articulate the 'truth' of his text, but *all* of them − and this is Derrida's point − made possible by something in the logic, the syntax or the structural resources of his writing. The Nazi perversion of Nietzschean themes was no mere accident of history but an episode in some sense prepared for and scripted in advance. Such 'perverse simplifications' obey a certain law, Derrida thinks, a law whose effects can best be observed in the various ideological programmes that have set themselves up in Nietzsche's name. It is wrong to suppose that writings 'live on' (*scripta manent*), their meaning always there to be consulted in cases of doubt, preserved from age to age by a body of self-authorized interpreters. As with Nietzsche, so with a text like Rousseau's *Social Contract,* or indeed a document of epochal significance like the American Declaration of Independence. There is always the possibility of some radical new reading that would utterly change — for better or worse — the way that such writings impinge upon our social and political practices. But this is not to license a relativist euphoria, a free-for-all approach that would brook no constraints upon the 'freeplay' of interpretative discourse. For it is still possible to perceive and deconstruct the various forms of angled misreading which make up this history of ideological claims-to-power.

One of Derrida's essays on Hegel ('From Restricted to General Economy', in *Writing and Difference*) shows how such variant interpretations can take hold of certain elements in the text and deploy them to radically divergent ends. In *Otobiographies* this lesson is extended to those post-Hegelian thinkers who inherit both the powers and the inbuilt aporias of dialectical reason. It is not by accident, Derrida writes, but by a kind of 'structural destiny' (*structure destinale*) that there comes about this contest of readings in the name of a Hegel, a Nietzsche or a Heidegger. Which means that no reading is ideologically innocent, but that all must take responsibility for the effects — the ethical or the socio-political effects — that follow from them. The risk of putting one's name to such writings is not the kind of risk that absolves the signatory from ever being called upon to justify what is written. Rather it is the kind that Freud, for instance, took when he launched the psychoanalytical project as an enterprise marked from the outset by quarrels, dissensions and struggles for power over a body of texts which bore his name but which could never be reduced to the paternal law of absolute origins and presence. In 'Coming into One's Own' Derrida describes the curious sequence of after-effects and delayed repetitions which made up one episode in this history.[4] The episode has to do with Freud's investment in a certain train of speculative thought; with the way this impinged upon his family life and relations with his children and grandchildren; with the future of the psychoanalytical movement and with Freud's desire to manipulate that future through various kinds of preemptive

205

strategy. Derrida's point — to summarize very crudely — is that no separation is possible between these various aspects of the Freudian case history. What is in question is a highly 'speculative' venture in both root senses of the word: a theoretical enterprise that also involves risking one's name, the name of both Freud the jealous paterfamilias and Freud the inventor of psychoanalysis. In a text like *Beyond the Pleasure Principle* these multiple dimensions are joined in a narrative which cannot be reduced either to 'theory' on the one hand or 'autobiography' on the other.

Derrida's several texts on Freud — like his various readings of Nietzsche — trace out this pattern of alternating risk and attempts at hermeneutic mastery. In 'Freud and the Scene of Writing' his topic is the series of inscriptionalist models and metaphors to which Freud had recourse in describing the economy of psychic drives and desires.[5] Freud never wholly relinquished the idea that psychoanalysis might one day become a species of applied science; that the hermeneutic aspects of interpretation might at last give way to a neurophysiological account of the mind and its workings. His efforts in this direction (notably the unfinished 'Project for a Scientific Psychology') tended to picture the mind as a field of competing energies and forces that could best be described in mechanistic terms. But as this project came to seem increasingly unworkable, so Freud fell back on his alternative model, that of the unconscious as a kind of subliminated *script,* a process whose effects could only be reckoned with by deploying certain metaphors of writing. Such was Freud's idea — albeit a passing fancy — when he compared the unconscious to a 'Mystic Writing Pad', a device involving a stylus and waxed paper which enabled inscriptions to be preserved (as it were) in a latent or invisible form long after they had apparently been erased from its surface. In a typical argumentative move, Derrida claims that the use of this image is far from a mere *jeu d'esprit* on Freud's part, offering as it does his most suggestive and carefully worded account of the unconscious as a kind of 'writing-machine'. Freud will never abandon what Derrida calls his 'neurological fable', the projected scientific version of psychoanalysis which would put an end to such speculative models and metaphors. But this project will remain forever unachieved, its failures made up for only by recourse to a different, grammatological idiom. In which case, Derrida suggests, the pertinent question is not so much whether the psyche is indeed 'a kind of text', but, more radically, 'what is a text, and what must the psyche be if it can be represented by a text?' (*Writing and Difference*, p. 199).

By the end of this essay Derrida has shown how ubiquitous are the metaphors of writing in Freud and how crucial the role they play in his various accounts of the unconscious activity manifest in language and dream. This is writing as *archi-écriture*, a writing that exceeds the classical opposition between self-present speech and mere written signs. For what Freud is forced to think − at whatever 'unconscious' level − is the necessity of a writing *before* speech, a psychic economy that can only be described in a language of traces, differences, inscriptions, subliminal marks and so forth. It is, Derrida writes, 'with a graphematics still to come, rather than with a linguistics dominated by an ancient phonologism, that psychoanalysis sees itself as destined to collaborate' (p. 220). And this because Freud can only think the unconscious in differential terms, as the name of whatever escapes, eludes or discomposes the logic of self-present waking thought. Such thinking involves a movement 'perhaps unknown to classical philosophy', that tradition which − from Plato down − has maintained the sovereignty of logocentric reason precisely by insisting on the derivative, supplementary character of the written. If it was Freud's great achievement − his 'Copernican revolution' − to invert the received order of priority between conscious and unconscious thought, he could do so only by constant resort to metaphors of a generalized writing. Without them he would have been unable to arrive at any workable account of desire, consciousness, perception and the way these operate to maintain a certain (distinctively Freudian) economy of psychic energies.

Most important here is the *differential* character of writing, its power to hold back, to postpone or to conserve (in latent form) what would otherwise be lost or exhausted in the moment of immediate perception. If such a moment were possible then it would fall outside any possible means of representation, any writing or theory whatsoever. But 'pure perception', says Derrida, 'does not exist: we are written only as we write, by the agency within us which always keeps watch over perception . . .' (*Writing and Difference,* p. 226). This 'agency' is that of repression and censorship, brought about by those mechanisms that Freud described in his writings on the topology of mind. It operates both within and outside the individual psyche, on the one hand as a system of checks and sanctions internalized by the superego, on the other as a projection into communal life of those same ineluctably thwarted desires. But everywhere in Freud – from the early *Interpretation of Dreams* to the late, sombre thoughts on civilization and its discontents – there is this same need to conceptualize the unconscious through metaphors and analogies based upon writing. 'The subject of writing [i.e. the subject who writes] is a *system* of relations between strata: the Mystic Pad, the psyche, society, the world' (pp. 226-7). And again: 'it is no accident that the metaphor of censorship should come from the area of politics concerned with the deletions, blanks, and disguises of writing . . . the apparent exteriority of political censorship refers to an essential censorship that binds the writer to his own writing' (p. 226). Thus the point at which psychoanalysis joins with a certain form of *Ideologiekritik* is also the point of its maximum investment in this whole metaphorics of writing and representation. It is here that an answer begins to take shape to those (mostly Marxist) opponents of deconstruction who deplore what they consider its 'textualist' obsession and indifference to political realities. As with Nietzsche, so with Freud as Derrida reads him: there is no question of affirming some delusive realm of 'pure' textuality beyond the claims of political or ethical life. To argue – as Derrida does – that such issues should be raised *in and through* the problematics of writing is not to deny that writing takes effect in far-reaching practical ways.

'Coming into One's Own' is very much about these worldly after-effects of the Freudian text. It asks, first, what relation obtains between the founding of a discipline (psychoanalysis) and the various events, 'personal' and otherwise, that make up its subsequent history. That Freud went to such lengths to assert his proprietory stake in the enterprise — that he often sought to withhold his authorizing *name* from deviant schools or trends — might be taken as a sign that psychoanalysis was the product of one man's obsessive fantasy, possessing no claim to genuine 'scientific' status. Classically, after all, 'the establishment of a science . . . should have been able to do without the family name Freud. Or able, at least, to make forgetting that name the necessary condition and the proof that science itself is handed on, passed down' ('Coming into One's Own', p. 142). The passing-down of Freudian wisdom was, on the contrary, a business fraught with private and public rivalries, a series of transactions that themselves call out for analysis in Freudian terms. Derrida's reading focuses on that well-known passage from *Beyond the Pleasure Principle* where Freud describes how his grandson would play at throwing a reel-and-thread out of his cot and then repeatedly drawing it back with evident pleasure and relief.[6] The sounds he uttered in the course of this game Freud interpreted as 'fort . . . da' ('gone . . . there'), suggesting a certain compulsive need to reenact the trauma of his mother's periodic absence in order to reassure himself that she, like the bobbin, would always come back in the end. Now Freud puts forward this hypothesis in the context of some far-reaching speculations on the balance of pleasure-seeking and self-denying impulses in the human psyche, on the death-instinct and the tendency of civilization to evolve increasingly repressive forms of institutional control. In thus giving rein to his speculative thoughts, Freud becomes involved — as Derrida reads him — with the same kind of calculated risk that his grandson initiates in the fort-da game. That is to say, he is advancing a provocative thesis, one that goes beyond any possible 'facts of the case', but which still seeks assurance in a certain recuperative gesture or movement. Like little Ernst, he wants to venture on to dangerous ground, experience the provisional loss of mastery, so long as he can pull on the string, so to speak, and recover his powers of theoretical command.

This pattern is repeated in the complex of relationships that extends to Freud's family and his various (more or less orthodox) colleagues and disciples. On the one hand Freud wants to exercise paternal power, to keep psychoanalysis firmly in the grasp of an authorizing word – or name – that would be his, and his only, to bestow. But on the other he is compelled to risk this name in all kinds of speculative enterprise, some of them leaving it a hostage to fortune at the hands of unauthorized interpreters. The Pleasure Principle is a point of departure for Freud's journey into strange seas of thought that lie beyond anything yet mapped out in his various accounts of the unconscious and its libidinal economy. It involves him in a game of uncanny repetitions where the notion of desire as a pleasure-seeking instinct, a straightforward quest for satisfaction, is oddly intertwined with death, self-denial and everything that appears to thwart such a quest. Up to a point, Derrida's reading might be said to draw upon 'autobiographical' sources: on the fact of Freud's own terminal illness, already far advanced as he planned and revised this essay; the death of his favourite daughter Sophie, the mother of grandson Ernst; on his ambivalent feelings toward Ernst's father, Freud's son-in-law and Sophie's husband, with whom Freud entered into a jealous struggle for 'sole possession' of his dead daughter. Sophie's 'definitive *fortgehen*' is perhaps what precipitates this whole strange 'game' of absences and deaths acted out in the guise of a child's self-comforting fantasy. Then again there was the fate of his other grandson Heinerle, Ernst's younger brother, who died after an operation at about the same time as Freud underwent surgery for his malignant condition. In Heinerle's death – so a letter records – Freud saw prefigured the end of all his progeny and also found the cause of his own stoic indifference – 'people call it courage' – toward the fact of his approaching death. And these multiplied sufferings in the private sphere were projected on to Freud's growing doubt as to the power he possessed of keeping psychoanalysis 'in the family', preventing its kidnap by revisionist interpreters outside the authorized circle. Thus it was that he turned to Marie Bonaparte, a trusted representative of the 'old alliance', one whose loyalty 'in some way renewed involvement by declaring it past'.[7] The only means of warding off these threats to his authority was by investing in the future of a psychoanalysis that would have taken full account of a mortal expenditure 'beyond the pleasure principle'. In the end, Derrida argues, we cannot draw a line between the theories advanced in this text and the complex of 'autobiographical' motives that went into its writing. 'In every detail we can see the super-position of the subsequent description of the *fort/da* (on the grandson's side of the house of Freud) with the description of the speculative game, itself so assiduous and so repetitive, of the grandfather in writing *Beyond the Pleasure Principle*' ('Coming into One's Own', p. 145).

This essay of Derrida helps to pinpoint at least two very common misunderstandings of what 'deconstruction' amounts to in the close reading of texts. It is *not* the kind of ironcast explanatory theory that would ultimately reduce all writing to the rehearsal of a few 'logocentric' or self-mystifying themes which deconstruction could then infallibly bring to light. On the contrary, it is a *speculative* enterprise, like Freud's, involved with all the risks that inevitably follow from advancing hypotheses far beyond the limits of safe explanation. Nor is deconstruction implacably opposed to the use of biographical evidence in the building up of a case history whose reading may require all manner of 'supplementary' source material. Unlike the American New Critics, Derrida rejects any parcelling out of separate linguistic domains, such that poetry (for instance) would enjoy a certain privileged ontological status, not to be confused with those other kinds of writing (history, biography etc.) which interpreters mistakenly call upon for 'evidence' in support of this or that reading. Such orthodox vetoes are themselves a species of logocentric thinking, one that seeks to authorize a high valuation of poetic language through a rhetoric of figures (ambiguity, paradox, irony and so forth) that would finally point back to an ultimate presence, an authority vested in the *logos* of poetry itself.[8] 'Coming into One's Own' is a thoroughly intertextual reading, one that draws upon numerous episodes from 'the life' in order to interpret, explain or illuminate 'the work'. But it does so by way of deconstructing those categories, refusing to ack-nowledge any distinction between, on the one hand, 'life' and 'work', and on the other the various activities of theory, speculation, biographical conjecture engaged in both by Freud *and* his latter-day critics and interpreters.

Psychoanalysis is all these things at once. It is the name of a legacy, a textual archive, whose reading has been subject – as it was for Freud himself – to the rival claims of 'scientific' method and a different, broadly 'hermeneutic' mode of approach. Both projects were involved in Freud's great plan to assert his peculiar authority as founder of an orthodox and self-perpetuating movement. 'This is what the grandfather calls "a game", when all the strings are brought together and held in one hand, with the parents needed neither as workers nor as players' ('Coming into One's Own', p. 125). But this is to ignore the *overdetermined* character of Freud's speculations, his involvement in a history of family and wider (institutional) kinships and rivalries that cannot be declared simply extraneous to the reading of his 'authorized' texts. Whose is it, Derrida asks, this endlessly repeated 'fort-da', this speculative movement that marks the inception of a certain psychoanalysis, but which also runs the risk of losing control over the future of the whole risky enterprise? 'Ernst's? That of his mother, linked with his grandfather in the reading of his own *fort:da*? That of . . . the father of psychoanalysis? Of the author of *Beyond the Pleasure Principle*? But how can we have access to him without a ghostly analysis of all the others?' (p. 136). So crucial is this game to the entire elaborate structure of Freud's argument that it becomes strictly impossible to decide just how much belongs to his 'private' case history and how much to the history of psychoanalysis as a science, a movement, a heritage of concepts. In his writing, 'there are at least three agencies or personae of the same "subject": the speculator-narrator, the observer, and the grandfather' (p. 126).

This is *not* to agree with those hard-headed critics of psychoanalysis who reject its truth-claims on the ground that all the 'evidence' adduced by Freud is a product either of his own obsessions or of those that prevailed among his patients, his colleagues and the Angst-ridden victims of Viennese *fin-de-siècle* society. Rather, it is to point toward a quite different way of conceiving the relation between knowledge and experience, one that would question such crude attempts to discredit 'mere' autobiography. The fact that an author inscribes certain details of his own life-history in a self-professed 'scientific' text is no reason to conclude that the document in question is 'without truth-value, without value as science or as philosophy'. On the contrary, its value may lie precisely in its power to suspend this delusive opposition and inaugurate a reading attentive to the various points of exchange, of intertextual crossing and confusion, between life and work. 'This text is auto-biographical, but in a completely different way from what was believed before . . . a domain opens up in which the "inscription" of a subject in his text is also the necessary condition for the pertinence and performance of a text, for its worth beyond what is called empirical subjectivity . . . The notion of truth-value is utterly incapable of assessing this performance' (p. 135). *Beyond the Pleasure Principle* defeats such reductive readings because it puts its own truth-claims at risk in the game for which Freud's grandson provided the speculative model. And this risk includes the future of psychoanalysis, the authority of Freud as its founding father, and the status of explanatory theories in general. Such theories 'depart in a speculative rhetoric' which may – in certain cases – yield large dividends, but which cannot guarantee any safe return on the original investment. 'Where is the truth when we are talking about the elaboration of a *fort-da* from which everything is derived, even the concept of truth?' (p. 141).

Foucault, Descartes and the 'crisis of reason'

In Derrida's writings on Nietzsche and Freud one can trace a similar pattern of shifting priorities. The effect is to qualify, though not to abandon, his stress on the irreducibility of writing, the fact that there is no 'outside' to the text, no ultimate appeal to 'lived' experience. I have already (in Chapter 6) given reasons for rejecting the simplified polemical response to this position which treats it as merely a species of modish 'textualist' solipsism. My arguments there had to do with the issues of truth, knowledge and representation bequeathed to modern philosophy in the wake of Kant's 'Copernican revolution'. But there is also the question — more urgent, perhaps — as to what might be the *ethical* bearings of deconstruction if its claims were taken up into our thinking about law, morality and social practice. We can perhaps best approach this question through a reading of Derrida's 'Cogito and the History of Madness', a critique of Michel Foucault's influential book *Madness and Civilization.*[9] His object here is to demonstrate the strict impossibility, in textual or logico-discursive terms, of Foucault's having actually achieved what his argument sets out to achieve. That is to say, this is a classic deconstructionist reading, pointing out the blindspots (or moments of aporia) produced in the course of Foucault's exposition. But there is more at stake here than a mischievous desire to go one better in the drive to dismantle received ideas of knowledge and truth. Indeed, it is Derrida's contention that this project — as Foucault conceives it — involves contradictions that amount virtually to a form of intellectual bad faith. In this respect his essay looks forward to those later writings (like 'The Principle of Reason') where Derrida stresses the need to keep faith with a certain post-Kantian tradition of 'enlightened' critique. It is therefore an important text for understanding the ethical implications of Derrida's thought.

What chiefly engages his attention here is Foucault's claim to have written, not a 'history of psychiatry' (that is, an account from *within* the regime of 'rational' psychiatric thought), but 'a history of madness itself, in its most vibrant state, before being captured by knowledge' (*Writing and Difference*, p. 34). Derrida's response is to show (*via* a reading of Foucault on Descartes) that thought is self-deluded if it tries to achieve a standpoint 'outside' or 'above' the very discourse of philosophic reason. Foucault seizes upon that moment when Descartes, in his first *Meditation,* entertained the 'hypothesis of insanity' as a means of strategically exposing to doubt all our commonplace certitudes about knowledge, experience and waking reality. Of course the whole purpose of this calculated risk, this experiment in hyperbolic doubt, was to reconfirm the sovereignty of reason by grounding it on the single, indubitable fact: 'I think, therefore I am' (*Cogito, ergo sum*). Foucault reads this episode as an allegory of modern (post-Cartesian) thought in its relation to madness as the feared and excluded 'other' of rational discourse. The correlative in socio-practical terms is that progressive isolation (or internment) of unreason whose history Foucault reads in the various institutions – the prisons, hospitals, psychiatric clinics – set up to contain or to study its effects. Madness is defined precisely on the terms laid down by an increasingly assertive and self-confident reason. It is the re-pressed dark side of an enlightened tradition which nonetheless needs to confirm its own normality by constantly rehearsing such rituals of exclusion. Thus Foucault reads the first *Meditation* as an allegory of reason at the moment of establishing its will-to-power over truth. From this moment there will always be a discourse on madness, but a discourse that perpetually upholds and reinforces the laws of rational thought. To speak or to write *on the side* of unreason is a gesture henceforth unthinkable within this juridico-discursive regime. Unless, that is, one adopts Foucault's radically antinomian position, renouncing the authority of knowledge and truth in order to write an authentic 'history of madness' that would break altogether with this enlightenment paradigm.

Derrida's counter-argument once again comes down to a form of transcendental *tu quoque*. That is, he denies that it is possible for Foucault to advance a single proposition in support of his case without rejoining the discourse of reason by adopting its language and discursive strategies. And this is not just a matter of some local confusions or corrigible weaknesses in Foucault's argument. Quite simply, it is a condition 'inherent in the essence and the very project of all language in general; and even in the language of those who are apparently the maddest; and even and above all in the language of those who, by their praise of madness, by their complicity with it, measure their own strength against the greatest possible proximity to madness' (*Writing and Difference*, pp. 54-5). Foucault would claim to be taking a stand against reason in its legislative aspect; revealing the Cartesian moment of 'insanity' as a covert policing operation, a prelude to internment, always safely under control by the agencies of rational thought. On the contrary, says Derrida: Foucault has performed 'a Cartesian gesture for the twentieth century', one that is all the more deceptive for flatly denying (unlike Descartes) the fact of its investment in the discourse of reason. For Foucault is undeniably *making sense* of this history, casting it in a perfectly intelligible narrative form and drawing argued conclusions on the basis of well-documented evidence. He is thus – for all his gestures of a contrary intent – finding room for the Cartesian discourse on madness within a thoroughly rational framework of discursive procedures. Only by picking out isolated episodes, like Descartes' moment of hyperbolic doubt, and by ignoring their place in his own strategy of argument, can Foucault pretend to be speaking in the name of madness or unreason.

Foucault took this critique as occasion for a contemptuous dismissal of Derrida's entire project.[10] He attacked deconstruction as a mere rhetorical bag of tricks, a neat little 'pedagogy' secure in its knowledge that nothing exists outside the text. And his argument would seem to have persuaded others – notably Edward Said – that there is ultimately a choice to be made between these two divergent paths of post-structuralist thought.[11] On the one hand is a strategy (Foucault's) which requires an active engagement with the politics of knowledge, refusing to draw any line between texts and the various legitimizing discourses of power, truth and representation. On the other is a mode of rhetorical close-reading (Derrida's) which rules out such interests from the start by declaring them a species of naive referential delusion. But this is to ignore the whole thrust of Derrida's repeated demands that we try to think beyond such disabling assumptions as that which would treat 'the world' and 'the text' in binary, disjunctive terms. What is really at issue in his quarrel with Foucault is *not* deconstruction's retreat into a realm of euphoric textual freeplay where political realities no longer obtrude. We have seen how Derrida's readings of Nietzsche and Freud effectively rebut this charge by insisting on the 'worldly' consequences and effects that follow from the act of writing. And this would certainly apply in the context of his argument with Foucault, where the stake *on both sides* is a set of institutionalized relations between power, knowledge and the discourse of reason. Foucault's extreme epistemological scepticism leads him to equate knowledge with power, and hence to regard all forms of 'enlightened' progress (in psychiatry, sexual attitudes or penal reform) as signs of an increasing sophistication in the applied technology of social control. Derrida, by contrast, insists that there is no opting out of that post-Kantian enlightenment tradition, and certainly no question of our now having emerged into a post-modern era where its concepts and categories lack all critical force. On the contrary: it is only by working persistently *within* that tradition, but *against* some of its ruling ideas, that thought can muster the resistance required for an effective critique of existing institutions.

Thus Derrida takes issue with Foucault on two main grounds. First, there is no such clear demarcation in Descartes' text between the discourse of reason and the hyperbolic doubt that threatens – *genuinely* threatens – the philosophic enterprise. If Foucault has failed to register the sheer unsettling force, the 'mad audacity' with which Descartes conjures up his demon, it is perhaps because we are nowadays 'too well assured of ourselves and too well accustomed to the framework of the Cogito, rather than to the critical experience of it' (*Writing and Difference*, p. 56). This experience goes far beyond the limits of that safe, self-preserving exercise of reason that Foucault reads in the first *Meditation*. Its risk is played down through Foucault's desire to fit Descartes into a narrative history whose theme is the repression of madness and unreason at the hands of enlightenment and progress. But in so doing he is constrained to ignore those 'critical' moments of Cartesian doubt when the security of every last rational belief was genuinely called into question. Thus Foucault wards off the threat of unreason by precisely that kind of accommodating gesture which he thinks he has discovered in Descartes. A strange compulsion seems to operate here, whereby reason is perpetually obliged to confront the possibility of madness, but only by way of reconfirming its own explanatory power. Thus the second objection to Foucault's account is that he fails to recognize the oscillating rhythm, the unending 'dialogue', as Derrida describes it, between 'hyperbole and the finite structure, between that which exceeds totality and the closed totality' (p. 60). An adequate reading of Descartes' text would register the force of his hyperbolic doubt as that which suspends (momentarily at least) the decidable opposition between reason and unreason. It would *not*, like Foucault, declare this opposition henceforth redundant, or claim to have come out on the far side of enlightened rational discourse. 'To all appearances it is reason that he [Foucault] interns, but, like Descartes, he chooses the reason of yesterday as his target and not the possibility of meaning in general' (p. 55). It is not so much that Foucault 'misinterprets' Descartes as that he fails to perceive how his own reading strategy repeats the same pattern of co-implicated insight and blindness.

There is an ethical as well as a political dimension to Derrida's quarrel with Foucault. It has to do with that strain of theoretical anti-humanism which marked the emergence of post-structuralist thinking in the late 1960s. Thus Foucault has a much-quoted passage in *The Order of Things,* describing 'man' – or the imaginary self-possessed subject of humanist discourse – as a figure drawn in sand at the ocean's edge, soon to be erased by the incoming tide.[12] This dissolution is seen as the upshot of a large-scale cultural mutation whereby the human sciences have come to recognize that 'man' is nothing more than a figure composed by certain (mainly nineteenth-century) discourses of knowledge. Such illusions are no longer tenable for an age that has witnessed – among other things – the rise of structural anthropology, the 'linguistic turn' across a wide range of disciplines, and the loss of any comforting faith in *history* as the universal ground and telos of human understanding. Nietzsche and Saussure are the chief instigators of this passage 'beyond' the naive metaphysical certitudes of earlier thought. Saussure points the way toward an all-embracing theory of language and discursive formations that would leave no room for the individual subject as origin or locus of meaning. Nietzsche sets the terms for a sceptical critique of those philosophies, from Plato to Hegel, which identify truth with the bringing-to-light of a distinctively human self-knowledge.

This anti-humanism takes different forms in the various

branches and disciplines of post-structuralist thought. For Althusser, it marks the emergence of a genuinely 'scientific' Marxism, purged of those humanist (or ideological) residues which show up in the texts of other, less rigorous thinkers.[13] In Foucault and Barthes it is proclaimed as an imminent 'death of the author', an end to that old, repressive regime which identified the true meaning of a text with the animating presence of authorial intent. Thus Foucault envisages a Nietzschean 'genealogy' of discourses which would study the shifting configurations of knowledge and power without any reference to individual authors. And Barthes — in *S/Z* (1970) and subsequent texts — explores to the limit those freedoms opened up by deposing the Author from his erstwhile position of ultimate authority and power.[14] Deconstruction is often seen as yet another product of this anti-humanist ethos, with its will to undermine all the sources of 'transcendental' knowledge and meaning vested in the language of Western metaphysics. Among those sources is undoubtedly the figure of the Author, one whose continuing presence in the text can always be invoked (as Searle invokes Austin) in order to rule out 'perverse' or uncanonical readings.

To be sure, Derrida has done much to encourage this view of deconstruction as collaborating cheerfully in the overthrow of 'man' and all his works. But he also sees problems — very real and far-reaching problems — with any claim that thought has at last come out on the far side of a humanist (or anthropocentric) ideology. In 'The Ends of Man' (*Margins of Philosophy*) Derrida examines a series of pronouncements, from Nietzsche, Heidegger, Sartre and others, which take it for granted at least that the question may be raised — intelligibly raised — as to whether such an 'end' is in sight. On the contrary, he argues: such pronouncements are always marked by a failure to interrogate their own root assumptions, their involvement with a language everywhere coloured by humanist themes and motifs. One cannot simply 'decide to change terrain, in a discontinuous and irruptive fashion, by brutally placing oneself outside, and by affirming an absolute break and difference' (*Margins*, p. 135). Such premature assertions of the 'end of man' will always be affected by the same kind of unperceived paradox or aporia as overtakes

Foucault's discourse on madness and reason. That is to say, they ignore the simple fact that no case can be argued, no proposition stated — however radical its intent — without falling back on the conceptual resources vested in natural language. And that language is in turn shot through with all the anthropocentric, 'metaphysical' meanings which determine its very logic and intelligibility. Any claim to have broken once and for all with the humanist 'sciences of man' is a claim which can only be self-deluding and devoid of critical power. 'The simple practice of language ceaselessly reinstates the new terrain on the oldest ground . . . thereby inhabiting more naively and more strictly than ever the inside one declares one has deserted' (p. 135).

Foucault's anti-humanist rhetoric goes along with his declared object of discovering a new discursive 'terrain', one that would enable him to take a stand *outside and against* the hegemonic truth-claims of reason. And this would mean abandoning the modern tradition of 'enlightened' ethical thought, the tradition that has attempted — at least since Kant — to ground the principles of morality in the exercise of enlightened thought. Kant's overriding concern was to establish a public sphere of agreed-upon (rational) laws and constraints, such that the individual subject would rejoice to concur in rules laid down for the communal good. By this means he sought to transcend the kind of drastic Hobbesian antinomy that treated social existence as a mere aggregate of isolated wills pursuing their own self-interest at others' expense and only held in check by the authority vested in an arbitrary sovereign power. Hence Kant's insistence that ethical judgement is exercised in the *interest* of a rational being, but one whose choices are dictated by the laws of its own intelligible nature, and not by some external ('heterono-mous') source of compulsion. As Gilles Deleuze writes, summar-izing Kant: 'When reason legislates in the practical interest, it legislates over free and rational beings, over their intelligible existence . . . It is thus the rational being that gives itself a law by means of its reason.'[15] And the converse of this is the Kantian argument that to act *against* the dictates of moral reason is to cut oneself off from the rational community, or socialized 'kingdom of ends', which alone gives meaning to human actions and motives. When we choose against the law, Deleuze explains, 'we do not cease to have an intelligible existence, we merely lose the condition under which this existence forms part of a nature and composes, with the others, a systematic whole. We cease to be subjects, but primarily because we cease to be legislators . . .'[16] And this because the individual, in so choosing, surrenders his or her moral autonomy and consents to take a law from the determining conditions of narrow or material self-interest.

Post-structuralism abandons the Kantian position and, along with it, the manifold problems and complications to which it gives rise. On the one hand post-structuralism involves that 'decentring' of the subject in relation to language that is proclaimed by Foucault, Lacan and Barthes; a knowledge brought about by the recent (post-Nietzschean, post-Saussurean) recognition that subjectivity is constituted *in and through* language, rather than providing its ultimate source and ground. On the other it signals a decisive break with the kinds of problem typically thrown up by the discourse of Kantian 'enlightened' liberal reason. These problems are henceforth regarded, not as crucial issues in the working-out of a coherent moral or political creed, but as symptoms of a merely local and transitory stage of discursive production. They are taken to belong to that episode of thought which produced 'man' – the transcendental subject – as a figment of his own unconscious linguistic devising. Thus the Kantian antinomies amount to nothing more than (in Foucault's metaphor) a momentary 'fold' in the fabric of knowledge, an episode brought about by the enlightenment need to think of man as the rational, autonomous dispenser of his own moral laws.

I have argued that Derrida cannot be understood as simply going along with this anti-enlightenment drift in the discourse of post-structuralism. One way of grasping his opposition to it is by comparing the course of Deleuze's productions since that early book on Kant (published in 1963). There his main object was to bring out some of the problems that develop as Kant strives to adjudicate the rival claims of the various faculties that enact this imaginary courtroom scene. They operate – according to Deleuze – on a system of 'rotating' chairmanship, established in order to prevent any single (heteronomous) voice of authority from exerting some ultimate power, and thus undermining the community of free and equal discourse 'before the law'. Thus the whole conceptual edifice of Kantian critique − his epistemology and ethics alike − can be viewed as the inward or reflective counterpart of a liberal-democratic 'parliament' of faculties, set up to ensure the sovereignty of reason. Derrida develops this idea quite explicitly in his own recent texts on the politics of knowledge and the place of philosophy in settling various litigious boundary-disputes.[17] What is important about these texts − I have argued − is their insistence that such questions must still be *thought through* with regard to their present-day social and ideological effects. This was also the case with Deleuze when he wrote his book on Kant. At least for the purposes of cogent exposition he could offer a faithfully Kantian gloss on the problems and antinomies encountered in the course of establishing this parliament of knowledge. But in his later writings (notably the *Anti-Oedipus,* co-authored with Félix Guattari) Deleuze breaks altogether with the paradigms of enlightened reason and adopts a heady post-structuralist style of apocalyptic discourse.[18] In short, he abandons the immanent critique of Kantian concepts and categories for a language that celebrates our emergence into an age when reason itself can at last be seen as nothing more than an agency of social repression. Like Foucault, Deleuze equates knowledge with power, and rejects any kind of philosophical critique that would *theorize* their relation from the standpoint of enlightened reason.

To put it like this is of course to ignore some significant differences of view. Deleuze was no more a typecast 'post-structuralist' than he had been an orthodox neo-Kantian in the earlier book. The *Anti-Oedipus* takes up an embattled stance against just about every variety of present-day 'advanced' critical thought, including − most insistently − Lacanian psycho-analysis. It treats them as mere reinforcements of a bad social order which they tend to perpetuate even by supplying the concepts and categories by which to understand it. Thus psychoanalysis props up the institutions of state and familial power precisely insofar as it accords a privileged explanatory role to notions like that of the Oedipus Complex. Such theories are devoid of radical force because (so Deleuze and Guattari argue) their analyses are fatally complicit with the forms of societal repression whose workings they claim to expose. It is in order to forestall such unlooked-for effects that the *Anti-Oedipus* adopts a style of radically *un*theoretical language, a rhetoric of 'schizoid' (polymorphous) desire supposedly beyond reach of explanatory concepts. It thus takes a stand squarely opposed to Lacan's insistence on the socializing agency of language, the induction of the subject into an order of instituted power and authority by way of 'successfully' passing through the Oedipal phase.

Nevertheless it is clear that Deleuze and Guattari represent a dissident fraction *within* the post-structuralist enterprise, rather than occupying a wholly separate terrain. Their rhetoric of polyperverse 'schizo-desire' envisages a breakdown in the order of self-possessed 'rational' subjectivity which in turn promises an end to the regime of repressive social constraints. In his study of Kant, Deleuze could still expound the antinomies of pure and practical reason in a way that made (Kantian) logical sense of them, even while revealing their inbuilt aporias. That is to say, his argument proceeded on the twofold assumption (1) that *reasons* could be given for Kant having pursued this course of enquiry, and (2) that the autonomous, self-acting subject of Kantian discourse was at least an intelligible notion. Thus Deleuze spells out the paradoxical injunction: 'This is what "subject" means in the case of practical reason . . . the same beings are subjects and legislators, so that the legislator is here part of the nature over which he legislates.'[19] But when Deleuze comes to write the *Anti-Oedipus* he has reached a position from which such ideas could only seem a species of legitimizing ploy in the service of repressive rationality. There is no longer any point in engaging that enlightenment tradition on ground which would always have been staked out in advance by the thought-police of an entrenched philosophical and socio-political order.

Epistemology and ethics: Husserl, Levinas

This is where deconstruction parts company with the wider post-structuralist enterprise. For Derrida, the realm of ethical discourse is that which exceeds all given conceptual structures, but exceeds them through a patient interrogation of their limits, and not by some leap into an unknown 'beyond' which would give no purchase to critical thought. This is the theme that runs through the otherwise diverse essays assembled in *Writing and Difference*. Two of them ('Force and Signification' and 'Genesis and Structure') have to do with the effects of structuralist thinking in criticism, philosophy and the sciences of man. There is a sense, Derrida writes, in which 'a certain structuralism has always been philosophy's most spontaneous gesture' (p. 159). That is to say, philosophers have sought to *conceptualize* knowledge and experience by setting up various systematic frameworks that would finally contain and adjudicate their rival claims. Structuralism is in this sense the inheritor of all those epistemological projects, from Plato to Kant and Husserl, which have tried to fix limits for the discourse of knowledge and the truth-claims of universal reason. And literary criticism, at least since Aristotle, has simply taken over these ambitions, insofar as it has worked with a handful of concepts (*mimesis,* form, 'metaphorical' versus 'literal' meaning) whose line of descent is philosophical through and through. Thus the structuralist approach to literary texts is something like a limit-point of traditional criticism, an approach that reveals with exceptional clarity its inbuilt strains and aporias.

In a striking image, Derrida compares the upshot of structuralist readings to 'the architecture of an uninhabited or deserted city, reduced to its skeleton by some catastrophe of nature or art' (*Writing and Difference,* p. 5). The virtue of such readings is to highlight the essentially abstract or 'lifeless' character of the landscape thus revealed. 'The relief and design of structures appears more clearly when content, which is the living energy of meaning, is neutralized' (p. 5). What structuralism necessarily leaves out of account is the *excess* of meaning over form, the fact that certain elements (of 'force' or 'signification') must always escape its otherwise lucid vigil. Thus structuralism effectively delimits its own project — and the project of philosophy at large — insofar as it fails to register this fact. 'By virtue of its innermost intention, and like all questions about language, structuralism escapes the classical history of ideas which already supposes structuralism's possibility, for the latter naively belongs to the province of language and propounds itself within it' (p. 4). This is why Derrida pursues the dialogue between structuralism and phenomenology, a dialogue whose terms he takes over from Husserl and interrogates most closely in 'Genesis and Structure'. For Husserl represents the furthest point yet reached in the conflict of interpretations between structuralism (in this extended usage) and whatever lies beyond the grasp of structural explanations. The sense of this 'beyond' is very different from anything suggested by Foucault, Deleuze or the adepts of post-structuralist apocalyptic discourse. It involves a knowledge of what Derrida calls — in one of his most densely packed sentences — 'the principled, essential, and structural impossibility of closing a structural phenomenology' (p. 162). If there is any way out of this deadlocked position it will *not*, clearly, lie in the direction of a new epistemology, a theory of knowledge that would somehow accommodate or reconcile the two sets of claims. It is not that Husserl, through some oversight or error, has simply failed to take such a step. Rather he has shown, with exemplary rigour, that the step cannot be taken; that phenomenology and structuralism are caught up in an endless process of reciprocal questioning which allows of no final synthesis. Only by pressing this aporia to the limits of conceptual explanation can philosophy begin to perceive what lies beyond. And this — as Derrida argues — will take us into the domain of ethics, rather than epistemology.

Derrida describes Husserl's project as forcing him to navigate a path between 'the Scylla and Charybdis of logicizing structuralism and psychologistic geneticism' (p. 158). On the one hand Husserl wanted to establish that the truths of a science like geometry were *a priori* truths, unchangeably vested in the nature of human reason. He therefore set out to re-think its grounding assumptions in such a way that their history and genesis — the record of geometrical 'discovery', from Euclid down – could be thought of as somehow prefigured in its origins, simply awaiting their historical turn. For Husserl, it is imperative to save such primordial intuitions by explaining (1) how their logic is reactivated in each subsequent reflection on that founding moment; (2) how geometry only has a 'history' insofar as it involves thinking back to a pure point of origin; and (3) how the *a priori* character of geometric truth is ideally unaffected by errors and distortions attendant on the process of historical transmission. In short, Husserl thinks of geometry as the paradigm or test-case for a method – that of transcendental phenomenology – which might secure science (and all forms of knowledge) against the threat of an unbridled relativism. And if this can be established, then the way is clearly open for philosophy to regain its authentic (post-Kantian) vocation. It would point toward the ultimate grounding of epistemology in a grasp of those constitutive structures of knowledge and perception which cannot be doubted since experience itself is strictly unthinkable without them.

Husserl's project in *The Origin of Geometry* therefore presents a very striking example of logocentric reason. It is a philosophy at once turned back toward origins and seeking to enclose all the history of thought in a moment of pure, self-present understanding. I shall not attempt to summarize all the detailed arguments that Derrida brings to bear in his reading of this text.[20] They turn on the fact that Husserl cannot conceptualize geometry or the source of its 'primordial intuitions' without, in the process, deploying a language of inscription, writing or graphic representation. And this affects not only the ideal objectivities of geometric truth but also that concept of a timeless access to such truths through the perfectly *repeatable* interplay of present intuition and past discovery. According to Husserl, 'traditionality is what circulates from one to the other, illuminating one by the other in a movement wherein consciousness discovers its path.' But in fact, as Derrida argues, it is only in terms of writing – of inscriptions cut off from any intuitive or self-present source – that Husserl can represent geometry as a form of universal knowledge. 'The possibility of writing will assure the absolute traditionalization of the object, its absolute ideal Objectivity . . . Writing will do this by emancipating sense from its actually present evidence for a real subject and from its present circulation within a determined community.' And this because writing alone is capable of conferring that 'ideal' permanence, removed from the accidents of history and change, that Husserl is so determined to establish. Without this recourse to an inscriptionalist idiom there would be no conceiving of geometry as a realm of absolute, *a priori* truth.

In 'Genesis and Structure' Derrida traces the constantly oscillating movement of thought by which Husserl attempts to steer a path between these twin necessities. 'Structure' pertains to everything on the side of ideality, permanence and objective knowledge; to everything, in short, that has need of *writing* to guarantee its proper status. 'Genesis' denotes that other dimension of Husserlian enquiry, concerned to explain how such knowledge is possible in terms of an intuitive coming-to-truth whose logic would yet be a product of *a priori* reasoning. If 'motifs of conflict or of tension appear numerous' in Husserl's text, this is not through some repeated error of judgement but according to the strictest order of necessity, inscribed in the very nature of his project. Husserl's is 'a philosophy of essences always considered in their objectivity, their intangibility, their apriority; but, by the same token, it is a philosophy of experience, of the temporal flux of what is lived, which is the ultimate reference' (*Writing and Difference*, p. 156). In this respect Husserl is the last and (as Derrida would claim) the most rigorous thinker of those who have inherited the great founding oppositions of Western intellectual history. Any attempt to surpass phenomenology can only go by way of a structuralist critique which in turn must come up against the inbuilt limits of its own conceptual heritage. Some, like Hegel, have thought to transcend the antinomies of Kantian reason by appealing to history, dialectics and change as the means by which thinking perpetually overcomes these aporias of its own creating. But Hegel's philosophy is itself a series of elaborate conceptual techniques for reducing whatever exceeds its grasp to an order of structural necessity expressed in world-historical terms. One can read Hegel otherwise, read him 'against the grain', so to speak, as Derrida does in his essay 'From Restricted to General Economy' (in *Writing and Difference*). Then it will appear that the Hegelian text has a figural logic and a wayward 'economy' of meaning which everywhere exceed the laws laid down for its own dialectical passage from stage to stage. These laws are implicit in Hegel's idea of the *Aufhebung,* that speculative movement of thought by which philosophy both conserves and transcends the contradictions encountered on its journey to truth. Derrida's reading brings out the extent to which this is an arbitrary movement, one reading among many, though one that is expressly sanctioned by all the resources of Hegelian dialectic. 'Since no logic governs, henceforth, the meaning of interpretation, because logic is an interpretation, Hegel's own interpretation can be reinterpreted − against him' (*Writing and Difference,* p. 260).

I have suggested − and it is time to make good the claim − that there is an ethical dimension to Derrida's writings which has yet to be grasped by most of his commentators. On the one hand he takes it as axiomatic that philosophy in the Western tradition has for so long been preoccupied with problems of knowledge, truth and reason (essentially *epistemological* problems) that there is no way of actively engaging that tradition except by continuing to think them through. In Kant, as we have seen, the two kinds of discourse − 'pure' and 'practical' reason − are involved in a constant reciprocal exchange, subject to the laws of enlightened reason. But this debate, though vital to the interests of philosophy, still has to exclude certain other voices, those that hail from outside the whole tradition of epistemological thinking, from Plato to Husserl. For Derrida, it is chiefly in Jewish writings − among them, those of Emmanuel Levinas − that this summons speaks most clearly.[21] There are many indications in his own work of Derrida's identifying closely with the heritage of Jewish thought, in particular the practice of extensive and multiplied commentary on the sacred texts of Jewish religion. What distinguishes such commentary from its orthodox Christian counterpart is precisely the emphasis placed upon *writing* as an endlessly productive signifying practice irreducible to some ultimate, self-evident truth.

Christian doctrine was shaped at an early stage by its exposure to Greek philosophical influences, tending to equate the Word of God with the *Logos* of revealed divine purpose. In Jewish tradition, on the contrary, there grew up a habit of treating the manifold commentaries as sacred texts in their own right, each adding to the store of received wisdom and requiring yet further attention from the scribes and exegetes. Christianity engendered an attitude of principled mistrust toward the written word, regarding it as a necessary evil, a token of man's unredeemed nature and his fallible grasp of God's will. The *opacity* of writing — its physical embodiment as mere inert marks on a page — thus came to signify the weaknesses of human understanding, the necessity of falling back upon man-made sources of knowledge. Writing was a strictly *instrumental* medium, a mortal script whose small claim to truth lay in its self-effacing readiness to yield up meanings 'written in the soul' by some higher, ineffable power. Thus Plato could be 'saved' for Christian tradition by stressing those common points of doctrine which converged on the idea of spiritual truth as something beyond the physical realm and — by the same token — beyond reach of writing in its literal aspect. The relation between commentary and sacred text reproduces that between the text itself and the ultimate, self-authorizing Word of God. It is a relation of strictly one-way dependence, with writing cast always in a derivative, supplementary role. Thus Christianity raises to its highest point of principle that logocentric bias which Derrida traces down through the history of Western thought.

To set the Jewish against the Graeco-Christian tradition is implicitly to foreground the matter of writing and its place in the economy of knowledge and truth. Derrida adopts various techniques for reminding the reader of his own close involvement with Rabbinical sources and traditions. These may take the form of riddling autograph signatures ('Reb Derissa'), of allusion to the methods of Talmudic commentary, or of multiple insets and other such graphic devices which refuse any clear demarcation between 'primary' and 'secondary' texts. Susan Handelmann, in her book *The Slayers of Moses*,[22] has given an admirably detailed account of how this Jewish speciality of textual exegesis surfaces in the writings of Freud, Derrida and other figures in the modern hermeneutic tradition. Its chief effect is to loosen the hold of that Christian (or logocentric) habit of thought which subdues writing to the service of a truth equated with speech, presence and origins. Thus in Derrida the rigours of deconstruction go along with an element of calculated textual 'play' whose aim is precisely to unfix and perturb our received ideas of what reading is all about.

But there is another aspect to the Jewish influence on Derrida's writing, one that brings us closer to the ultimately ethical nature of his enterprise. His essay on Levinas ('Violence and Metaphysics') takes an epigraph from Matthew Arnold's *Culture and Anarchy*. 'Hebraism and Hellenism — between these two points of influence moves our world. At one time it feels more powerfully the attraction of one of them, at another time of the other; and it ought to be, though it never is, evenly and happily balanced between them' (quoted in *Writing and Difference*, p. 79). And the essay closes with a sentence from Joyce, 'most Hegelian of modern novelists', who writes in *Ulysses*: 'Jewgreek is Greekjew. Extremes meet' (p. 153). What is 'Hegelian' here — and in the passage from Arnold — is also what marks the Hellenizing strain that unites their intellectual heritage. It is the desire to *reconcile* oppositions and differences through a movement of thought that would finally reduce them to aspects of a single, comprehensive vision. Such, after all, was Arnold's evangelizing message to Victorian England in the face of widespread social unrest. The middle classes had brought this threat upon themselves by pursuing an ethic of religious and worldly self-interest to the exclusion of everything else. They had cultivated the 'Hebraic' (or Judaeo-Christian) virtues — hard work, thrift, ethical individualism — and ignored that other, 'Hellenic' tradition which stood for the disinterested pursuit of knowledge, beauty and truth. Only by an infusion of Hellenic 'sweetness and light' — a newly awakened interest in poetry and the life of the mind — could the Victorian bourgeoisie achieve the kind of *cultural* hegemony that would overcome those looming forces of destruction.

Arnold's vague talk of 'balancing' these rival claims disguises the fact that such an outcome can only be envisaged through the kind of detached, contemplative thought that belongs wholly to the 'Hellenic' way of ideas. To sublimate the knowledge of real social conflicts by appealing to a realm of pure, disinterested 'culture' is itself a fine example of Hegelian speculative logic at work. And the subsequent, short-lived episode of British Hegelianism — influenced by the Oxford Idealist, F.H. Bradley — showed exactly this combination of a high-minded ethical creed linked to an all-embracing dialectics of knowledge and experience.[23] So Derrida's epigraph from Arnold carries a considerable weight of implied ideology. It stands for that power of logocentric thinking to absorb all differences into itself by viewing them as mere stages or signposts on the way to some grand conceptual synthesis. Philosophy has developed plentiful techniques for coping with whatever is perceived as external to its own sovereign domain. Emblematic of this process is the encounter with the so-called 'Eleatic Stranger' in Plato's *Sophist,* an encounter in which (as Derrida reads it) there still persist 'traces of an alterity that refuses to be totally mastered'.[24] But the thrust of dialectical reason, from Socrates to Hegel, is the effort to comprehend everything on terms which philosophy will always have laid down in advance. And this applies even to what might seem the most resistant categories, like those of a radically empiricist or materialist cast. As soon as they enter the discourse of philosophy — whether Kantian, Hegelian or Marxist — these categories are subject to a kind of conceptual sea-change which renders them henceforth intra-philosophical. What Derrida finds in Levinas is an attempt to *think the limits* of this tradition and to make out the points where it encounters the 'violence' of an alien (ethical) mode of thought.

For Levinas, the course of Western philosophical tradition is determined from the outset by its ancient Greek heritage. 'Philosophy employs a series of terms and concepts — such as *morphe* (form), *ousia* (substance), *nous* (reason), *logos* (thought) or *telos* (goal), etc. — which constitute a specifically Greek lexicon of intelligibility.'[25] Like Derrida, he sees a systematic relationship or complicity between these terms, since they all point toward a moment of ultimate, self-present truth when reason would grasp the encompassing logic of its own nature and history. What is *intelligible* to thinkers in this Greek tradition is whatever lends itself to the various 'totalizing' methods and strategies which thought has devised to maintain its grasp upon an otherwise recalcitrant world. Philosophy is a series of elaborate detours which all lead back to this reassuring point of origin. Even where it thinks to reintroduce an historical dimension as the ground of all knowledge – as Hegel did in reacting against the timeless, *a priori* truth-claims of Kantian reason – philosophy can only conceptualize history on the model of an endlessly circular return to its own first principles. To equate truth with self-presence is always to have known *in advance* what the prospects were at any given stage on the road to enlightened understanding. There is nothing that could come as a salutary shock from outside this domain of speculative reason. For the only kind of knowledge that *counts* philosophically is that which finds its place in the grand dialectical scheme and thus has a claim to world-historical status. 'However different the two terms of a relation might appear . . . or however separated over time . . . they can ultimately be rendered commensurate and simultaneous, the same, englobed in a history which totalizes time into a beginning or an end, or both, which is presence.'[26] Thus Hegel's excursion into history – including the history of cultures remote from any mainstream Hellenizing influence – still leads up to the apotheosis of an Absolute Reason which has always foreknown every episode along the way.

And so it has come about – according to Levinas – that Western philosophy has developed chiefly as a form of *epistemological* enquiry, a quest for accurate knowledge of the world as perceived by the isolated subject.[27] This primary stress on the relation between knower and known (or mind and object) has effectively marginalized that other kind of discourse whose challenge can only be grasped through the encounter between self and human other. Not that philosophy has simply ignored such questions or failed to find room for ethics *within* its various epistemological projects. Indeed, as we have seen, it was a major requirement of that tradition – from Plato to Kant and beyond

232

— that ethical theory should be harmonized with the truth-claims of a reason that acknowledged no limits to its proper domain. But it is precisely this assumed order of priorities that Levinas questions on behalf of an ethics which would *not* be thus subject to the governing interests of epistemological enquiry. Such a project only comes into view, he argues, at the point of encounter with an otherness, a radical 'alterity', which exceeds all the concepts and categories devised to keep thinking on a path of safe return to its own, self-identical logic. 'The inter-human is thus an interface: a double axis where what is "of the world" qua *phenomenological intelligibility* is juxtaposed with what is "not of the world" qua *ethical responsibility*.'[28] Phenomenology represents — for Levinas as for Derrida — the most advanced and sophisticated stage yet reached in the effort to provide indubitable grounds for the exercise of human understanding. But this position is attained only at the cost of confirming philosophy in its narrowed, epistemological mode of enquiry. In Husserl it takes the form of a rigorous reflection on the powers and limits of a 'transcendental' ego whose activity is directed toward objects in the field of first-hand perceptual experience. Heidegger and Sartre attempted to extend this activity into a domain of ethical reflection where the issue of human concern for others played a more central role. But they failed in this endeavour, Levinas argues, insofar as they sought an understanding of the other based on the primordial experience of the self. Thus in Sartre, 'the phenomenon of the other was still considered, as in all Western ontology, to be a modality of unity and fusion, that is a reduction of the other to categories of the same.'[29]

Derrida is by no means an uncritical exponent of Levinas's texts. For one thing, he perceives the impossibility of mounting such a radical critique while perforce continuing to use the language, the sedimented concepts and categories, of Western intellectual tradition. 'By making the origin of language, meaning, and difference the relation to the infinitely other, Levinas is resigned to betraying his own intentions in his philosophical discourse' (*Writing and Difference*, p. 151). And Derrida likewise questions Levinas's claim to have delimited Husserlian phenomenology as a mode of thought which would have to be surpassed by any authentic enquiry into ethical values. Levinas seeks to identify those points at which Husserl allegedly drew back into a sphere of 'egological' reflection where ethics could only be conceived as a kind of reciprocal self-knowledge. 'To make the other an alter ego, Levinas says frequently, is to neutralize its absolute alterity' (*Writing and Difference,* p. 123). But there is no way of raising these questions, Derrida argues, without first passing through the necessary rigours of phenomenological thought. 'One could neither speak, nor have any sense of the totally other, if there was not a *phenomenon* of the totally other, or evidence of the totally other as such. No one more than Husserl has been sensitive to the singular and irreducible style of this evidence, and to the original non-phenomenalization indicated within it' (p. 123). This squares with what I have said about Derrida's stress on the need to keep faith with enlightened reason, to think through the problems of epistemological tradition, even while essaying that tradition's limits. His own early texts on Husserl are evidence enough of Derrida's close and productive engagement with phenomenological thought. His counter-argument to Levinas – like his case against Foucault in 'Cogito and the History of Madness' – comes down to this essential point. Deconstruction can have no *critical* purchase on the texts of Western logocentric reason if it thinks to move decisively 'beyond' tradition by a leap on to different ground.

Nevertheless it is clear that Levinas exerted a deep and lasting influence on Derrida's thought. In Levinas, he writes, all the concepts of Western philosophy 'are dragged toward the *agora,* summoned to justify themselves in an ethico-political language that they have not always sought – or believed that they sought – to speak, summoned to transpose themselves into this language by confessing their violent aims' (p. 97). That Derrida's work has been received with such open hostility – especially by philosophers in the mainstream Anglo-American line of descent – is perhaps a sign of this 'violence' aroused by any challenge to the protocols of rational debate. Here one is reminded of Kant's attack on the mystagogues and those who adopt an 'apocalyptic tone' to disrupt the parliament of reason. Their worst crime, from Kant's point of view, is the confusion thus brought about between truths accessible to reasoned enquiry and truths of revealed moral law. The mystagogues offend against reason, morality and religion alike when they collapse the terms of this crucial distinction. As Derrida puts it, summarizing Kant: 'they do not distinguish between pure speculative reason and pure practical reason; they believe they *know* what is solely *thinkable* and reach through feeling alone the universal laws of practical reason' ('Of an Apocalyptic Tone', p. 12). Thus the real complaint is that these fake illuminati set up as purveyors of a truth vouchsafed to them alone, and denied to the genuine philosophers whose task it is to determine the proper limits and capacities of human reason.

This helps to explain what is at stake when philosophers – most recently, A.J. Ayer – dismiss Derrida as a mere rhetorician, a 'literary' gadfly whose ideas are beneath the notice of serious thinkers.[30] For Kant likewise, 'all philosophy is indeed prosaic', and any suggestion that thinking revert to its 'poetical' (pre-Socratic) origins is a mere affront to rational dignity and truth. The zealots of unaided intuition reveal their hand most clearly in resorting to metaphor as a substitute for reasoned argument. 'This cryptopolitics is also a cryptopoetics, a poetic perversion of philosophy' (p. 14). And this because metaphor – or 'poetic' language in general – claims access to a realm of intuitive truth unaccountable to plain prose reason. Once again, it is the Kantian 'parliament' of faculties – the discourse of free and equal voices under the law of reason – which shows itself quick to register this threat. What Kant so dislikes about the poet-philosophers is their habit of indulging a rhapsodic style which ignores all the rules of civilized parliamentary exchange. These purveyors of apocalypse 'scoff at work, the concept, schooling . . . to what is given they believe they have access effortlessly, gracefully, intuitively or through genius, outside of school' (p. 9). And this Kantian charge-sheet is regularly echoed by philosophers such as Ayer and Searle when they take it that Derrida's 'literary' style is ground enough for refusing to engage with him in serious, reasoned debate.

On the contrary, I have argued: deconstruction involves a labour of thought – an effort of rigorous demystification – which in many ways aligns it more closely with the Kantians than with their high-toned opponents. There is, Derrida writes, quite simply no escaping the 'law and destiny' of present-day enlightened thought. Such is the theme of his latest writings on the politics of knowledge, the 'principle of reason' and the role of university teaching and research. It is a superficial irony at most that Derrida should devote himself to defending philosophy's place in the French school and university curriculum while continuing to 'deconstruct' its traditional arguments and truth-claims. 'Who is more faithful to reason's call,' he asks, 'who hears it with a keener ear . . . the one who offers questions in return and tries to think through the possibility of that summons, or the one who does not want to hear any question about the principle of reason?' ('The Principle of Reason', p. 9). This should be read as a twofold challenge, on the one hand to philosophy, insofar as it remains constitutionally blind to its own governing interests and motives, but on the other – and more pointedly – to those forms of neo-pragmatist or 'postmodern' thinking that renounce reason itself. For Derrida, as for Levinas, there is an ethical injunction to challenge philosophy on terms which offer the maximum resistance to its powers of recuperative grasp. But this challenge can only be sustained through a close and reasoned engagement with the texts where philosophy stakes its claims to truth.

Certainly Derrida goes far toward dismantling that Kantian idea of philosophy which treats it as a locus of pure, disinterested enquiry, free from the pressures of state interference by virtue of its guaranteed non-participation in practical affairs. He shows how this rhetoric of disinterest serves both to elevate philosophy's self-image and, more crucially, to divert attention from its manifold stakes and interests in the world 'outside' the university. But to bring these arguments against the Kantian ideal – and to link that ideal with a certain epistemology of knowledge, reason and truth – is *not* to suggest that we henceforth abandon the whole project of enlightened critique. Such work must always involve, as Derrida writes, 'a double gesture, a double postulation: to ensure professional competence and the most serious tradition of the university even while going as far as possible, theoretically and practically, in the most directly underground thinking about the abyss beneath the university . . .' In this passage from 'The Principle of Reason' (p. 17), Derrida is alluding on the one hand to certain distinctive topographical features of the Cornell University campus, and on the other to that long tradition in philosophy, from Plato to Heidegger, which has sought to establish grounds or foundations for reason itself. That such grounds may turn out to be simply unavailable − products of the will-to-truth within language, metaphors masquerading as concepts − is the Nietzschean message most often extracted from Derrida's texts. But to take this message at face value is to fall in with those who refuse to *read* Derrida on account of his supposed irrationalism. For it may be in the questioning of reason itself − a questioning nonetheless patient and meticulously argued − that philosophy can best live up to its present responsibilities.

Chronology

1930   Born in El Biar, Algiers, of 'assimilated' Sephardic-Jewish parents ('all the family names are encrypted, along with several others, in *La Carte postale*').

1940–   War comes to Algeria; 'first concealed rumblings' of French-Algerian War of Independence. Racial tensions and growing signs of antisemitic prejudice and violence.

1942   Camus, *L'Etranger (The Outsider)* and *Le Mythe de Sisyphe (The Myth of Sisyphus)*.

1943   Sartre, *L'Etre et le néant (Being and Nothingness)*.

1945–   Allied victory; end to period of 'two-headed' administration (de Gaulle–Giraud) when 'racial laws were maintained for almost six months under a "free" French government'. Derrida enrolled at Jewish lycée but aware of mounting hostility and 'skipped classes for a year'. (Lévi-Strauss, 'Structural Analysis in Linguistics and Anthropology'. Sartre launches *Les Temps modernes*, a journal that grew out of the French Resistance movement and aimed to provide an incisive commentary on ideological issues in the post-war years. Camus involved at this early stage although clearly unsympathetic to some of Sartre's ideas.)

1947   Sartre publishes *Situations*, vol. I (essays on literature, politics and the post-war cultural climate). Also Camus, *La Peste (The Plague)*, an allegory of events and attitudes in France during the years of German occupation.

1948–   Attained baccalaureate; interest in philosophy first sparked when listening by chance to radio broadcast when a professor from the Grandes Ecoles preparatory programme 'introduced his class and spoke of a former student, Albert Camus'. Also much impressed by Sartre's role as engaged intellectual and activist; 'a model that I have since judged to be ill-fated and catastrophic, but one I still love . . .'

1950– Early studies in France; stays on to work at the Ecole Normale Supérieure with the Hegel scholar Jean Hyppolite. Intensive reading of Hegel, Husserl, Heidegger, Bataille, Blanchot and others. *Mémoire* (master's thesis) on meaning, structure and genesis in Husserl. Later the topic of two essays in Derrida's *Writing and Difference*. (Publication of Camus, *Aktuelles I: Chroniques 1944-48*.)

1951 Camus, *L'Homme Révolté (The Rebel)*. Marks the beginning of Camus's quarrel with Sartre (publicized in *Les Temps modernes*) on the question of 'authentic', individual choice versus the claims of party-line communist commitment.

1953 Roland Barthes, *Writing Degree Zero*; Jacques Lacan, 'The Function and Field of Speech and Language in Psychoanalysis'. Also Camus, *Aktuelles II: Chroniques 1948-53*.

1955 Hyppolite, *Studies on Marx And Hegel*; Claude Lévi-Strauss, *Tristes Tropiques*.

1956– One-year Visiting Scholarship at Harvard. Publication of Jakobson and Halle, *Fundamentals of Language*.

1957– Planning to write thesis for state doctorate on 'The Ideality of the Literary Object', inspired by reading of Husserl and phenomenological aesthetics. Work on this project abandoned as Derrida moved toward the deconstructive standpoint enounced in *Speech and Phenomena*. Growing sense of the problems created for philosophy (or a certain canonical idea of philosophy) by the confrontation with literature, writing and its own inescapably textual character. (Publication of Barthes's *Mythologies* and Lacan's most influential essay, 'The Agency of the Letter in the Unconscious, or Reason since Freud'.)

1958– Derrida will look back on the decade up to 1968 in France as 'the most static period of the Gaullist republic'. He will also associate this period with something in the nature of 'classic' or high French structuralism, that 'immobility' of system and concept that sought to place limits on the differential play of meaning. (Lévi-Strauss publishes *Structural Anthropology*; Camus the third volume of his *Aktuelles*, the *Chroniques Algériennes*.)

1960– Taught at the Sorbonne for the next four years; continued work at the problematic interface of phenomenology, structuralism and literary theory.

1961 Michel Foucault publishes *Madness and Civilization*.

1962– End of Algerian War of Independence. First major publication: Edmund Husserl, *L'Origine de la géométrie*, trans. with a long introductory essay by Derrida. Awarded the Prix Cavaillès for this work.

1955– Taught History of Philosophy at the Ecole Normale Supérieure. (Publication of Barthes's *Elements of Semiology*. Also Derrida's association with the journal *Tel Quel*, marking the emergence of a new French criticism opposed to the claims of positivist literary scholarship and open to the influences of semiology, Marxism, psychoanalysis and the structuralist 'sciences of man'.)

1966 Louis Althusser, *For Marx*; Emile Benveniste, *Problems of General Linguistics*; Foucault, *The Order of Things*; Lacan, *Ecrits*. Barthes's *Critique et vérité* issues a shrewdly provocative challenge to the guardians of critical orthodoxy.

1967 Undoubtedly the single most significant year in terms of Derrida's publishing and reception-history. Three major books: *La Voix et le phénomène* (on Husserl), *De la grammatologie* and *L'Ecriture et la différence*. Also initial reactions to the paper 'Structure, Sign and Play in the Discourse of the Human Sciences', which Derrida had given at a Johns Hopkins conference during 1966, and which marked the first impact of deconstruction among North American literary critics.

1968   Year of *les évènements*, the student rising in Paris, at first welcomed by leftist intellectuals as heralding the downfall of de Gaulle's government. Eventually quelled by limited concessions, including the establishment of new, more liberal universities like Paris-Vincennes. Failure of working-class and union activists to rally behind the student cause. Deepening divisions within the French Communist Party, with criticism of leading intellectuals (Althusser among them) for having neither foreseen this crisis nor, in the event, given it their unqualified support. Signalled the beginning of a widespread disenchantment with Marxism among French intellectuals and (later) the rise of a fashionable group (the *Nouveaux Philosophes*) who gave voice to that mood during the next decade.

1970   Publication of Barthes's *S/Z*; clear signs of Derrida's influence in the way Barthes has moved from structuralist narratology to a mode of reading that renounces such reductive methods and celebrates the plural (*scriptible* or 'writerly') text.

1971   Paul de Man, *Blindness and Insight: Essays in the Rhetoric of Contemporary Criticism*.

1972   Derrida publishes *Positions* (a volume of interviews), *La Dissémination* and *Marges de la philosophie*. Henceforth divides his time between teaching in Paris and various American universities, including regular visiting appointments at Johns Hopkins and Yale. Close collaboration with various translators results in a series of essays intended mainly for his American readership. (Deleuze and Guattari publish *L'Anti-Oedipe*.)

1973   Appearance of *Speech and Phenomena*, the first of Derrida's major works in translation. (Baudrillard publishes *The Mirror of Production*, a text symptomatic of the general trend toward post- or more overtly anti-Marxist positions. Derrida's work not a part of this trend, despite his involvement with the *Tel Quel* group [among them Julia Kristeva and Philippe Sollers] whose political allegiances will prove, to say the least, highly volatile.)

1974   Publication of *Glas*, Derrida's most 'literary' work to date, in the form of a Joycean intertextual commentary on Hegel, Genet and the problematic border-line between literature and philosophy. Can be see as a delayed outcome of Derrida's suggestion, in his first work on Husserl, that thinking must in some sense choose between the quest for pure, univocal concepts and the Joycean path of unlimited semiotic 'freeplay'. Misunderstood by those who take him to have followed this second course exclusively and lost all interest in 'serious' philosophical work. Hence what appears as a widening rift between Derrida's influence on American literary criticism and his continuing work on the texts of Kant, Hegel and others in the 'mainstream' philosophical tradition.

1975– Involved with the collective GREPH (Groupe de Recherches sur l'Enseignement Philosophique), set up to examine institutional aspects of the teaching of philosophy and – more urgently – to resist French government proposals for eliminating philosophy from the final-year lycée course.

1976   *Of Grammatology* appears in the landmark translation by Gayatri Chakravorty Spivak. (Foucault publishes Volume I of his *History of Sexuality*.)

1977 Derrida's exchange with John R. Searle on the topic of Austin and speech-act philosophy. Marks a further stage in the deepening resistance or baffled antagonism to Derrida's work among Anglo-American philosophers.

1979 *Spurs: Nietzsche's Styles.* Also the essay 'Living On: Border-lines', in a kind of loose-knit Yale manifesto (*Deconstruction and Criticism*) which lends credence to the widespread idea that Derrida, Hartman, Hillis Miller, Paul de Man and Harold Bloom somehow represent a united front of avant-garde literary theory. This idea will persist despite increasing evidence to the contrary. (Publication of Paul de Man, *Allegories of Reading*, and Jean-François Lyotard, *La Condition postmoderne*.)

1980 Derrida, *La Carte postale de Socrate à Freud et au-delà*.

1982 *Margins of Philosophy* translated by Alan Bass. Contains a number of essays (notably 'White Mythology: Metaphor in the Text of Philosophy') which go clean against the account of deconstruction given by many of its literary-critical exponents. Nevertheless Derrida finds himself frequently at the centre of much-publicized debates that have more to do with American academic rivalries than with anything in the nature of his own work.

1983– Derrida invited to play a coordinating role in the International College of Philosophy, a Paris-based communal venture set up to encourage work in areas of interdisciplinary study and research that find no place in more conventional curricula. Follows on very much from his involvement with GREPH; intended to open up philosophy (broadly defined) to those with some specific interest or project in mind, but not necessarily possessing any of the standard academic credentials. Derrida remains closely involved with the College, although his administrative role has now been taken over by Jean-François Lyotard.

1984– Publication of several texts (including 'The Principle of Reason') which attempt to re-focus the interests of 'American deconstruction' on issues of politics, teaching and ideological criticism. Signs of an increasing converg- ence between Derrida's work in France and America.

1986 Appearance of three English-language books on Derrida (Gasché, Harvey and Llewelyn: see Bibliography, pp. 257-63), all of which address his *philosophical* concerns and therefore mark a decided shift in the Anglo- American response to his work.

1987– Accepts an appointment as regular Visiting Professor at the University of California, Irvine. *Glas* appears in an English translation (with companion volume of textual exegesis and commentary) by John P. Leavey and Richard Rand.

(Biographical data from various sources, including the three interviews with Derrida [Kearney, Salusinszky and Wood, eds.], cited in this volume, p. 247. I am also much indebted to the record of his intellectual projects and involvements narrated in Derrida, 'The Time of a Thesis: Punctuations' [see note, p. 247]. J.G. Merquior's book *From Prague to Paris* (London: Verso, 1986) has a useful calendar of major publications in the structuralist and post-structuralist line of descent.)

Notes

1. Introduction

1. A translation of this interview may be found in David Wood (ed.), *Derrida and Différance* (University of Warwick: Parousia Press, 1985), pp. 107-27.
2. See Derrida, 'Devant la Loi', in A. Phillips Griffiths (ed.), *Philosophy and Literature* (Cambridge University Press, 1984).
3. Interview in Wood (ed.), *op. cit.*, p. 123.
4. Derrida, 'The Time of a Thesis', in Alan Montefiore (ed.), *Philosophy in France Today* (Cambridge University Press, 1983), pp. 34-50.
5. For a brief account of this work, see Derrida's 'On the University', an interview with Imre Salusinszky, *Southern Review* (Adelaide), vol. XIX, no. 1 (1986), pp. 3-12.
6. See the essay 'Différance', most readily available in Derrida's *Margins of Philosophy*, trans. Alan Bass (Chicago University Press, 1982), pp. 3-27.
7. Richard Rorty, 'Deconstruction and Circumvention', *Critical Inquiry*, vol. XI (1984), pp. 1-23.
8. See Derrida's interview with Richard Kearney in Kearney (ed.), *Dialogues with Contemporary Continental Thinkers* (Manchester University Press, 1984), pp. 83-105; p. 100.

2. Philosophy/Literature

1. See interview with Salusinszky, cited above.
2. Derrida, 'Letter to a Japanese Friend', in David Wood (ed.), *op. cit.*, pp. 1-8.
3. See especially Geoffrey Hartman, *Saving the Text: Literature/ Derrida/Philosophy* (Baltimore: Johns Hopkins University Press, 1981).
4. Interview with Kearney, *op. cit.*, p. 98.

Notes

3. Derrida on Plato: Writing as Poison and Cure

1. Derrida, 'Plato's Pharmacy', in *Dissemination*, trans. Barbara Johnson (London: Athlone Press, 1981), pp. 61-171. All further references given by page number in the text.

2. Plato, *Phaedrus and the Seventh and Eighth Letters*, trans. and intro. Walter Hamilton (Harmondsworth: Penguin, 1973). See especially pp. 95-9 for Socrates' discussion of writing and its harmful effects.

3. For a collective statement on this and other issues in the teaching of philosophy, see GREPH, *Qui a peur de la philosophie?* (Paris: Flammarion, 1977).

4. A sizable literature has grown up around the problems of translating Derrida's texts, and on the issues that deconstruction raises for the practice of translation in general. See especially Joseph F. Graham (ed.), *Difference in Translation* (Ithaca, NY: Cornell University Press, 1985). This volume contains both French and English versions of Derrida's 'Les Tours de Babel', an essay whose title ('tours' = 'towers', 'turns' or 'tropes') gives some indication of its theme.

5. The classic statement of this orthodox New Critical position may be found in W.K. Wimsatt, *The Verbal Icon: Studies in the Meaning of Poetry* (Lexington: University of Kentucky Press, 1954).

6. Derrida, 'The Double Session', in *Dissemination, op. cit.*, pp. 173-286. All further references given by page number in the text.

7. On Derrida's *Glas*, see Geoffrey Hartman, *Saving the Text, op. cit.*, and – for a useful summary account – Jonathan Culler's *On Deconstruction* (London: Routledge and Kegan Paul, 1982). Vincent Leitch also has some good points to make in *Deconstructive Criticism: an Advanced Introduction* (London: Hutchinson, 1983).

8. Angela Carter, *Nights at the Circus* (London: Picador, 1983), p. 103.

9. Ibid, p. 109.

10. For a brief and clear-headed discussion of these issues, see Alan R. White, *Truth* (London: Macmillan, 1970).

11. William Empson, *Seven Types of Ambiguity* (Harmondsworth: Penguin, 1961).

12. Notably W.K. Wimsatt in *The Verbal Icon, op. cit.*

13. Plato, *The Republic*, trans. H.D.P. Lee (Harmondsworth: Penguin, 1955), pp. 278-86.

4. Speech, Presence, Origins: from Hegel to Saussure

1. Derrida, *Of Grammatology*, trans. Gayatri Chakravorty Spivak (Baltimore: Johns Hopkins University Press, 1976). All further references given by page number in the text.
2. Derrida, 'Living On: Border-lines', in Bloom, Miller, Hartman *et al.* (eds.), *Deconstruction and Criticism* (New York: Seabury Press, 1979), pp. 75-176.
3. Derrida, 'The Pit and the Pyramid: Introduction to Hegel's Semiotics', in *Margins of Philosophy*, *op. cit.*, pp. 69-108.
4. Hegel, *Phenomenology of Spirit* (Oxford: Clarendon Press, 1977).
5. Derrida refers in particular to I.J. Gelb, *A Study of Writing: the Foundations of Grammatology* (University of Chicago Press, 1952). Although Gelb uses the term in its more traditional (restricted) sense, it was his work — Derrida records — that provided the first impetus toward *Of Grammatology*. More recent titles in which the word figures (e.g. Gregory Ulmer, *Applied Grammatology*, Baltimore: Johns Hopkins, 1985) are written very much under Derrida's influence and no doubt mark a decisive shift in its currency and range of application.
6. Ferdinand de Saussure, *Course in General Linguistics*, trans. Wade Baskin (London: Fontana, 1974).
7. Ibid, p. 84.
8. A more detailed account of these matters can be found in Jonathan Culler, *Saussure* (London: Fontana, 1976).
9. Roland Barthes, *Mythologies*, trans. Annette Lavers and Colin Smith (London: Jonathan Cape, 1972).
10. See especially Roman Jakobson, *Phonological Studies* (The Hague: Mouton, 1962).
11. Saussure, *op. cit.*, p. 76.

5. Rousseau: Writing as Necessary Evil

1. In Paul de Man, *Allegories of Reading: Figural Language in Rousseau, Nietzsche, Rilke, and Proust* (New Haven: Yale University Press, 1979).
2. See Jean-Jacques Rousseau, *Essay on the Origin of Languages*, trans. John H. Moran (New York: F. Ungar, 1967).
3. Derrida cites numerous texts in his account of Rousseau's social and political thought. See Rousseau, *Political Writings*, trans. and ed. Frederick Watkins (New York: Thomas Nelson and Sons, 1953).

Notes

4. The reader may wish to look up the words 'supplement', 'supplementary' and 'supplementarity' in the most recent Supplement (Se-Z, 1986) of the *Oxford English Dictionary*. Apart from citing Derrida to good effect, these entries suggest that even lexicography has taken a deconstructive turn.

5. For a useful account of these developments, see John Passmore, *A Hundred Years of Philosophy* (Harmondsworth: Penguin, 1970).

6. See, for instance, Michel Foucault, 'What Is an Author?', trans. Kari Hanet, *Screen*, vol. XX, no. 1 (1979), pp. 13-33, and Roland Barthes, 'The Death of the Author', in *Image-Music-Text*, trans. Stephen Heath (London: Fontana, 1977), pp. 142-8.

7. See Jacques Lacan, *Ecrits*, trans. Alan Sheridan (London: Tavistock, 1977) and *The Four Fundamental Concepts of Psychoanalysis*, trans. Sheridan (London: Hogarth Press, 1977; reprinted Penguin, 1979). Among the more accessible studies are Anika Lemaire, *Jacques Lacan*, trans. David Macey (London: Routledge and Kegan Paul, 1977), and Juliet Flower MacCannell, *Figuring Lacan: Criticism and the Cultural Unconscious* (London: Croom Helm, 1986).

8. See especially Roman Jakobson, 'Closing Statement: Linguistics and Poetics', in Thomas A. Sebeok (ed.), *Style in Language* (Cambridge, Mass.: MIT Press, 1960), pp. 350-77. David Lodge makes extensive and systematic use of Jakobson's ideas in his book *The Modes of Modern Writing* (London: Edward Arnold, 1977).

9. See Jacques Lacan, 'Seminar on "The Purloined Letter" ', trans. Jeffrey Mehlman, *Yale French Studies*, no. 48 (1972), pp. 38-72. For Derrida's response, see 'The Purveyor of Truth', *Yale French Studies*, no. 52 (1975), pp. 31-114.

10. Barbara Johnson, 'The Frame of Reference: Poe, Lacan, Derrida', in Geoffrey Hartman (ed.), *Psychoanalysis and the Question of the Text* (Baltimore: Johns Hopkins University Press, 1978), pp. 149-71. A revised version appears in her book *The Critical Difference: Essays in the Contemporary Rhetoric of Reading* (Johns Hopkins, 1980).

11. See, for instance, Roger Scruton, *The Meaning of Conservatism* (Harmondsworth: Penguin, 1980) for a statement of this New Right political creed. Some of the best recent essays on the topic may be found in Ruth Levitas (ed.), *The Ideology of the New Right* (Cambridge: Polity Press, 1986). See also Christopher Norris, 'Aesthetics and Politics: Reading Roger Scruton', in *The Contest of Faculties: Philosophy and Theory after Deconstruction* (London:

Methuen, 1985), pp. 123-38.

12. T.S. Eliot, 'The Metaphysical Poets', in *Selected Essays* (London: Faber, 1964), pp. 241-50.

13. See particularly Kelvin Everest, *Coleridge's Secret Ministry: the Context of the Conversation Poems* (Brighton: Harvester, 1979).

14. Claude Lévi-Strauss, *Tristes Tropiques*, trans. John Russell (London: Hutchinson, 1966).

15. On this and related topics, see G. Charbonnier, *Conversations with Claude Lévi-Strauss*, trans. John and Doreen Weightmann (London: Jonathan Cape, 1969). The most accessible brief introduction is Edmund Leach, *Lévi-Strauss* (London: Fontana, 1970).

16. On *bricolage*, see Lévi-Strauss, *The Savage Mind* (London: Weidenfeld and Nicolson, 1966).

17. Derrida, 'Structure, Sign and Play in the Discourse of the Human Sciences', in *Writing and Difference*, trans. Alan Bass (London: Routledge and Kegan Paul, 1978), pp. 278-93. All further references are given in the text.

18. The proceedings of this conference — including Derrida's 'Structure, Sign and Play' — were published in Richard Macksey and Eugenio Donato (eds.), *The Structuralist Controversy: the Languages of Criticism and the Sciences of Man* (Baltimore: Johns Hopkins University Press, 1970).

6. Derrida and Kant: the Enlightenment Tradition

1. Derrida, *Positions*, trans. Alan Bass (London: Athlone Press, 1981), p. 74.

2. See Derrida, *The Archeology of the Frivolous: Reading Condillac*, trans. John P. Leavey (Pittsburgh: Duquesne University Press, 1980).

3. Derrida, *Positions*, *op. cit.*, p. 74.

4. Derrida, interview with Richard Kearney, *op. cit.*, p. 124.

5. G.E. Moore, 'Proof of an External World', in *Philosophical Papers* (London: Allen and Unwin, 1959).

6. Barry Stroud, *The Significance of Philosophical Scepticism* (London: Oxford University Press, 1984), p. 122.

7. Ibid, p. 171.

8. Ibid, p. 195.

9. Derrida, 'Economimesis', *Diacritics*, vol. XI, no. 2 (1975), pp. 55-93.

10. Immanuel Kant, *Critique of Judgement*, trans. J.H. Bernard (New York: Hafner Press, 1974).
11. Derrida, *Positions*, *op. cit.*, p. 63.
12. Ibid, pp. 73-4.
13. Ibid, p. 73.
14. See Richard Rorty, 'Philosophy as a Kind of Writing', in *Consequences of Pragmatism* (Minneapolis: University of Minnesota Press, 1982), pp. 89-109.
15. See, for instance, Rorty, 'Overcoming the Tradition: Heidegger and Dewey', in *Consequences of Pragmatism*, *op. cit.*, pp. 37-59.
16. For a powerful critique of post-structuralist thinking from precisely this angle, see Gillian Rose, *Dialectic of Nihilism* (Oxford: Basil Blackwell, 1984).
17. See Jean-François Lyotard, *The Post-Modern Condition: a Report on Knowledge*, trans. Geoff Bennington and Brian Massumi (Manchester University Press, 1983). Also Lyotard and Jean-Loup Thébaud, *Just Gaming*, trans. Wlad Godzich (Manchester University Press, 1986).
18. Rorty, 'Idealism and Textualism', in *Consequences of Pragmatism*, *op. cit.*, pp. 139-59.
19. Lyotard, *The Post-Modern Condition*, *op. cit.*, p. 64.
20. Derrida, 'The Principle of Reason: the University in the Eyes of its Pupils', *Diacritics*, vol. XIX (1983), pp. 3-20. All further references given by page number in the text.
21. Charles Sanders Peirce, *Values in a Universe of Chance* (Stanford University Press, 1958), p. 332. The passage is quoted by Derrida in 'The Principle of Reason', cited above, p. 9.
22. Derrida, 'No Apocalypse, Not Now (full speed ahead, seven missiles, seven missives)', *Diacritics*, vol. XX (1984), pp. 20-31. All further references given by page number in the text.
23. See, for instance, the two recent volumes edited by Nigel Blake and Kay Pole, *Dangers of Deterrence* and *Objections to Nuclear Defence* (London: Routledge and Kegan Paul, 1983, 1984).
24. The classic statement of this position may be found in Theodor Adorno and Max Horkheimer, *Dialectic of Enlightenment*, trans. J. Cumming (New York: Herder and Herder, 1972).
25. See Jürgen Habermas, *Knowledge and Human Interests*, trans. Jeremy Shapiro (London: Heinemann, 1971); *Theory and Practice*, trans. John Viertel (London: Heinemann, 1974); *Communication and the Evolution of Society*, trans. Thomas McCarthy (London: Heinemann, 1979).

26. Some of the best informed discussion of these issues may be found in recent numbers of the journal *New German Critique*.

27. Derrida, 'White Mythology', in *Margins of Philosophy, op. cit.*, pp. 207-71.

28. Derrida, 'The Supplement of Copula', in *Margins of Philosophy, op. cit.*, pp. 175-205; p. 177.

7. Letters Home: Derrida, Austin and the Oxford Connection

1. Jacques Bouveresse, 'Why I Am So Very UnFrench', in Alan Montefiore (ed.), *Philosophy in France Today* (Cambridge University Press, 1983), pp. 9-33; p. 24.

2. Ibid, p. 20.

3. Ibid, p. 25.

4. See Richard Rorty, 'Keeping Philosophy Pure' and 'Professionalized Philosophy', in *Consequences of Pragmatism, op. cit.*, pp. 19-36 and 60-71.

5. See Derrida, 'Signature Event Context', *Glyph.* vol. I (Baltimore: Johns Hopkins University Press, 1977), pp. 172-97; John R. Searle, 'Reiterating the Differences', *Glyph*, I, pp. 198-208; and Derrida's response to Searle, 'Limited Inc abc', *Glyph*, vol. II (1977), pp. 162-254. All further references to 'Limited Inc' are given by page number in the text.

6. See, for instance, Christopher Norris, *Deconstruction: Theory and Practice* (London: Methuen, 1982), pp. 108-15; Gayatri Chakravorty Spivak, 'Revolutions That As Yet Have No Model: Derrida's "Limited Inc" ', *Diacritics*, vol. X (1980), pp. 29-49.

7. Derrida, *La Carte postale de Socrate à Freud et au-delà* (Paris: Aubier-Flammarion, 1980).

8. See Derrida, *La Carte postale, op. cit.*, pp. 101-18 in particular.

9. Derrida, *La Carte postale*, pp. 92 *ff.*

10. Shoshana Felman, *The Literary Speech-Act: Don Juan with J.L. Austin; or, Seduction in Two Languages*, trans. Catherine Porter (Ithaca, NY: Cornell University Press, 1983).

11. Stanley Cavell, *Must We Mean What We Say?* (London: Oxford University Press, 1969), p. 43.

12. Henry Staten, *Wittgenstein and Derrida* (Lincoln: University of Nebraska Press, 1984), p. 75.

13. Derrida, *La Carte postale, op. cit.*, p. 108 (my translation).

14. Derrida, 'Speculer – sur "Freud" ', in *La Carte postale*, pp.

275-357. Translated as 'Speculating – on Freud', *Oxford Literary Review*, no. 3 (1978), pp. 78-97.

8. Nietzsche, Freud, Levinas: on the Ethics of Deconstruction

1. H.L.A. Hart, *Essays in Jurisprudence and Philosophy* (Oxford: Clarendon Press, 1983).
2. Derrida elaborates on this metaphor in his essay 'Living On: Border-lines', in *Deconstruction and Criticism, op. cit.*, pp. 75-176.
3. Martin Heidegger, *Nietzsche* (Pfüllingen: Neske, 1961).
4. Derrida, 'Coming into One's Own', in Geoffrey Hartman (ed.), *Psychoanalysis and the Question of the Text, op. cit.*, pp. 114-48.
5. Derrida, 'Freud and the Scene of Writing', in *Writing and Difference, op. cit.*, pp. 196-231. All further references are given in the text.
6. Sigmund Freud, *Beyond the Pleasure Principle*, in *On Metapsychology: the Theory of Psychoanalysis*, vol. XI of the Pelican Freud Library, ed. Angela Richards (Harmondsworth: Penguin, 1984), pp. 275-337. See especially pp. 283-7.
7. See Ronald W. Clarke, *Freud: the Man and the Cause* (London: Jonathan Cape, 1980) for details of this and other fraught passages in Freud's dealing with his colleagues, students and disciples. The letters to and from his early associate Wilhelm Fliess are among the many 'correspondences' that Derrida draws upon in *La Carte postale*.
8. See especially W.K. Wimsatt, *The Verbal Icon, op. cit.*
9. Michel Foucault, *Madness and Civilization*, trans. Richard Howard (New York: Pantheon, 1965). For Derrida's critique, see 'Cogito and the History of Madness', in *Writing and Difference, op. cit.*, pp. 31-63.
10. Foucault's response to Derrida appeared as an appendix to the second edition of *Folie et Déraison* (Paris: Gallimard, 1972), pp. 583-603.
11. See Edward Said, 'The Problem of Textuality: Two Exemplary Positions', *Critical Inquiry*, vol. IV (1978), pp. 673-714.
12. Foucault, *The Order of Things: an Archaeology of the Human Sciences*, trans. Alan Sheridan (New York: Random House, 1970), closing sentence.
13. See, for instance, Louis Althusser, *For Marx*, trans. Ben Brewster (Harmondsworth: Penguin Books, 1969). Catherine Belsey's *Criti-*

cal Practice (London: Methuen, 1980) offers a lucid account of Althusser, Lacan and other proponents of this anti-humanist theoretical line.

14. See also Barthes, 'The Death of the Author', in *Image-Music-Text*, *op. cit.*

15. Gilles Deleuze, *Kant's Critical Philosophy: the Doctrine of the Faculties*, trans. Hugh Tomlinson and Barbara Habberjam (London: Athlone Press, 1984), p. 32.

16. Ibid, pp. 32-3.

17. See, for instance, Derrida, 'The Principle of Reason', *op. cit.*; also his essay 'Of an Apocalyptic Tone Recently Adopted in Philosophy', trans. John P. Leavey, *Oxford Literary Review*, vol. VI, no. 2 (1984), pp. 3-37.

18. Gilles Deleuze and Félix Guattari, *Anti-Oedipus: Capitalism and Schizophrenia* (New York: Viking, 1977).

19. Deleuze, *Kant's Critical Philosophy*, *op. cit.*, p. 36.

20. Derrida, *Edmund Husserl's 'Origin of Geometry': an Introduction*, trans. John P. Leavey (Pittsburgh: Duquesne University Press, 1978).

21. See Derrida, 'Violence and Metaphysics: an Essay on the Thought of Emmanuel Levinas', in *Writing and Difference*, *op. cit.*, pp. 79-153.

22. Susan Handelmann, *The Slayers of Moses: the Emergence of Rabbinic Interpretation in Modern Literary Theory* (Albany, NY: State University of New York Press, 1982).

23. For more in this connection – notably the influence of Bradleian idealism on modern Shakespearian studies – see Terence Hawkes, *That Shakespeherian Rag: Essays on a Critical Process* (London: Methuen, 1986).

24. Derrida, interview with Kearney, *op. cit.*, p. 96.

25. Richard Kearney, interview with Emmanuel Levinas, in Kearney, *op. cit.*, pp. 45-63; p. 55.

26. Ibid, p. 55.

27. Emmanuel Levinas, *Totality and Infinity*, trans. A. Lingis (Pittsburgh: Duquesne University Press, 1979).

28. Kearney, interview with Levinas, *op. cit.*, p. 56.

29. Ibid, p. 58.

30. A.J. Ayer, *Wittgenstein* (London: Weidenfeld and Nicolson, 1984), p. 159.

Bibliography

Derrida: Principal References

This section lists only the principal works of Derrida cited in the text. Other references may be found in the Notes (pp. 247-55, above).

'*Speech and Phenomc 'a' and Other Essays on Husserl's Theory of Signs* (1967), trans. David B. Allison (Evanston, Ill.: Northwestern University Press, 1973).

Edmund Husserl's 'Origin of Geometry': an Introduction (1962), trans. John P. Leavey (Pittsburgh: Duquesne University Press, 1978).

Of Grammatology (1967), trans. Gayatri Chakravorty Spivak (Baltimore: Johns Hopkins University Press, 1976).

Writing and Difference (1967), trans. Alan Bass (London: Routledge and Kegan Paul, 1978).

Spurs: Nietzsche's Styles (1972), trans. Barbara Harlow (Chicago University Press, 1979).

Dissemination (1972), trans. Barbara Johnson (London: Athlone Press, 1981).

Positions (1972), trans. Alan Bass (London: Athlone Press, 1981).

Margins of Philosophy (1972), trans. Alan Bass (Chicago University Press, 1982).

Glas (Paris: Galilée, 1974; also Paris: Denoel/Gonthier, 1981).

La Carte postale de Socrate à Freud et au-delà (Paris: Aubier-Flammarion, 1980).

Otobiographies: l'enseignement de Nietzsche et la politique du nom propre (Paris: Galilée, 1984).

'Signature Event Context', *Glyph*, vol. I (Baltimore: Johns Hopkins University Press, 1977), pp. 172-97.

'Limited Inc abc' (response to John Searle), *Glyph*, vol. II (Baltimore: Johns Hopkins University Press, 1977), pp. 162-254.

'Living On: Border-lines', in *Deconstruction and Criticism* (New York: Seabury Press, 1979), pp. 75-176.

257

Bibliography

'Economimesis', *Diacritics*, vol. XI, no. 2 (1981), pp. 3-25.

'The Principle of Reason: the University in the Eyes of its Pupils', *Diacritics*, vol. XIX (1983), pp. 3-20.

'Of an Apocalyptic Tone Recently Adopted in Philosophy', trans. John P. Leavey, *Oxford Literary Review*, vol. VI, no. 2 (1984), pp. 3-37.

Derrida: Selected Reading

There is room here only for a brief survey of texts not included in the list of references above. I have chosen items with a view to (1) their importance for a basic grasp of Derrida's work; (2) their relevance to the lines of argument pursued in this book; and (3) their usefulness in challenging some of the misconceptions that have grown up around his texts.

'Entre crochets' and 'Ja, ou le faux-bond' (two-part interview), *Diagraphe*, nos. 8 and 11 (April 1976 and March 1977), pp. 97-114 and 83-121.

'Ou commence et comment finit un corps enseignant', in Dominique Grisoni (ed.), *Politiques de la philosophie* (Paris: Bernard Grasset, 1976), pp. 55-97.

'Scribble', preface to Warburton, *Essai sur les hieroglyphes* (Paris: Aubier-Flammarion, 1977).

'Fors: the English words of Nicolas Abraham and Maria Torok', trans. Barbara Johnson, *Georgia Review*, vol. XXXI, no. 1 (1977), pp. 64-116.

'The Retrait of Metaphor', *enclitic*, vol. II, no. 2 (1978), pp. 5-34.

La Vérité en peinture (Paris: Flammarion, 1978).

'The Law of Genre', trans. Avital Ronnell, *Critical Inquiry*, vol. 1 (1980), pp. 55-81.

'The Parergon', *October*, no. 9 (1979), pp. 3-40.

'Title (to be specified)', *Substance*, no. 31 (1981), pp. 5-22.

'Les Morts de Roland Barthes', *Poétique*, 47 (September 1981), pp. 269-92.

'Télépathie', *Furor*, 2 (February 1981), pp. 3-41.

Affranchissement du transfert et de la lettre (Paris: Editions Confrontation, 1982). Responses to *La Carte postale*, along with Derrida's comments.

Interview with Christie V. MacDonald in *Diacritics*, vol. XII (1982), pp. 66-76.

'The Time of a Thesis: Punctuations', in Alan Montefiore (ed.),

Philosophy in France Today (Cambridge University Press, 1982).

'Comment juger Jean-François Lyotard', Colloque à Cérisy, 1982; forthcoming.

'Geschlecht — différence sexuelle, différence ontologique', *Research in Phenomenology*, vol. XIII (1983), pp. 68-84.

'La langue et le discours de la méthode', *Recherches sur la philosophie et le langage*, no. 3 (1983), pp. 35-51.

'Mes Chances/My Chances', in Joseph Smith and William Kerrigan (eds.), *Taking Chances* (Baltimore: Johns Hopkins University Press, 1984).

'An Idea of Flaubert: "Plato's Letter" ', trans. Peter Starr, *Modern Language Notes*, vol. XCIX (1984), pp. 748-68.

Feu la cendre (Firenze: Sansoni, 1984). French text with Italian translation by Stefano Agosti.

Signéponge/Signsponge, trans. Richard Rand (New York: Columbia University Press, 1984). Commentary on writings of Francis Ponge: French text with English translation.

'Devant la loi', in A. Phillips Griffiths (ed.), *Philosophy and Literature* (Cambridge University Press, 1984).

La Faculté de juger (Paris: Minuit, 1985).

The Ear of the Other: Otobiography, Transference, Translation: Texts and Discussions with Jacques Derrida, trans. Peggy Kamuf (New York: Schocken Books, 1986).

Parages (Paris: Galilée, 1986).

Mémoires (for Paul de Man), trans. Cecile Lindsay, Jonathan Culler and Eduardo Cadava (New York: Columbia University Press, 1986).

'Shibboleth' (on Paul Celan), in Geoffrey Hartman and Sanford Budick (eds.), *Midrash and Literature* (New Haven: Yale University Press, 1986), pp. 307-47.

'The Age of Hegel', trans. Susan Winnett, *Glyph*, vol. 1 (new series, 1986), pp. 3-43.

Glas, trans. John P. Leavey and Richard Rand (Lincoln, Nebraska: University of Nebraska Press, 1987).

Books and Articles on Derrida

(i) Introductory

Jonathan Culler, 'Jacques Derrida', in John Sturrock (ed.), *Structuralism and Since: from Lévi-Strauss to Derrida* (London: Oxford University Press, 1979), pp. 154-80.

Bibliography

―――― *On Deconstruction* (London: Routledge and Kegan Paul, 1982).

David Couzens Hoy, 'Deciding Derrida: on the Work (and Play) of the French Philosopher', *London Review of Books*, vol. IV, no. 3 (February/March 1982), pp. 3-5.

Christopher Norris, *Deconstruction: Theory and Practice* (London: Methuen, 1982).

Richard Rorty, 'Philosophy as a Kind of Writing', in *Consequences of Pragmatism* (Minneapolis: University of Minnesota Press, 1982), pp. 89-109.

David Wood, 'An Introduction to Derrida', *Radical Philosophy*, no. 21 (1979), pp. 18-28.

(ii) More advanced

Thomas J. Altizer *et al.*, *Deconstruction and Theology* (New York: Crossroads, 1982).

A.J. Cascardi, 'Skepticism and Deconstruction', *Philosophy and Literature*, vol. VIII (1984), pp. 1-14.

Jonathan Culler, 'Meaning and Convention: Derrida and Austin', *New Literary History*, vol. XIII (1981), pp. 15-30.

Robert Denoon Cumming, 'The Odd Couple: Heidegger and Derrida', *Review of Metaphysics*, vol. XXXIV (1981), pp. 487-521.

Robert Detweiler (ed.), *Derrida and Biblical Studies* (Chico, Cal.: Scholar's Press, 1982).

Terry Eagleton, 'Marxism and Deconstruction', *Contemporary Literature* (Fall, 1981), pp. 477-88.

Lucette Finas, Sarah Kofman, Roger Laporte and Jean-Michel Rey, *Ecarts: quatre essais à propos de Jacques Derrida* (Paris: Fayard, 1973).

Les Fins de l'homme: a partir du travail de Jacques Derrida (Paris: Galilée, 1981).

Stanley Fish, 'With the Compliments of the Author: Reflections on Austin and Derrida', *Critical Inquiry*, vol. VIII (1982), pp. 693-721.

John Frow, 'Foucault and Derrida', *Raritan*, vol. V, no. 1 (1985), pp. 31-42.

Rodolphe Gasché, 'Deconstruction as Criticism', *Glyph*, vol. VI (1979), pp. 177-216.

―――――*The Tain of the Mirror: Derrida and the Philosophy of Reflection* (Cambridge, Mass.: Harvard University Press, 1986).

Geoffrey Hartman, 'Monsieur Texte: on Jacques Derrida, his *Glas*',

Bibliography

Georgia Review, vol. XXIX, no. 4 (1975), pp. 759-97.

———'Monsieur Texte II: Epiphany in Echoland', *Georgia Review*, vol. XXX, no. 1 (1976), pp. 169-204.

Irene E. Harvey, *Derrida and the Economy of Différance* (Bloomington: Indiana University Press, 1986).

Marian Hobson, *Jacques Derrida* (London: Croom Helm, forthcoming).

Sarah Kofman, *Lectures de Derrida* (Paris: Galilée, 1984).

Mark Krupnick (ed.), *Displacement: Derrida and After* (Bloomington: Indiana University Press, 1983).

John P. Leavey, 'Jacques Derrida's *Glas*: a Translated Selection and Some Comments on an Absent Colossus', *Clio*, vol. XI (1982), pp. 327-37.

John Llewelyn, *Derrida on the Threshold of Sense* (London: Macmillan, 1986).

Robert Magliola, *Derrida on the Mend* (West Lafayette, Ind.: Purdue University Press, 1984).

Stephen Melville, *Philosophy Beside Itself: on Deconstruction and Modernism* (Minneapolis: University of Minnesota Press, 1986).

Floyd Merrell, *Deconstruction Reframed* (West Lafayette, Ind.: Purdue University Press, 1985).

J. Hillis Miller, 'Tradition and Difference', *Diacritics*, vol. II, no. 4 (1972), pp. 6-13.

Christopher Norris, 'On Marxist Deconstruction: Prospects and Problems', *Southern Review* (Adelaide), vol. XVII (1984), pp. 203-11.

———'Names' (on Derrida's *Signsponge*), *London Review of Books*, vol. VIII, no. 3 (1986), pp. 10-12.

———'On Derrida's "Apocalyptic Tone": Textual Politics and the Principle of Reason', *Southern Review* (Adelaide), vol. XIX, no. 1 (1986), pp. 13-30.

Andrew Parker, 'Taking Sides (on History): Derrida Re-Marx', *Diacritics*, vol. XI (1981), pp. 57-73.

Michael Ryan, *Marxism and Deconstruction: a Critical Articulation* (Baltimore: Johns Hopkins University Press, 1982).

Hugh J. Silverman and Don Ihde (eds.), *Hermeneutics and Deconstruction* (Albany: State University of New York Press, 1985).

Henry Staten, *Wittgenstein and Derrida* (Lincoln: University of Nebraska Press, 1984).

Gregory L. Ulmer, *Applied Grammatology: Post(e)-pedagogy from Jacques Derrida to Joseph Beuys* (Baltimore: Johns Hopkins University Press, 1985).

Bibliography

David Wood, 'Derrida and the Paradoxes of Reflection', *Journal of the British Society for Phenomenology*, vol. XI, no. 3 (1980), pp. 225-36.

———'Style and Strategy at the Limits of Philosophy', *Monist*, vol. LXIII, no. 4 (1980), pp. 494-511.

Ann Wordsworth, 'Derrida and Criticism', *Oxford Literary Review*, vol. III (1978), pp. 47-52.

Edmond Wright, 'Derrida, Searle, Contexts, Games, Riddles', *New Literary History*, vol. XIII (1982), pp. 463-77.

(iii) Deconstruction and literary theory

Jonathan Arac (ed.), *The Yale Critics: Deconstruction in America* (Minneapolis: University of Minnesota Press, 1983).

G. Douglas Atkins and Michael L. Johnson (eds.), *Writing and Reading Differently: Deconstruction and the Teaching of Composition and Literature* (Lawrence, Kansas: University Press of Kansas, 1985).

Elizabeth Bruss, *Beautiful Theories: the Spectacle of Discourse in Contemporary Criticism* (Baltimore: Johns Hopkins University Press, 1982).

Christopher Butler, *Interpretation, Deconstruction and Ideology* (London: Oxford University Press, 1984).

William E. Cain, *The Crisis in Criticism: Theory, Literature and Reform in English Studies* (Baltimore: Johns Hopkins University Press, 1984).

Jonathan Culler, *The Pursuit of Signs: Semiotics, Literature, Deconstruction* (London: Routledge and Kegan Paul, 1981).

Paul de Man, *Blindness and Insight: Essays in the Rhetoric of Contemporary Criticism*, second edition, expanded and revised (London: Methuen, 1983).

Robert C. Davis and Ronald Schleifer (eds.), *Rhetoric and Form: Deconstruction at Yale* (Norman: University of Oklahoma Press, 1985).

Terry Eagleton, *Literary Theory: an Introduction* (Oxford: Basil Blackwell, 1984).

———*Against the Grain: Essays 1975-85* (London: New Left Books/ Verso, 1986).

John Fekete, *The Structural Allegory: Reconstructive Encounters with the New French Thought* (Manchester University Press, 1984).

Shoshana Felman (ed.), *Literature and Psychoanalysis: the Question of Reading – Otherwise* (Baltimore: Johns Hopkins University Press, 1982).

Bibliography

Howard Felperin, *Beyond Deconstruction: the Uses and Abuses of Literary Theory* (Oxford: Clarendon Press, 1985).

Michael Fischer, *Does Deconstruction Make Any Difference?* (Bloomington: Indiana University Press, 1985).

Eugene Goodheart, *The Skeptic Disposition in Contemporary Criticism* (New Jersey: Princeton University Press, 1985).

Josué V. Harari (ed.), *Textual Strategies: Perspectives in Post-structuralist Criticism* (London: Methuen, 1979).

David Couzens Hoy, *The Critical Circle: Literature and History in Contemporary Hermeneutics* (Berkeley and Los Angeles: University of California Press, 1978).

Ann Jefferson and David Robey (eds.), *Modern Literary Theory: a Comparative Introduction*, second edition, expanded and revised (London: Batsford, 1986).

John P. Leavey, Jnr, *Glassary* (Lincoln: University of Nebraska Press, (1987).

Frank Lentricchia, *Criticism and Social Change* (University of Chicago Press, 1983).

Richard Machin and Christopher Norris (eds.), *Post-Structuralist Readings of English Poetry* (Cambridge University Press, 1987).

Christopher Norris, *The Deconstructive Turn: Essays in the Rhetoric of Philosophy* (London: Methuen, 1984).

————*The Contest of Faculties: Philosophy and Theory after Deconstruction* (London: Methuen, 1985).

William Ray, *Literary Meaning: from Phenomenology to Deconstruction* (Oxford: Basil Blackwell, 1984).

Edward Said, *The World, the Text and the Critic* (London: Faber and Faber, 1984).

Imre Salusinszky, *Criticism in Society* (London: Methuen, 1986).

Robert Scholes, *Textual Power: Literary Theory and the Teaching of English* (New Haven: Yale University Press, 1985).

Index of Names and Topics

(Since these authors and topics are all treated in relation to some aspect of his work, I have not thought it worthwhile to duplicate details by providing a comprehensive entry under 'Jacques Derrida'. For the same reason 'deconstruction' is not here but can be tracked easily enough through various related terms and ideas.)

Index

Topics

271